Hybrid Warfare:
A Collection of Scenarios

Edited by Adrian Borbély

Hybrid Warfare: A Collection of Scenarios
Published by DRI Press, an imprint of the Dispute
Resolution Institute at Mitchell Hamline School of Law

Dispute Resolution Institute
Mitchell Hamline School of Law
875 Summit Ave, St Paul, MN 55105
Tel. (651) 695-7676
ISBN-13: 979-8-9991171-0-6

Mitchell Hamline School of Law in Saint Paul, Minnesota has been educating lawyers for more than 100 years and remains committed to innovation in responding to the changing legal market. Mitchell Hamline offers a rich curriculum in advocacy and problem solving. The law school's Dispute Resolution Institute, consistently ranked in the top dispute resolution programs by U.S. News & World Report, is committed to advancing the theory and practice of conflict resolution, nationally and internationally, through scholarship and applied practice projects. DRI offers more than 30 dispute resolution courses each year in a variety of domestic and international certificate programs. Established in 2009, DRI Press is the scholarship dissemination arm of the Dispute Resolution Institute which brings significant conflict resolution work to a broad audience. For more information on other DRI Press publications, visit https://mitchellhamline.edu/dispute-resolution-institute/dri-press/

Interior Design by Erik Christopher/Ugly Dog Digital
Cover design by Karin Preus/Acorn Design.

Hybrid Warfare: Textile Art

On this page and between sections later in this book, an artist illustrates the complexity of efforts to cause economic and political disruption, by weaving phrases from a Chinese military text into the interleaving and interlocking strands of fibers.

Some further details are on the relevant pages.

From a series of weavings by Rachel Parish, with quotes from Qiao and Wang's Unrestricted Warfare (People's Liberation Army Publishing House, Beijing 1999.) Here: *"This information is not information", "Undermine the legitimacy of key institutions", "Remember your future", "Paralyze decision making", "A society of excrescence", "Encourage social discord", and "Delay recognition an attack is underway".* Original size 119" x 20". In color at https://rachelparish.com/projects/gentle-and-kind-things/

Even if fiction sometimes meets realty,
this collection is a work of fiction –
and should be treated as such.

We dedicate this volume to Bill Zartman (1932-2025), one of the conflict management field's greatest thinkers. Scenario 12 is merely one example of how he continued to contribute, long after "retirement age," as a force in the field, and a major contributor to Project Seshat.

CONTENTS

ACKNOWLEDGMENTS

Adrian Borbély

This collection is the first of its kind, and although hybrid warfare is becoming more and more widespread in the news and in the academic literature, we owe this book to the work of true precursors.

I would like first to acknowledge Chris Honeyman. Chris is a true innovator and entrepreneur. For decades, he has been building communities around large projects in negotiation and conflict management, working with different partners including in the Canon of Negotiation initiative and then in the Rethinking Negotiation Teaching book series. He has been able to gather around him a network of academics and practitioners of the highest quality.

Through a series of conversations between Chris and Calvin Chrustie, the idea emerged of an academic community gathering conflict management scholars and security practitioners around the study of this new threat to Western societies: Hybrid Warfare. Calvin is also an innovator, with an indefatigable willingness to spread wisdom on hybrid warfare threats, not only to decision-makers but also to the whole-of-society and the broad academic community.

This book is the direct outcome of these exchanges. First, Chris and Calvin honored me with their confidence to edit this book. Second, the commonality among almost all contributors to this book is that they have known Chris and/or Calvin for years, have trust in them and have responded positively to their call for action on this new topic of study.

I also want to acknowledge the other leaders of this burgeoning community, namely Andrea K. Schneider (now the Executive Director of the initial project's successor, the Council for Countering Hybrid Warfare – CCHW), Cynthia Alkon, Art Hinshaw, Janice Fischer and Sanda Kaufman, all members of the steering committee of CCHW. Together with Chris, they are central to the development of our academic understanding of hybrid warfare.

I would like also to recognize everyone who has shown interest in conversing with us, from Governments, law firms, company and NGO C-Suites and especially at NATO Headquarters. The fact that you have looked at our work with such benevolence and support is the best motivation to keep going. Your validation is priceless, as it shows that we are contributing to building a more informed, more secure world.

Nothing would have been feasible without a publisher. A heartfelt thank you to Sharon Press and her team at DRI Press, for their support and enthusiasm for this project.

Finally, I want to thank every contributor to this book for their immeasurable support and kindness. To every co-author of a case or a chapter, everyone cited in thank-you footnotes and everyone who made contributions that are less obvious: THANK YOU!

FOREWORD:
A NATO PERSPECTIVE

Vlasta Zekulic, PhD
Branch Head, Strategic Issues and Engagements
Supreme Allied Commander Transformation
NATO

In an age where the boundaries of warfare are increasingly blurred – where cyberattacks, proxy forces, disinformation campaigns, economic coercion and conventional military tactics converge – understanding the conceptual frameworks that govern such complexity has never been more urgent. Hybrid warfare is not just a military strategy; it is a legal and ethical frontier that challenges the very foundations of the international rules-based order. This collection of scenarios offers an invaluable lens through which to examine how states and non-state actors alike are navigating – and often testing – the limits of existing norms. Each case contributes to a deeper understanding of how international law and other schemas of conflict management are being interpreted, challenged, and, in some instances, reshaped.

NATO has been tracking and developing options against this coercive and ambitious type of war since 2009, when NATO troops in Afghanistan suffered under attacks by multiple adversarial forces and proxies that were not clearly identifiable or attributable, and against whom the typical kinetic military force was not easily applied due to the high risk of collateral casualties. The use of hybrid tools increased radically in 2014 in conjunction with Russia's illegal annexation of Crimea. The speed and efficiency of these relatively bloodless operations, which relied heavily on psychological and information warfare, sent a shock wave across security communities. By the spring of 2015, this in turn triggered the development of NATO and EU strategies to counter hybrid warfare.[1] Writing those strategies was a painful and tedious process.

First, we needed to understand if what we were seeing was truly a new form of warfare, or merely an evolution of "politics by other means." We were fully aware of the former Soviet Union "active measures" that aimed to break NATO from within by attacking

---

[1] For NATO: https://www.nato.int/cps/en/natohq/topics_156338.htm
For the EU: https://eur-lex.europa.eu/legal-content/EN/TXT/?uri=CELEX:52016JC0018

all its weak points and undermining the mutual confidence of the Allies in each other and in NATO as a whole. After reviewing all the intelligence and piecing together what had played out, the verdict was in: while the aims were not new, the tools available to achieve them had changed so profoundly that hybrid warfare now equates in severity to any other form of war.

The key new criteria included:

- Clearly set **goals** and end-states that predominantly focus on coercion, control and disruption of the existing international order.

- Dedicated and carefully designed **weapons** of hybrid warfare in the form of disinformation, corruption and disruption, just to name a few; and

- Carefully selected **battlefields** to maximize the effectiveness of their campaigns and their weapons, while staying hidden and below the threshold of open conflict. Those battlefields are predominantly perceptions, beliefs, values, and the decision-making calculus of both our citizens and our decision makers.

Secondly, we needed to design and develop effective tools to fight such campaigns. If hybrid actors aim to attack and exploit vulnerabilities and weaknesses, we believed that the militaries themselves would likely not be attacked, but actors, organizations and infrastructure that may have a significant impact on and/or enable the military's ability to fight will be. This is what we need to protect.

However, in our attempt to do so, the planning teams discovered, while reviewing NATO Cold War archives, that old plans and the related civil preparedness could not be effectively resurrected, for three simple reasons. First, the NATO borders are now far more to the East and encompass nations that during the Cold War were NATO's adversaries and thus have no baseline or experience in the Western system of preparedness. Second, most of the critical infrastructure that used to be owned by governments is now in private hands. Negotiating with private firms and finding the way ahead to protect access to critical services has proven to be rather challenging. Lastly, the collective consciousness of people has shifted, and a heavy cloak of disbelief that war of any kind – hybrid or kinetic – could be 'for real', after years of peace dividends, had to be cleared.

The final challenge in designing NATO's response against hybrid warfare was awareness that most of the collective defense mechanisms were almost forgotten, as a whole generation of NATO military officers and strategic planners had spent their careers fighting in the expeditionary operational theaters across the Balkans, Afghanistan and Iraq, and not contemplating how to design deterrence and defense against Russia. This was particularly true in relation to non-military defenses, civilian preparedness and resilience. The team understood that resilience against hybrid warfare and preparedness to counter it had to be re-invented, not resurrected. So, we did.

Within the span of a year, we had written the Strategy on NATO's Role in Countering Hybrid Warfare, redefined what it means to be resilient from NATO's perspective, and designed seven baseline requirements of how to achieve it.[2] Over the next several years, we also agreed that a hybrid attack can trigger the famous 'Article 5' of the collective defense, deployed 'Counter hybrid support teams' to several Allied nations, and wrote the 'playbook' on comprehensive preventive and response measures against hybrid attacks.[3]

We believed we were doing a great job until we first met with Chris Honeyman and Calvin Chrustie, two of the contributors to this important book. We spent hours discussing how NATO's views match and contrast with their own, and we gained a full understanding of how their group's insights needed to be collated together and presented to a broader audience. We in NATO were particularly struck by two elements: first the passion of this remarkable group of mostly non-military, non-government experts for the challenges that hybrid warfare poses, and second, their focus on how hybrid warfare is playing out in the legal and business arenas, as well as in nonprofits, universities, municipalities, hospitals and more. In all the years of our work on countering hybrid threats, we broadly understood, for instance, that "lawfare" can be one of its manifestations (see scenario #3); but that was mostly perceived through the lens of China's build-up of First Island Chain fortifications. This book is written to ensure that such misconceptions, in relation not just to lawfare but to many other hybrid warfare tools and tactics, will at least begin to encounter organized teaching tools designed to help the West learn how to confront them.

The authors of these scenarios are a remarkable collage of experts from many areas of work, who have been studying how hybrid warfare plays out in real life. While we in NATO tend to focus more on **identifying** elements of hybrid campaigns launched against our governments or organizations, **recognizing** what are the goals and aim of the attack, what it is that the attackers wish to disrupt, destroy or curtail, and **attributing** the perpetrators of the hybrid campaigns, a number of scenarios in this book follow other patterns. Some of the scenarios may leave you thinking, what *is* the aim of this adversarial action? – or is it just another common, though immoral, business practice?

But that is exactly where the danger and gravity of hybrid warfare hides: in the gray zone between business, law, security and other silos. Our adversaries are exploring every vulnerability and weakness, every gap and crack they can find to achieve their goals. Truly, not everything is hybrid warfare. But we are in an age when any strength can be turned into a weakness, and where anything that can help humankind can also harm it. When it is becoming harder and harder to decipher what is right and what is wrong, whom to trust, or even what is really going on, one needs to at least ask the following questions: "Is this a hybrid attack? Who is attacking what? Why?" Guiding questions in

---

[2] https://www.nato.int/cps/en/natohq/topics_132722.htm

[3] https://www.nato.int/docu/review/articles/2021/03/19/enlarging-natos-toolbox-to-counter-hybrid-threats/index.html

each of the chapters will help you work through the ambiguity of the situations described and come to your own conclusions.

Moreover, in NATO, we are predominantly focusing on those hybrid attacks that aim to affect public will, and to manipulate strategic choices of our citizens and decision makers, in order to shape perceptions, alter consciousness and challenge the strategic calculus that underlies national and international security. But this book broadens the scope of the perceptible attacks. I found that the most valuable element of this book is that it takes its audience to so many different settings and lays out examples showing how they can also be used to inflict economic pressure, e.g. in scenario #8 (Trouble in Agudama-Epie) or scenario #11 (Rare Earth Elements); how they vary geographically, such as in scenarios #2, #8 and #12, and can be applied across all Instruments of Power, such as in scenarios #1, #4, or #7. Together they showcase how different hybrid campaigns can play out and exploit vulnerabilities in each specific area and prime our thinking to other possible scenarios of disruption.

For these reasons, whether you are new to this subject or a seasoned expert, I am confident that you will find something here that resonates deeply. This book is not just informative, it is transformative and gives any reader full appreciation of the complexity, ambiguity and danger that hybrid warfare poses.

Midnight in a Kaleidoscope:
Conflict Management and Hybrid Warfare

Adrian Borbély & Chris Honeyman

Why a book of scenarios about hybrid warfare designed for non-military people?

Fair question! The short answer is that one characteristic of hybrid warfare, which will become apparent in the scenarios which follow, is that it affects us all: everyone should feel concerned. A central condition of below-the-surface foreign aggressions is that they are not limited to a classical battlefield, i.e., a localized region where armed forces shoot at each other trying to take each other's positions. In hybrid warfare, society as a whole is the battlefield.

Below, we will discuss in broad terms the current state of relevant teaching in several key fields and articulate our conception of what is now needed to address hybrid warfare. But first, it is essential to note the rising public perception of hybrid warfare; to discuss at least briefly how our societies got to this point; and to assess what is currently being done about it. In all these areas, for reasons which follow, our focus will be on those parts of Western societies and economies which do not have the resources of national governments.

Public perceptions of hybrid warfare (ca. early 2025)

"Grey zone conflict" and "hybrid warfare"[1] are just two among several terms currently used to depict the same thing – assaults against a nation, its citizens and its private enter-

---

[1] Confusion over these and other terms is common; see Leonard Lira's and Bryan Reyes' chapter for an explanation of how such overlapping terms developed. We endorse their recommendation that in future, those discussing this whole topic area could clear the decks by adopting a newer catchall term, "hybrid conflict." However, fifty Project Seshat contributors, in numerous discussions over several years, settled on "hybrid warfare" as a working expedient, and we decline to suddenly disturb that. We are accordingly using "hybrid warfare" for the time being, throughout this book.

prises, as well as public and NGO actors.[2] These attacks may or may not involve a military component and may be executed by entities seemingly unconnected to another country's national security forces. Even after an attack, its true intent may remain quite obscure. For example, the well-known Colonial Pipeline attack of 2021, which resulted in widespread economic damage after a pipeline carrying 45% of the U.S. East Coast's oil supply was shut down for nearly a week, was claimed by the attacker to be a purely money-oriented attack with no broader consequences intended.[3] Reportedly the attack was facilitated by such poor security practices at the pipeline company that the theft of a single password was all that was needed, suggesting in turn that such a major attack could conceivably have been mounted by a relatively "amateur" group.[4] Yet the group involved is widely believed to be based in Russia, where government support of such private crime groups is widely known,[5] and denial of all sorts of government-supported hybrid attacks has become routine.

A scant five years ago as of writing this, "hybrid warfare" was still an obscure enough concept that when contacted by Honeyman during the fall of 2019, hardly any among dozens of conflict management veterans admitted to having even heard the term before. But now it is increasingly recognized as a matter of public concern; for example, a November 2023 daylong public event on the subject, mounted by London's Imperial War Museum, sold out.[6] The UK Ministry of Defence's pithy quote on the flyer for that event read: "The international consensus on hybrid warfare is clear; no one understands it, but everyone agrees it is a problem."

This book's particular intent is to shed light on attacks targeting entities beyond national governments, for several reasons. First, campaigns of hybrid warfare coordinate activities among private, government and nonprofit entities. They routinely use tools aimed at nonmilitary targets, including cyber tools, public or commercial corruption, transnational organized crime, disinformation campaigns, and various other methods.[7] And deception, including denial that any such attack is underway, is a standard element

---

[2] Hybrid warfare is still a new enough topic that many audiences require a basic explanation. This discussion has been adapted for the present book from prior related publications designed for other audiences; see e.g. Chris Honeyman and Rachel Tan Xi'En, 'A New Management System, for a New Type of Conflict? Singapore's Possible Role in Managing Grey Zone Conflict in International Commerce' (Dispute Resolution Review (Australia) Vol. 4/2: 99-119 and directed to a public policy audience); Chris Honeyman and Andrea Kupfer Schneider, 'Hybrid Warfare: Fighting Back with Whole-of-Society Tactics.' (2023) 30 On Track 6 (for a Canadian military audience); Chris Honeyman and Andrea Kupfer Schneider, 'Introduction: Negotiation Strategies for War by Other Means' (2023) 24 Cardozo Journal of Conflict Resolution 487 (in an American legal and dispute resolution context.) It also draws extensively on previous writings by several security colleagues quoted below, particularly Christopher Corpora, Leonard Lira and Steven Desjardins.

[3] Freed, A.A. blog: Inside the DarkSide Ransomware Attack on Colonial Pipeline.
 https://www.cybereason.com/blog/inside-the-darkside-ransomware-attack-on-colonial-pipeline

[4] "One password allowed hackers to disrupt Colonial Pipeline, CEO tells senators." https://www.reuters.com/business/colonial-pipeline-ceo-tells-senate-cyber-defenses-were-compromised-ahead-hack-2021-06-08/

[5] See e.g. Galeotti, M. 2018. *The Vory: Russia's super mafia*. New Haven: Yale.

[6] From Sniper to Smartphone: Hybrid Warfare and the New Face of Conflict' Imperial War Museum (Web Page): www.iwm.org.uk/events/from-sniper-to-smartphone.

[7] Galeotti, M. 2023. *The Weaponization of Everything: A Field Guide to the New Way of War*. New Haven: Yale.

in creating an atmosphere of ambiguity, and in parallel, the attacker's desired state of mind among defenders: doubt and confusion.[8] Additionally, it is evident that Western intelligence, military and other security agencies are not (yet) effectively organized to respond strategically or coherently to such actions impacting non-military sectors.[9]

Hybrid warfare in history

It is important to emphasize that what we are seeing today as hybrid warfare is new in its variety, as well as the sheer volume of activity, and of course in many of the specific techniques used – but not in its essence. In a previous Project Seshat publication,[10] Christopher Corpora noted that present-day hybrid warfare has many precedents:

> ... Hybrid Warfare and Gray Zone Conflict are recent terms used to understand and explain an age-old human social phenomenon – attaining dominance and influence without throwing a punch or firing a shot. Versions of this strategic concept have existed throughout history, but they have been evolving more rapidly in the modern era. Asymmetric Warfare, Military Operations Other Than War (MOOT-WA), Irregular Warfare and Active Measures are a few of the terms used over the past 50 years to describe non-conventional strategies and tactics for weakening an enemy, ideally limiting the amount of conventional force needed to win. Softening an enemy through psychological or physical deception led to many great classical victories in war – ranging from Egyptian fighters in baskets, through Alexander's famous deception in the conquest of Punjab, to the Trojan Horse. The price of war increasingly became a point of focus, as the costs rose, in terms of both blood and treasure, forcing policymakers to think carefully about direct combat as a viable option to gain power and pursue their interests. Hybrid Warfare and Gray Zone Conflict are updated versions of this indirect aggression – using unconventional means and targeting a broader community outside the traditional combatant space and enabled largely through the internet (or cyberspace as some call it). The creation and growth of the internet over the past 40 years provided a new domain for contestation, joining air, land, sea and space as places for international competition. It also is a space of easy intersection with the private sector,

---

[8] Christopher A. Corpora, How to Undermine a Nation-State in 120 Days: Mediation and Negotiation in a Hybrid Warfare World (2023) 24 Cardozo Journal of Conflict Resolution 503. See also Steven Desjardins, Hybrid Warfare – Is it New, is it Real, and What are the Threats, Vulnerabilities, and Implications for Defence and the Military? 30 On Track, Winter 2023

[9] Scott Tait, Hybrid Warfare: the New Face of Global Competition, Financial Times: https://www.ft.com/content/ffe7771e-e5bb-11e9-9743-db5a370481bc.

[10] Corpora, above at fn 8. (Internal citations omitted.)

which is the domain where most Hybrid War actions occur – ranging from indirect manipulation through disinformation operations to cyber blackmail and denial operations. The locus of these Hybrid War activities purposefully targets "civilian" and "commercial" interests to instigate chaos and create unignorable disruptions, where scarce public resources must be expended to respond, and private legal actions are required to address the impact... Hybrid warfare, as the latest term or euphemism for actions other than the use of conventional violence to advance national interests, has grown rapidly in importance since the end of the Cold War, coinciding with the advance of cyber and communications technologies. State and non-state actors now use the tactics associated with hybrid warfare to:

- Undermine an adversary's ability to pursue its own interests and/or thwart the attackers.

- Reduce public and market confidence in the adversary at all necessary levels – global, regional and local.

- Instigate confusion, chaos and internal conflict to deflect an adversary's attention, resources and self-confidence.

- Promote state and organizational interests in opposition to the adversary's potential gains.

Historically, the kinds of deception and sabotage described above resulted in eventual fighting. This strategy has always involved the strategic positioning to develop and leverage non-conventional means or tactics to weaken an opponent, preferably with little to no attribution – allowing for success by default, with tumult inside an adversary's camp. Sun Tzu makes one of the earliest mentions of this strategy, saying, "To subdue the enemy without fighting is the acme of all skill," and, "The supreme art of war is to subdue the enemy without fighting." Another long-respected military theorist, Carl von Clausewitz, said, "[t]he best form of defense is attack" and, "[a]ll war presupposes human weakness and seeks to exploit it." Although his own intentions were literal, the broader application of this idea provided a theoretical space to spark more purposeful thinking about taking offensive actions in advance of direct conflict, either to soften the adversary or to sufficiently deter it from contesting an issue. Clausewitz also recognized the relationship between politics and war, calling the latter an extension of the former. Hybrid Warfare occupies a space between conventional politics and war, which is why many of the tactics are shared across the domains. Deception, disinformation and sabotage are all important competencies for the modern political operator. The increased capability and public reliance on the internet have increased the span and effect of such techniques. The outcomes are seen daily across various media and polemic websites.

Similarly, Steven Desjardins[11] points out that:

> ... Much of what we now experience and refer to as hybrid warfare has been and remains an integral part of the fabric of inter-state competition and warfare. Hostile actors strive to change the global order of things without provoking open kinetic hostilities... Leveraging all forms of national power, in a coordinated and synchronized manner, is not new. Mixing and matching elements of national power to deceive, deny, delay, destroy and disrupt an adversary is not new. The substantive changes we experience in today's security environment are economic globalization, changes in the information environment, increased societal interfaces and emerging technologies. These have very substantively amplified whole new realms of societal vulnerabilities to hybrid threats, and they have very substantively empowered and facilitated access to hybrid means for hostile state and non-state actors to employ to generate ambiguity and achieve strategic, operational, and tactical effects.

Outlining a series of technological developments, Desjardins goes on to state that:

> ... The mixing and matching, coordinating and synchronizing of conventional and unconventional elements of national power, along with leveraging ambiguity in targeting these against societal interfaces to defeat, disrupt, deny or degrade an opponent's decision-making processes and ability to act, is more accessible than previously. It is also executed with much greater speed, reach, depth and persistence, and this pays dividends despite being easier, cheaper, and less risky than kinetic operations.

And in a detailed review of the military and security literature related to hybrid warfare,[12] Leonard Lira and Bryan Reyes note that:

---

[11] Desjardins, above at fn 8. (Internal citations omitted.)

[12] We took this quote from the unpublished paper that was used as a basis for drafting two chapters of this book, the Lira and Reyes terminology chapter, as well as the selected readings bibliography presented at the end of this volume.

... Initially, hybrid threats were only seen as asymmetric strategies employed by non-state actors such as terrorist groups residing in countries like Lebanon, Syria, Pakistan, Afghanistan, or Iraq. Scholars observed that these groups would blend conventional and irregular capabilities specifically targeted at US vulnerabilities to draw out conflict in hopes to achieve their goals. However, the invasion of Ukraine by Russia, and earlier examples of Russian hybrid attacks employed against Estonia, and Georgia, demonstrated a shift from only non-state actors employing hybrid threats to state actors colluding with non-state actors to employ these techniques in conflict. The shift of state actors purposefully engaging in grey zone conflicts demonstrates the dilemma of how to respond to low aggression conflicts that fall below traditional threshold descriptions of warfare. Aggressors employing hybrid threats in the grey zone could operate within the wording of international treaties and laws like UN Security Council's Article 51 guarantee of self-defense and NATO's Article 5 mutual defense treaty and not trigger a united international response. Other challenges to international laws, such as China's build-up of artificial islands to extend their claims to the South China Sea, diminished the integrity of international laws. These examples exposed 'weaknesses' in international security regimes and allowed adversaries to exploit blurred lines of sovereignty, rules, and laws, to gain an advantage.

Current responses to hybrid warfare, effective and otherwise

Responses from the targeted entities are often unhelpful and ineffectual, ranging from denying the occurrence of any attack to threats of retaliation, or proposing increasing defense expenditures at the government level or severing all dealings with countries responsible for these attacks.[13] Although each of these reactions may have its place, none of these responses has proven generally effective. Thus, it is imperative to develop a comprehensive approach so that hybrid warfare can be better comprehended as a category and managed on an overarching level – as distinct from countermeasures that are overtly retaliatory on a military scale.

At the same time, as Corpora and Desjardins note above, the direct roles and vulnerability of all kinds of non-governmental entities have vastly increased. For one thing, in a globalized economy, "business and NGO executives, and critically, their lawyers, are routinely engaged in negotiations of all kinds, with suppliers, customers, municipalities, potential merger partners and more. These dealings do not have to be visibly cross-border

---

[13] See articles cited in note 2.

transactions to have hybrid warfare connotations."[14] For instance, if a seemingly "domestic" company with which a city government is contracting for water or other utilities, transportation, communication networks, or a myriad of other services, is covertly influenced by a foreign government, the city might become a target without recognizing the opponent's intention or even its existence.[15] Dealings with innocent third parties can have the same effect in the private sector. A conspicuous example was the NotPetya virus, which was used by Russia in a cyberattack on Ukraine in 2017 – and which was so over-effective that it spread to thousands of companies that were not targets at all. In the most startling result, the infection of a single computer at a Ukrainian branch office of Maersk, the world's largest shipping firm, spread throughout the firm's internal networks, and resulted in the entire company effectively shutting down for an extended period.[16]

Meanwhile there is compelling evidence not only that the private and nonprofit sectors are significant target areas in hybrid warfare,[17] but that they are even less prepared for this than governments. What's more, many of these attacks appear to operate by perverting transactions that, to Western parties, may look like ordinary commercial dealings, such as in supply chains, licensing and other domains.

Efforts to respond to hybrid warfare at the strategic level are ongoing, with recent events, particularly the Russian invasion of Ukraine, elevating their prominence. However, the critically important tactical and operational responses often occur in widely dispersed corporate boardrooms, law offices, municipal government or university offices, etc. Many who are unwittingly involved in a hybrid warfare attack have little or no understanding of the phenomenon, and even those who are aware of an attack are often poorly informed about what actions they can take.[18]

As Corpora and Desjardins point out, efforts to undermine a perceived rival nation without triggering open warfare are not new; such practices date back thousands of

[14] Chris Honeyman and Andrea Kupfer Schneider, 'Introduction: Negotiation Strategies for War by Other Means' (2023) 24 Cardozo Journal of Conflict Resolution 487.

[15] See the discussion of the SolarWinds attack in Leslie, A. 2023. 'Redefining Contours of "Business as Usual" and the Potential Role of the Military.' In Hybrid Warfare: Fighting Back with Whole-of-Society Tactics, 30 On Track 28, Winter 2023.

[16] Daniel E. Capano, 'Throwback Attack: How NotPetya accidentally took down global shipping giant Maersk', Industrial Cybersecurity Pulse (online at 30 September 2021): https://www.industrialcybersecuritypulse.com/threats-vulnerabilities/throwback-attack-how-notpetya-accidentally-took-down-global-shipping-giant-maersk/

[17] Case after case the evidence has accumulated in recent years. For those still inclined to treat the stories as anecdotal, we can recommend Qiao Liang and Wang Xiangsui, *Unrestricted Warfare* (Beijing: People's Liberation Army Publishing House, 1999). There is no more authoritative source than these two Chinese army colonels, who originally set forth what has since transparently become China's strategy for hybrid warfare against the West. A selection of short phrases from Qiao and Wang (as used throughout the book by an artist who created a series of weavings to illustrate hybrid warfare) will give the general idea: "erode economic strength", "this war is not a war", "a borderless battlefield", "this information is not information", "undermine the legitimacy of key institutions", "remember your future", "paralyze decision making", "encourage social discord", "delay recognition an attack is underway", and last but not least, "Some morning you may awake to find that the gentle and kind things around you have begun to have lethal and offensive characteristics." See also 'Gentle and Kind Things', Rachel Parish (Blog Post), https://rachelparish.com/projects/gentle-and-kind-things/

[18] Calvin Chrustie, 'Mind the Hybrid Warfare Gap' (2023) 30 On Track 12

years. Yet there is something new here. Sanda Kaufman distinguishes the new style of attack from long-used methods of undermining opponents in these terms:

> ... Perhaps a key difference between hybrid warfare and historic deceptive methods of prevailing over enemies is the use of sophisticated technologies applied to ever more complex situations. Hybrid warfare technologies include acting covertly at great distances from the targets (e.g., the disabling of some of Iran's nuclear facilities using a computer virus), using information – correct or not – to target and rally various groups unaware of the real intent (e.g., youth destroying culturally valuable objects as a means of fighting against climate change), dividing and weakening various opponent groups (e.g., polarizing parts of societies), and even reaching out to the very young to addict them to social media activities and ideas that brainwash, or even to drugs.[19]

Current related teaching in business, law and other professional schools

We believe not only that the topic of hybrid warfare matters to us all, but that it is currently in an educational blind spot, stuck in an intermediate zone between macro/systemic risks on the one hand, and micro risks on the other hand.

When it comes to macro risks, European business and law students are routinely taught about geopolitics, while their American counterparts are in general much more focused on affairs within their home country. Across these domains, such teachings remain mostly disconnected from their future fields of action: throughout the West, geopolitics is taught as an element of context, rarely as something that could intrude into everyday operations. As such, in business schools, geopolitics is taught because it is useful for making sound decisions on financial markets, to help tailor the right international supply chain, or to decide whether to enter a new market. However, students – and professionals alike – are not told that geopolitics may directly impact them, or their organization, as a target or as an accessory to morally-disputable activities.

Regarding micro risks, business and law students are taught that compliance is a requirement to avoid legal troubles, as well as business and reputation costs. Most of them are also made aware of everyday risks such as occupational illnesses, cashflow issues and contractual incidents (e.g., late deliveries' impact on a supply chain) – and how to respond to them.

What sits in between such "regular" risks (micro) and exceptional risks (macro) may, in general, be in a blind spot for future business leaders, managers and lawyers. It is in such an intermediate layer that hybrid warfare hides.

---

[19] Sanda Kaufman, How Should the Whole-of-Society Respond to Hybrid Warfare? (2023) 30 On Track 47

Meanwhile, future diplomats and military officers are taught that countries compete with one another using four distinct instruments (acronym DIME). A thumbnail sketch might look something like this:

- Diplomacy: traditionally, diplomats interact with governments and among them; they pass messages to each other and report home about foreign government policies, society's impulses and economic development trends. Diplomats are also used to building coalitions and confidentially expressing warnings and threats.

- Information: each country builds its own narrative and communicates it on the international scene through its culture and the internationalization of their economic champions. The line between this and propaganda is difficult to ascertain. On a different level, diplomats also gather information about the state of the world and the actions of various foreign governments. Information also includes intelligence and, hence, spying activities.

- The military serves both as a dissuasion mechanism and a way to advance a state's interests. Today, it is used as the last option, when everything else has failed. Countries invest heavily in their armed forces. In addition to their classical roles, military forces are also used to preserve peace, for emergency crisis response and for humanitarian purposes (also by third parties to tip the balance in favor of the friendlier party in open conflicts).

- Economic: countries cooperate and compete economically, within the rules of the World Trade Organization and various bilateral and regional economic exchange treaties. They may use private companies and/or public sector entities. Countries measure their influence on the international scene based on their GDP and their trade surplus or deficit. Sovereign debt is also exchanged, with or without strings attached.

Traditionally, each of these instruments has its own rules, the most well-known being the rules of war established through various treaties and international conventions. Players are accustomed to the rules of their own field of action, while the other fields may be totally foreign to them. In a European business school, students will learn about Economic, maybe a bit about Information (through academic exchange programs) and Diplomatic (through geopolitics courses). Law students may not hear much about any of the four instruments.

Hybrid warfare, turbocharged by globalization and information technology, is blurring lines and has created a less-regulated environment where new forms of influence and power are at play. One common factor is that these do not have to comply with the rules of war and as such may have a broader base of possible targets. In effect, warfare, previously limited for practical purposes to military and political circles, may now spill over to all of society.

In this new environment, public planning, business and law students – and citizens in general – should be taught that geopolitical games may infiltrate their everyday lives. But so far, they rarely are. Hence the idea behind this book.

Examples of warfare pervading society are numerous:

- Lawyers may register companies that are fronts for foreign State-supported activities (including criminal networks), and then work diligently to keep them "below the radar" by staying, as far as possible, in apparent compliance with local laws.

- Entrepreneurs looking to finance their start-up through global finance and venture capital may be unaware that foreign States may use such financial mechanisms to hijack patented technology, or to preserve their own, national companies.

- Public services may be the target of disinformation campaigns or cyberattacks by foreign States looking to cause chaos within a competing country's population.

- In court, lawyers may be defending people who are in fact foreign assets, or be representing, consciously or unconsciously, foreign agents using "lawfare" to advance foreign interests (e.g., to silence opponents among its diaspora).

- No matter who you work for, cyber incidents may be triggered by State-sponsored cybercriminals looking to access sensitive data – or trying to force you to pay a ransom to finance their other unlawful activities, or even their armed forces.

- Data theft may, on the one hand, be a purely criminal endeavor (aiming to capture a ransom payment). On the other hand, once harvested, such data may be copied over to a foreign nation's intelligence services and reused to sway public opinion, or to target individuals to use to their own advantage, sometimes as "useful idiots."

- On social media, people may be induced to push opinions that are in fact propaganda tailored by a delinquent foreign nation.

- Elections, supposed to be free and fair, may be subjected to external forces (disinformation, illegal financing and/or corruption) to pursue goals such as destabilization or the installation of "friendly" leadership.[20]

- Participation in a demonstration or resistance movement may in fact have been incited by a foreign nation looking to gridlock an adversary.

- Law enforcement personnel may try to dismantle transnational criminal activities (such as drug trafficking, or money laundering) without awareness of the links between these criminals and foreign states.

- University researchers may be collaborating with scientists who are secretly funneling data and knowledge to a foreign nation's army labs.[21]

- Journalists who are close to uncovering hybrid warfare mechanisms at play (or even their family members) may be threatened, or sued, to silence them or to deter other journalists from investigating.

And this list is far from exhaustive.

In other words, the world is not only more dangerous than what initially meets the eye, but the dangers directly affect a far broader swath of the population than has previously been the case.

When one of these mechanisms comes into someone's view, there is still a strong tendency to approach the risk as isolated, instead of taking a systemic approach that would include all hybrid warfare at play simultaneously. The same myopia applies to the links between kinetic actions (armed forces in action) and hybrid warfare mechanisms (e.g., cyberattacks). Taken by itself, for instance, any one such action might seem, if not innocuous, at least limited in its possible harms. "Yes, a Russian cybercriminal group attacked our company. So what? We've paid the ransom / fixed our servers / restored our data / improved our internet security, and this has happened before to lots of companies." However, if the attacking group is backed by Russian military intelligence; if it has also attacked other companies in a domain that may have strategic significance; and if, in parallel, other actions, such as disinformation campaigns, are launched on our country – well, taken together, these events paint a completely different picture, do they not? Students in many fields now need to be trained to evaluate that picture, and to respond effectively as part of their future employment – but to begin with, they must be trained even to perceive that picture.

---

[20] Recent examples include Georgia (https://www.politico.eu/article/georgia-elections-marred-by-intimidation-and-interference-observers-warn/) and Romania (https://www.ifes.org/publications/romanian-2024-election-annulment-addressing-emerging-threats-electoral-integrity).

[21] See e.g. https://www.striderintel.com/newsroom/strider-technologies-launches-new-tailored-platform-to-safeguard-academic-research-from-emerging-global-threats/

All these reflections should lead us to an unsettling conclusion: the line between war and peace is now blurred. We may be officially at peace with nations that use hybrid warfare to destabilize us, working hard to stay beneath the level of conspicuousness that would trigger a reaction from us. This should in turn lead to some difficult conversations: are we truly at peace with Iran? With China? Are Iran, Russia, or North Korea just messing with their immediate neighbors, or engaged in what amounts to a global war against the western world? In the answers to these questions lie strategic challenges that need to be addressed.

Add to this that what constitutes hybrid warfare may be subject to definition issues. Beyond the definitions and descriptions above, and broadly speaking, some common indications of a hybrid warfare incident include:

- Some illegal activity is taking place, or a democratic instrument is hijacked to serve the interests of some to the detriment of others.

- The incident benefits the interests of a foreign nation.

- That foreign nation may be pulling the strings, despite its public denial.

- The incident takes place in a context of distrust, exacerbated competition and/or latent or open conflict between the country of the target and the suspected attacking nation.

The fact that several such mechanisms are at play concurrently is a particularly strong indicator that we may be in a hybrid warfare situation.

Hybrid warfare is also a moving target. It relies on public policy weaknesses (permissive laws) and on information technologies. It thrives in the freedom space that our Western democracies represent. And its elements evolve fast. Progress made in one area may even inadvertently open another door for new destabilization mechanisms. We are writing these lines in January 2025: we can confidently expect some new avenues for hybrid warfare actions to appear shortly, even as some existing ones may be effectively closed.

The role of expertise in conflict management and negotiation

Some will undoubtedly ask:[22] *What do negotiation and conflict management have to do with any of this?*

To anyone who has been following the news these past years, it should be self-evident that the expertise and diligence of military and security forces, even with their vast budgets, have not been enough to forestall a rapid rise in attacks on Western populations via their economic, social and political infrastructures. But there are many lenses through

---

[22] It is worth noting that most of the conflict management experts Honeyman initially approached asked exactly this question, and/or its corollary "What does any of this have to do with my work?" The answers apparently convinced them, because the vast majority of those canvassed subsequently joined Project Seshat.

which conflict has been studied, and multiple disciplines in which knowledge and skills have led to the development of different tools for working on, with or through conflict.[23]

By 2019, there was at least one security expert (Calvin Chrustie) who had enough experience of how other kinds of conflict management experts worked to see how working with them might help. Project Seshat was formed specifically to create such a working collaboration, starting with an arena for security experts and legal, negotiation and other conflict management scholars to meet and discuss possibilities. During the fall of 2019, Honeyman recruited about 40 conflict management experts from a wide range of fields for the new project; Chrustie meanwhile worked to recruit a dozen security experts willing to engage with these unfamiliar species of professionals, and though some of them required more convincing than others, he eventually succeeded.

These two worlds have rarely interacted in the past, and people with expertise on both sides are rare indeed, so we would like to commend all our colleagues in that effort for their openness to working in an unfamiliar way. We would also like to express our gratitude for their level of real commitment: their efforts over years have not only been for zero pay, but at their own expense for several related costs, such as travel to meetings. If any further difficulty were needed, the project formally launched just weeks before the covid pandemic struck. Once drawn into the discussion, however, the group was not easily daunted, and by the fall of 2020, following copious and trenchant advice from many project members, the project steering committee was able to publish an article laying out the strategy the group had developed to make some progress in the face of these hurdles.[24]

This centered on using remote meeting technology to form and support five teams, each of which was chartered to write one realistic hybrid warfare scenario. Each team included a cross-section of conflict management expertise from multiple fields, along with at least two security experts (with quite different backgrounds from each other.) It speaks for itself as to the effectiveness of this approach that the teams ultimately produced not five, but eight scenarios, which became the foundation for this book. Borbély has since recruited authors for four additional scenarios which round out the topic areas addressed in this work.

We believe the result is the most comprehensive and realistic scenario-based approach now available for the study of hybrid warfare, and for improving the potential for using knowledge and skills far removed from military and security training to help deal with it. Indeed, among many recent books on hybrid warfare there are very few actual teaching texts of any kind.

---

[23] For example, Honeyman is also co-editor of *The Negotiator's Desk Reference* (DRI Press 2017), the most comprehensive work yet attempted in the search for an overall understanding of human conflict and what can be done about it. The salient point here is that this two-volume reference not only required over a hundred expert contributors to write it but that they came from some 40 different scholarly disciplines and practice specialties.

[24] Honeyman, C., Chrustie, C., Schneider, A.K., Fraser, V. and Jordaan, B. 2020. Hybrid Warfare, International Negotiation, and an Experiment in 'Remote Convening'. Negotiation Journal, Fall 2020. This article also discussed some further details of the case design strategy which we are not repeating here.

And yet, hybrid warfare demands that we continuously revisit, challenge, and improve our theories regarding negotiation and conflict management. For those – and they are many – who believe "negotiation" and "conflict management" apply primarily to the relationship between the principal parties and/or their named agents, such as attorneys, we offer some simple, yet (we hope) thought-provoking questions:

- Since the puppet master stays hidden and denies any involvement, and since the attacker himself may be an underling or subcontractor who may not be told the big picture behind his actions, whom could we negotiate with?

- Since the attacker's bosses' true objective may be to sow chaos through the attack, while it is the underling who seeks to get money or some form of promotion, when the attack has taken place, what is left to negotiate? In other words, when a maniac takes hostages, we can offer to trade for the hostages with what the offender truly wants – money, freedom… But if those really behind the attack have reached their objective as soon as the attack is effectuated, there may be nothing useful to us left to trade for.

- We may be dealing with bad-faith actors who will never reveal their true interests and objectives. How do we integrate "unspeakable interests" in negotiation?

- Would our collaborative negotiation and conflict management methods work between "the parties" in *any* hybrid warfare scenario?

Clearly theories around interests, or Best Alternatives to a Negotiated Agreement (BATNA), need revision to prove useful in hybrid warfare scenarios.

Yet even with this new set of challenges, in other ways, negotiation and conflict management skills may be key if we want to create resilient societies and organizations. When a crisis hits, people need to interact (sometimes for the first time) both to coordinate and to prioritize. These processes require the skills of a thoughtful negotiator. The "behind the table" parties to these negotiations need to discipline themselves to postpone assigning blame until the impact of the crisis has been evaluated, controlled and erased. They need to communicate with other key stakeholders (lawyers, insurance companies, clients, suppliers, staff…). And these "behind the table" negotiations will likely be essential even where negotiation between the principal parties is impossible.[25]

Even before a crisis strikes, organizations which take to heart these concerns and redesign themselves for the necessary collaborations will be better equipped. Such resilience may indeed be the best anticipation mechanism. And in this area, the already-

---

[25] Art Hinshaw, Adrian Borbély and Calvin Chrustie, Where is Negotiation in Hybrid Warfare? 24 Cardozo Journal of Conflict Resolution 517.

worked-out teachings about the importance of preparation, as well as many other aspects of negotiation, stand ready for adaptation.

To be more specific, we believe that guarding against attacks, even more than formulating effective responses to an attack, is where the field of conflict management / negotiation really has the most to offer. Yet again, it must be emphasized that this requires a shift in thinking: the "negotiation" most directly relevant here is simply not the kind most people think of first, i.e. what happens directly at a bargaining table with "the parties." In hybrid warfare, for all the reasons noted above, direct negotiation between the attacker and the target is currently unlikely, with limited exceptions such as in ransomware attacks.[26] But the kind of preparation that skilled negotiators make for any such encounter is, if anything, more relevant than ever, and needs to be addressed on a much broader level.

Several articles cited here[27] and in the following footnotes show how conflict management scholars affiliated with Project Seshat have already begun to review existing conflict management literature and findings and to distinguish the parts that seem most useful in the hybrid warfare context. In this new environment, pursuing the path thus opened will involve consultation and cooperation among different professional communities on who assumes what roles and responsibilities as part of a broader conflict management strategy.[28]

We cannot emphasize too strongly that the "behind the table" negotiations – in other words, the negotiations between many players who are nominally on your own side – are where "the action" really is. These often-obscure negotiations are incredibly important in averting, preparing for, or responding to a hybrid warfare attack.[29] A hybrid warfare attack on a company that has not prepared adequately, by contrast, can create an atmosphere of defensiveness and mutual recrimination up and down the senior corporate ranks, or the equivalent in other types of organization. And this disunity is exactly what the attacker wants. So, these negotiations are where expertise in conflict management can make a real difference: not only to a company's preparation, but to its response to an emergent attack, and perhaps to its survival.

Too often ignored or short-circuited, preparation here includes a careful analysis of parties with whom a company or nonprofit should consider dealing. And because the real parties, goals and strategies in hybrid warfare are routinely disguised, that analysis is no simple matter. In the future, military and other security agency professionals, who

---

[26] This is not necessarily a permanent condition. A new article, discusses the possibility that this may change over time, and offers a possible venue. See Honeyman and Tan, above at fn. 2. available at https://drr.scholasticahq.com/article/140835-a-new-management-system-for-a-new-type-of-conflict-singapore-s-possible-role-in-managing-grey-zone-conflict-in-international-commerce

[27] Nancy A. Welsh, Sharon Press and Andrea Kupfer Schneider, Negotiation Theories Engage Hybrid Warfare, 24 Cardozo Journal of Conflict Resolution 543; Chris Honeyman and Ellen Parker, Thinking Ahead in the Grey Zone, 24 Cardozo Journal of Conflict Resolution 617.

[28] Cynthia Alkon and Sanda Kaufman, A Theory of Interests in the Context of Hybrid Warfare: It's Complex. 24 Cardozo Journal of Conflict Resolution 581.

[29] Hinshaw, Borbély and Chrustie above at fn. 25.

may have better access to early-warning sources that could help in this, can and should develop partnership roles with "domestic" firms, nonprofits, universities, hospitals, municipalities and other bodies which in the past have had little contact with the military. There are already some examples, such as, in the U.S., the FBI's Private Sector Office. But much more is needed.

It is worth noting that such prospective larger-scale collaborations themselves constitute one area that will clearly call for expertise in conflict management and negotiation. The creation and maintenance of the military / security / civil partnerships called for here will not be simple: in a common English phrase, these groups are "chalk and cheese", with at best limited experience and facilities for dealing productively with each other. Fortunately, getting dissimilar groups of people to work productively together toward their common good is at the very core of several kinds of negotiation expertise – among which public policy mediation is just the most obvious, and in which the last few decades have developed a corps of known-expert practitioners. Such partnerships will call for talent, consistent effort, and of course funding. But the conflict management field can at least offer one great strength: people who already know how to create effective collaborations between very different people.[30]

Many, many more challenges will undoubtedly appear, and as participants in our group have often remarked, if we don't apply an attitude of humility, our subject is one which will teach it to us. We know that this book is coming out while our collective reflections are still in their infancy. A more enduring academic-practitioner community still needs to be structured around such issues. We hope this book will form part of the impetus for it.

In the near term, companies, hospitals, nonprofits, think-tanks, municipalities and most other targets will continue to lack the resources of national governments in trying to ward off and resolve hybrid warfare attacks. But at least a start is now being made toward providing the foundational materials and courses.[31] These are intended to assist in orienting and preparing professionals in many organizations to become more effective at defending their organizations.

All the contributors to these pages hope that this book will help.

Note: From Project Seshat to the Council on Countering Hybrid Warfare

This book is the culminating product of Project Seshat. The project started in early 2020 (after six months' preparatory work) and immediately had to contend with the covid pandemic's restrictions. Its members met physically twice, in Canada in July 2022 and in Belgium in June 2023. The latter meeting was the first occasion for project members

---

[30] There are even examples of still more creative and perhaps rather startling combinations that have proved productive, e.g. one of uniformed professionals—in this case, police—working with an artist, two psychologists, a conflict management specialist, a sociologist, five poets and an emergency-room physician to design and enact a course for training rank-and-file officers in at least the basic skills of a hostage negotiator (see Rachel Parish and Jack J. Cambria, *The Other Side of The Door: The Art of Compassion In Policing*, DRI Press, 2020.)

[31] The first known for-credit course on the impact of hybrid warfare on law and lawyers' practice was taught in the fall of 2024, by Professor Cynthia Alkon, who heads the criminal law program at Texas A&M Law School.

to meet and exchange ideas with representatives of NATO and of diplomatic think-tanks interested in security issues.

Project Seshat, like its conflict management predecessor projects,[32] was designed to be nimble, adaptable, and open to including a wide variety of people, with a shared entrepreneurial spirit and sense of purpose. The main outcome of the project is, we believe, the first sustained academic effort at publishing on hybrid warfare beyond the realm of military or other security personnel. Prior to this book, Project Seshat produced, among other things, a special issue of the Canadian Defense Association Institute's journal *On Track* and a special issue of the *Cardozo Journal of Conflict Resolution* (both amply cited in this chapter). We would like to take this opportunity to thank everyone involved.

Some original members of Project Seshat have since worked to develop a more sustainable structure. In 2024, they founded the Council on Countering Hybrid Warfare (CCHW), and they are working toward institutionalizing it as a research initiative attached to the Cardozo Law School at Yeshiva University (New York City).

CCHW's explicit mission is to enhance the capacity and respond to the threat of hybrid warfare through a conflict management framework, inclusive of civil society and military cooperation. The Council assisted in formulating and presenting the program of the 2024 Vancouver International Security Summit[33] and is preparing several academic and professional events for the years to come.

Publication of this book marks the formal close of Project Seshat, and future related action along these lines will be by the Council on Countering Hybrid Warfare.

---

[32] See e.g. the Canon of Negotiation Initiative (2003–present) (discussed at https://www.convenor.com/canon-of-negotiation.html) and the Rethinking Negotiation Teaching project (2007–2013) (discussed at https://www.convenor.com/rethinking-negotiation-teaching.html). Together these projects have involved scholars and practitioners from more than forty fields and have produced over 350 published articles and book chapters.

[33] https://www.rebootcommunications.com/event/viss2024

FROM HYBRID WARFARE AND GREY ZONE CONFLICT TO "HYBRID CONFLICT": TERMINOLOGY AND IMPLICATIONS

Leonard L. Lira & Bryan Reyes

Editor's Note: The authors make a significant contribution by disentangling a set of overlapping terms that have confused many. Their recommended phrase "hybrid conflict" offers a way of encapsulating the larger picture and averting arguments rooted in differing professional literatures and cultures. This book, however, was assembled over years by nearly 50 people who reached a consensus that "hybrid warfare" could be used in a broader sense than its original military definition. Beyond this chapter, the book therefore honors their consensus for the time being, while endorsing a general shift to the new term for the future.

This chapter reviews the evolution of the concept of hybrid conflict. Hybrid conflict, a concept that merges elements of hybrid warfare and grey zone conflict, represents a multifaceted approach to understand modern conflict, and requires a multidisciplinary approach to understanding how this phenomenon impacts areas beyond military or international conflicts.

Evolution of the hybrid warfare / grey zone / hybrid conflict terminology

The concept of hybrid *warfare* has evolved significantly over the past two decades, particularly in the context of international relations and military strategy. In common military usage, "hybrid warfare" involves the simultaneous use of conventional military force, irregular tactics, cyber operations, and information warfare to achieve strategic objectives while operating below the threshold of open war. We therefore begin here with the traditional military distinction between "hybrid warfare" and "grey zone conflict." Many writers now use these (and other) terms interchangeably. We will argue that the term "hybrid conflict" is becoming a more encompassing and more useful one for addressing a rapidly shifting set of concepts.

Both "hybrid warfare" and "grey zone conflict" have not only been used interchangeably, but they have also led in turn to many other neologisms in the writings of defense intellectuals such as Frank Hoffman, Thomas X. Hammes, Nathan Freier, and many military and security specialists (Freier, 2009 & 2021; Wither, 2023). Furthermore, both terms have proliferated in the publications of think tank studies and military policy reports, with little theoretical development occurring in the peer-reviewed empirical literature. However, while both terms are related, they have different etymologies. It may help to disentangle some of the confusion over terms to discuss at least briefly how they originated.

Initially, hybrid warfare was primarily associated with military operations that combined conventional and unconventional tactics, often employed by non-state actors. Frank Hoffman (2007) introduced the term "hybrid warfare" to describe adversaries that "simultaneously and adaptively employ a fused mix of conventional weapons, irregular tactics, terrorism, and criminal behavior in the battlespace to achieve their political objectives."

The origins of hybrid warfare can be traced back to the Second Lebanon War in 2006, where Hezbollah's use of a combination of conventional military capabilities and irregular tactics challenged traditional military strategies (Brânda & Sauliuc, 2020). This event marked a turning point, leading to a greater recognition of the complexities involved in modern conflicts.

Early definitions of hybrid warfare focus on the militarized aspects of the activities between belligerents as "...a full range of different modes of warfare including conventional capabilities, irregular tactics and formations, terrorist acts including indiscriminate violence and coercion, and criminal disorder, conducted by a variety of non-state actors" (Hoffman, 2007, p. 8).

Over time, scholars challenged this one-dimensional definition of hybrid warfare by observing emerging state-sponsored hybrid threats emanating out of China, Russia, Iran, and North Korea. Particularly during the War on Terror and the mid-to-late 2010s influence of the Islamic State, non-state actors engaged in hybrid activities to expand their political reach and influence while aiming to operate over a broad geographic area. Another example, the annexation of Crimea following the 2014 Russia-Ukraine conflict, led scholars to use the term to identify combinations of conventional and unconventional tactics that synchronized horizontally and vertically the strategic instruments of power: Military, Political, Economic, Civil, and Informational – MPECI (Cullen & Reichborn-Kjennerud, 2017). The literature started to acknowledge more actors beyond political or military ones, including private civilians as well as multinational corporations, and began to consider additional domains such as cyberspace.

The evolution of "hybrid warfare", while related to the term "grey zone conflict", thus both preceded it and then developed parallel to it. The emergence of grey zone conflicts, which are traditionally characterized by actions that fall below the threshold of conventional military engagement, often involves a mix of political, economic, and informational strategies designed to achieve strategic objectives without triggering a full-scale war (Jordan, 2021). The ambiguity inherent in grey zone conflicts complicates the response strategies of states, as traditional military responses may not be appropriate or effective in these contexts. This has prompted a reevaluation of security strategies, with a focus on resilience and adaptability in the face of hybrid threats (Azad et al., 2022).

This evolution reflects a shift in the understanding of warfare, where the lines between war and peace, military, and non-military actions have become increasingly blurred (Vračar & Ćurčić, 2018; Wither, 2016 & 2023). Thus, grey zone conflicts involve actions that are coercive and aggressive yet remain below the threshold of formal warfare, creating ambiguity and complicating responses (Echeverria, 2016).

As such, definitions of grey zone conflicts also have evolved over time, and scholarly literature now uses the term "grey zone" to depict a blurred boundary between peace and war where adversaries exploit conditions to obtain desired goals without facing major repercussions or total war (Echeverria, 2016). For example, Morris et al., (2019) define grey zone conflicts as:

> An operational space between peace and war, involving coercive actions to change the status quo below a threshold that, in most cases, would prompt a conventional military response, often by blurring the line between military and non-military actions and the attribution for events.

Whereas Jordan (2021, p. 5) defines it as:

> Within the spectrum of political conflict, the gray zone is an intermediary space separating competition waged in accordance with conventional guidelines governing interstate politics from direct and continued armed confrontation. Gray zone conflict revolves around an incompatibility perceived as relevant at least in the eyes of the aggressor. The strategies used are multidimensional and synchronized (hybrid), and implementation is gradual, usually in the pursuit of long-term goals.

Both terms gained further prominence following Russia's annexation of Crimea in 2014, which highlighted the effectiveness of hybrid tactics in achieving strategic objectives without engaging in open warfare (Najžer, 2020; Oprea & Bercaru, 2023). Analysts have since argued that hybrid warfare is not merely a tactic of weakness, but rather a sophisticated approach that leverages local knowledge and escalation dominance that tempts but does not trigger a violent response (Lanoszka, 2016). This has led to a broader recognition of hybrid warfare and grey zone conflicts as a significant security challenge, prompting scholars and policymakers to explore its implications in the absence of a military context. For instance, the concept has been applied to analyze China's use of economic sanctions as a strategy to achieve its geopolitical objectives, particularly in the South China Sea (Wiśniewski, 2021).

Thus, both terms have since expanded to encompass a broader range of strategies and tactics utilized by state and non-state actors alike, particularly in the context of geopolitical competition, and which go beyond military applications. In fact, the concept of hybrid warfare and the metaphor of grey zone conflict have both permeated non-military sectors, such as business and law, thus expanding each phenomenon beyond the traditional (read: military) conceptual notions of war and peace.

The emergence of "hybrid conflict" as a more comprehensive term

In the business realm, hybrid strategies are increasingly seen as essential for navigating complex geopolitical landscapes. For example, business organizations are increasingly recognizing the importance of navigating grey zones – areas where traditional rules and norms may not apply. Dieuaide and Azaïs (2020) argue that these grey zones represent a continuum of social relations and power dynamics that can influence labor and employment relationships in the digital age. Therefore, companies and their lawyers must adapt to hybrid threats that blend economic coercion with traditional competitive practices, necessitating a nuanced understanding of both domestic and international legal frameworks (Duginets & Busarieva, 2021). This perspective highlights the necessity for businesses to adapt their strategies to operate effectively within these ambiguous environments, which can be likened to the strategic maneuvering seen in hybrid warfare.

Moreover, the legal implications of hybrid warfare and grey zone conflicts have garnered attention in scholarly discourse. The concept of "lawfare," which refers to the use of legal means to achieve military objectives, has gained traction as a form of hybrid warfare that can undermine adversaries without direct confrontation (Sari, 2020; Tropin, 2021). This approach underscores the importance of legal frameworks in countering hybrid warfare tactics, as states must navigate complex legal landscapes while responding to unconventional threats. The interplay between law and hybrid warfare illustrates how non-military sectors, like business, are increasingly influenced by the dynamics of hybrid conflict in the geopolitical setting. These developments together suggest to us that focusing on "hybrid conflict," as a more encompassing term, would help those who must deal with it steer past an unproductive overlap of other terms.

Current state of research

Research on hybrid conflicts (i.e., research encompassing both hybrid warfare and grey zone conflicts) continues to evolve, reflecting the changing nature of international relations and security dynamics. Scholars increasingly emphasize the need for interdisciplinary approaches to understand the multifaceted nature of hybrid warfare, which encompasses military, economic, and psychological dimensions, to name just a few areas where this phenomenon is being studied (Andrei, 2022; Dorosh et al., 2019). Scholars are increasingly examining the implications of hybrid warfare for state sovereignty, security policy, and international law. For instance, Kormych et al. (2023) highlight the legal dimensions of grey zone strategies, emphasizing the need for states to develop legal frameworks that can effectively address the challenges posed by hybrid conflict. This ongoing research underscores the complexity of hybrid conflict and the necessity for interdisciplinary approaches that integrate insights from military strategy, law, and international relations.

Conclusion

In conclusion, the concepts of hybrid warfare and grey zone conflict have undergone significant evolution, transitioning from a primarily military-focused framework to a multifaceted approach that encompasses a wide range of strategies and tactics. This evolution has implications not only for military operations but also for non-military sectors such as business and law, and we believe the term "hybrid conflict" responds to this evolution.

As the nature of conflict continues to change, ongoing research will be essential in understanding and addressing the challenges posed by hybrid warfare and grey zone conflicts. The state of research in this area is dynamic, with scholars exploring the intersections of military strategy, legal frameworks, and the implications for international relations and business, thereby contributing to a more comprehensive understanding of contemporary security challenges. Practitioners need to be aware of the latest developments in this research to implement practical and realistic responses to hybrid conflicts in their domains.

References:

- Andrei, C. (2022). The dimensions of military engineer support in the hybrid war. *International Conference KBO*, 28(3), 1-5. https://doi.org/10.2478/kbo-2022-0079

- Azad, T., Haider, M., & Sadiq, M. (2022). Understanding gray zone warfare from multiple perspectives. *World Affairs*, 186(1), 81-104. https://doi.org/10.1177/00438200221141101

- Brânda, O. E., & Sauliuc, A. L. (2020). Hybrid Threats on NATO's Eastern Flank- A Comparative Analysis. *International Conference KBO*, 26(1), 33–41. https://doi.org/10.2478/kbo-2020-0005

- Cullen, P.J., & Reichborn-Kjennerud, E.. (2017). Understanding hybrid warfare. *MCDC Countering Hybrid Warfare Project, Vol. 1.*

- Dieuaide, P., & Azaïs, C. (2020). Platforms of Work, Labour, and Employment Relationship: The Grey Zones of a Digital Governance. *Frontiers in Sociology*, 5(2), 2–2. https://doi.org/10.3389/fsoc.2020.00002

- Dorosh, L. and Ivasechko, O. (2019). Comparative analysis of the hybrid tactics application by the Russian federation in conflicts with Georgia and Ukraine. *Central European Journal of International and Security Studies*, 13(2), 48-73. https://doi.org/10.51870/cejiss.a130202

- Duginets, G., & Busarieva, T. (2021). Hybrid War As A New Form Of Interstate Confrontation. *Intellect* XXI, 3, 2021. https://doi.org/10.32782/2415-8801/2021-3.1

- Echevarria, A. J. (2016). Operating in the Gray Zone: An Alternative Paradigm for U.S. Military Strategy. *Strategic Studies Institute.* https://press.armywarcollege.edu/monographs/425

- Freier, N. (2009). The Defense Identity Crisis: It's a Hybrid World. *Parameters*, 39(3), 81–94. https://doi.org/10.55540/0031-1723.2483

- Freier, N. (2009). Hybrid threats and challenges: Describe... Don't define. *Small Wars Journal.* https://smallwarsjournal.com/2010/01/07/hybrid-threats-and-challenges-describe-dont-define/

- Hoffman, F. (2007). Conflict in the 21st Century: The Rise of Hybrid War. *Potomac Institute for Policy Studies.* https://www.potomacinstitute.org/images/stories/publications/potomac_hybridwar_0108.pdf

- Jordan, J. (2021). International competition below the threshold of war: toward a theory of gray zone conflict. *Journal of Strategic Security*, 14(1), 1-24. https://doi.org/10.5038/1944-0472.14.1.1836

- Kormych, B., Malyarenko, T., & Wittke, C. (2023). Rescaling the legal dimensions of grey zones: Evidence from Ukraine. *Global Policy*, *14*(3), 516–530. https://doi.org/10.1111/1758-5899.13233

- Lanoszka, A. (2016). Russian hybrid warfare and extended deterrence in eastern Europe. International Affairs, 92(1), 175-195. https://doi.org/10.1111/1468-2346.12509

- Morris, L. J., Mazarr, M. J., Hornung, J. W., Pezard, S., Binnendijk, A., & Kepe, M. (2019). Gaining competitive advantage in the gray zone: Response options for coercive aggression below the threshold of major war (RR-2942). RAND Corporation. https://www.rand.org/pubs/research_reports/RR2942.html

- Najžer, B. (2020). Russia and Hybrid Warfare. In The Hybrid Age: International Security in the Era of Hybrid Warfare (pp. 113–146). London: I.B. Tauris. Retrieved November 28, 2024, from http://dx.doi.org/10.5040/9780755602544.0012

- Oprea, G. & Bercaru, R. G. (2023). Frozen conflicts as a tool of the Russian hybrid warfare in the post-Soviet space., 146-167. https://doi.org/10.18485/isimod_strint.2023.ch9

- Sari, A. (2020). Legal resilience in an era of grey zone conflicts and hybrid threats. *Cambridge Review of International Affairs*, *33*(6), 846–867. https://doi.org/10.1080/09557571.2020.1752147

- Tropin, Z. (2021). Lawfare as part of hybrid wars: The experience of Ukraine in conflict with Russian Federation. *Security and Defence Quarterly*, *33*(1), 15–29. https://doi.org/10.35467/sdq/132025

- Vračar, M., & Ćurčić, M. (2018). The evolution of European perception of the term "hybrid warfare." *Vojno Delo*, *70*(1), 5–21. https://doi.org/10.5937/vojdelo1801005V

- Wither, J. K. (2016). Making Sense of Hybrid Warfare. *Connections. The Quarterly Journal (English Ed.)*, *15*(2), 73–87. https://doi.org/10.11610/Connections.15.2.06

- Wither, J. K. (2023). Hybrid Warfare Revisited: A Battle of 'Buzzwords.' *Connections. The Quarterly Journal*, *22*(1), 7–27. https://doi.org/10.11610/Connections.22.1.02

- Wisniewski, R. (2021). Economic Sanctions as a Tool of China's Hybrid Strategies. *Polish Political Science/Polish Political Science Yearbook*, *50*(3), 91–103. https://doi.org/10.15804/ppsy202133

General Teaching Note

Adrian Borbély

This chapter presents the overall philosophy of this book, as well as guidelines for instructors on how to use the scenarios in their classroom. The last section is specific to case #11 – Rare Earth Elements.

Philosophy of the book

This book is the first collection of teaching scenarios on the broad topic of hybrid warfare. They have been drafted by teams of negotiation and conflict management academics along with security specialists with intelligence, cybersecurity, law enforcement and/ or military experience. The scenarios emerged from conversations initiated by Chris Honeyman and Calvin Chrustie, who for several years gathered about 50 contributors from around the world. We are forever indebted to the authors for their groundbreaking work.

The authors initially participated in Project Seshat, now institutionalized as the Council for Countering Hybrid Warfare. This book supports the Council's mission to enhance the capacity to respond to the threat of hybrid warfare through a conflict management framework, inclusive of civil society, and of military cooperation. The authors believe that everyone who seeks to take an active role in society in our Western liberal democracies should become aware of hybrid warfare threats, and of how these threats may impact their jobs, and even their existence.

The scenarios are designed to be used as pedagogical tools in a broad variety of settings. For example, they may be used in courses dedicated to hybrid warfare; or they could become one topic in courses in various disciplines, such as law, business administration, public affairs, international relations, cybersecurity management, risk management, and others. They could also serve as background for discussions on complexity, and on tackling ensuing problems in negotiation and conflict management courses.

Instructors browsing through our collection may pursue different objectives:

- Present hybrid warfare in its full complexity.

- Select one hybrid warfare mechanism for in-depth scrutiny – for example, cyber ransoming or lawfare.

- Discuss the gray zone between open warfare and peace, and some of its potential implications; for example, how non-military institutions have become the target of nefarious actors pursuing military objectives, such as weakening the opponent State's economy, or dividing its citizens through hate-mongering propaganda.

- Present complex challenges, sometimes referred to as *wicked problems*, where the traditional cooperative methods prescribed by negotiation theory may not be effective, and holistic thinking is required.

These scenarios may prove useful not only for introducing students to hybrid warfare, but also for developing the kinds of strategic thinking required to respond to it. By design, the scenarios do not require students to have prior substantive knowledge to engage with them. A list of references is provided at the end of this book to help students and their instructors dive into the topic. Some of the scenarios require situation-specific references, which have been included. The scenarios may also be used to sharpen the skills of those who have prior knowledge of the topic of hybrid warfare, such as security personnel who have experienced similar situations in real life.

Please keep in mind that hybrid warfare is a complex phenomenon, which entails a variety of mechanisms to be used in conjunction with one another. Frequently, cyber, criminal, disinformation, lawfare and other tools are used concurrently toward the same objective. It is difficult (some would say, impossible) to paint a complete picture in a few pages of any single scenario. Therefore, each scenario unveils one or a few of these hybrid warfare methods and may remain implicit about the others, thereby trying to balance efficiency and depth by looking at the hybrid warfare iceberg from one specific angle.

Thus, each scenario takes one, or a few, hybrid warfare mechanism(s) as their starting point. The reader opens the black box of hybrid warfare by starting from the one issue he or she immediately faces – for example, a ransomware attack. Hence, each scenario may be used at two complementary levels: to look at the phenomenon described, or to take a broader perspective, including what may lie behind this phenomenon, to capture the broader logic of hybrid warfare.

Several scenarios may be used in conjunction with one another, as a way to promote a broader perspective. When assigning two or more scenarios to the same class, different groups of students may be asked to read several or all scenarios, but to focus on only one. The multiplicity of scenarios may serve to trigger debate among students, to reveal commonalities such as the complexity of hybrid warfare phenomena, as well as their situational specificities.

Most of the scenarios in the book are based – however loosely – on events which have already taken place. A few scenarios begin with past events, but as is the case in many complex conflicts, they continue in the present and likely in the future. Such is scenario #9 – Nord Stream, which presents historical facts as they happened, but was buffeted by events more recent than the scenario itself. A couple of scenarios – #5 and #11 – look to the future, anticipating what might happen and how those concerned should respond in the event of hybrid warfare attacks.

Some scenarios have translated real events into a different or a fictional setting, with actor names anonymized, although security experts may guess who the real actors are. This serves two purposes: 1) to make the case relatable to learners from different Western countries and 2) to protect the anonymity of people involved in the real story. Certain scenarios do not specify the country responsible for the hybrid attack; this serves to avoid pointing fingers at certain States, to prevent certain students from feeling targeted. In other cases, authors have relied on reports of similar behavior, and chose to reveal the identity of the attacker.

The collection: how to choose which scenario(s) to use?

We have organized this initial scenario collection into four broad, if imperfect categories:

1) **Individuals facing hybrid warfare**: in this first part, we follow individuals embroiled in hybrid warfare situations.

Scenario #1 "Halkan" transports us into the mind of the Chief Information Officer of a consulting company / defense contractor being hit by a cyberattack. Halkan's systems have been taken offline, and their potentially sensitive data may be in the hands of a hacker group that makes monetary and political demands.

Scenario #2 "Oil Development in Ogoniland" puts us in the shoes of Pere, a young Nigerian professional, hired by a Chinese company to interact with local communities around oil fields. Pere witnesses an oil spill, which leads him to face the full measure of the pressures at play, including brewing hybrid and kinetic warfare.

Scenario #3 "A National Crime Reporter" depicts a journalist's legal troubles deriving from his investigative work on the Chinese Communist Party's involvement in organized crime and the corruption of Western politicians. His targets end up using US laws and the US Court system to try and silence him, as well as his fellow journalists.

2) **Individuals being weaponized**: in this second part, individuals are not only targeted but also used, against their will, as agents of hybrid warfare by a foreign entity.

Scenario #4 "Disinformation" focuses on false information, transmitted via a bystander to a party at the negotiation table of an international trade agreement. The individual moves from the status of "useful idiot" to victim of blackmail: if she reveals her involvement, she may be considered a foreign Nation's asset.

Scenario #5 "Life in 2040" leads us to a scenario played out in the future. We follow Julie, who gets hired to negotiate land deals for what looks like a legitimate development project, but may instead be a front for a foreign nation taking hold of natural resources. She hesitates whether to blow the whistle and face potentially dire personal consequences.

3) **Business organizations in hybrid warfare**: in this third part, the focus is on corporations which are being targeted – or used – in hybrid warfare destabilization efforts.

Scenario #6 "NovaFeed" focuses on a media company, operated by Russian and Ukrainian immigrants to the USA, which is the target of a cyberattack by a Russian hacker group due to the stance they adopted toward Russia's invasion of Ukraine in 2022.

Scenario #7 "Money Does Not Come Free" tells the tale of a start-up manufacturing high-tech medical devices which could have military applications. Its founders' quest for funds in venture capital markets leads to the dilution of their capital, and to their invention eventually landing in the hands of a foreign Nation's armed forces.

Scenario #8 "Trouble in Agudama-Epie" follows a Nigerian petroleum executive, employed by a Chinese oil and gas company, who reflects on the narrow frontier between business and geopolitics. His employer seems to be part of a network of corporations seeking to advance China's national interests in Nigeria.

4) **Geopolitical cases**: this fourth and final part consists of scenarios that touch upon geopolitics and competing State interests.

Scenario #9 "Nord Stream" focuses on the pipelines built to deliver natural gas from Russia to Germany by circumventing Poland and the Ukraine. The pipelines were bombed shortly after Russia's invasion of Ukraine, demonstrating the geopolitical implications of this business venture.

Scenario #10 "No Good Deed Unpunished" looks at the project of siting a nuclear power plant in a Balkan country. The project reveals the Bosnian society's polarization, torn as it is between Russia and the EU. Financers, companies, and even some EU officials are drawn into the middle of a high-stakes dispute.

Scenario #11 "Rare Earth Elements" focuses on the global rush to capture rare earth elements and to secure their supply chains for our everyday and high-tech products. It takes a consultancy perspective, where negotiation and conflict management skills and processes are sought to support a global think-tank's work.

Scenario #12 "State Collapse" looks at four failed Nation States (Libya, Yemen, the Central African Republic, and Afghanistan) and at how their institutions were dismantled through a mix of kinetic and hybrid warfare. It aims to illustrate the crucial functions of a State and the consequences that ensue when the State becomes impaired.

Most scenarios have been written from a Western, liberal democracy perspective. Although these cases are grounded (explicitly or implicitly) in countries such as the USA, European Union member States, Australia, or New Zealand, they are easy to transpose into the context of other Western, liberal democratic countries. Three scenarios stand out as exceptions: #2 "Oil Development in Ogoniland" and #8 "Trouble in Agudama Epie" transport participants to Sub-Saharan African contexts. Scenario #12 "State Collapse" takes students to failing Nations in Africa and the Middle East.

Most scenarios start from one hybrid warfare method, and expand to the general phenomenon. Hence, if your interest is focused on one method, we suggest you start from the following scenarios:

- Cyberattacks and cyber ransoming: #1 "Halkan" or #6 "NovaFeed"

- Cyber security and private cyber hygiene: #4 Disinformation

- Use of criminal organizations to sustain State objectives: #2 Oil Development in Ogoniland or #10 No good deed unpunished

- Lawfare: #3 "A National Crime Reporter"

- Disinformation: #4 "Disinformation"

- Appropriation of natural resources: #5 "Life in 2040", #8 "Agudama Epie" or #11 Rare earth elements"

- Innovation theft: #7 "Money Does Not Come Free"

- Environmental threats: #2 "Oil Development in Ogoniland" and #5 "Life in 2040"

- Bombing of an industrial site: #9 "Nord Stream"

- Corruption: #3 "A National Crime Reporter"

- Murder: #10 "No Good Deed Unpunished"

For a bird's eye view of consequences of successful hybrid warfare, refer to scenario #12 "State Collapse."

Suggestions for how instructors might use the scenarios

Instructors may choose to use one, or several of the scenarios in the book, independently or in conjunction with one another. The possible combinations are numerous; therefore, this collection can be tailored to various teaching needs, depending on the context, the students' backgrounds, and the pedagogical points the instructor intends to drive across.

Each scenario is designed to promote an understanding of:

- Hybrid warfare in general – and hence, to illustrate security concerns inherent to the world we live in;

- Certain tactics that may be used in hybrid warfare settings, (e.g., lawfare) and their impact on the targeted organizations and people;

- The negotiation and conflict management mechanisms at play to prevent hits, react to crises and/or build resiliency in organizations and society.

Above all, the scenarios are designed to foster in-class discussion. Each case tells a story that aims to provoke reflection and debate.

Some scenarios ask learners to follow specific characters, and even put themselves in their shoes; others offer a more general, fly-on-the-wall perspective. Authors have considered that most students will be unlikely to enter careers in diplomacy or hostage negotiations. Most also tend to be ill-equipped regarding information in geography, history, cultures, and politics, which may impair their ability to understand possible dynamics of hybrid warfare and negotiation. Therefore, we suggest asking students to consider themselves potential stakeholders in the hybrid warfare situations described in the scenarios. This may lead them to wonder what information they would need in order to respond in constructive ways to hybrid warfare situations. It may also encourage them to collect and share information with their colleagues. This approach can help students learn how to think strategically, identify what they don't know and seek information, make wise and robust decisions, and evaluate the quality of others' decisions that affect them. Such skills come in handy in any negotiation, and even more so when hidden, nefarious actors are involved.

The scenarios share a common format:

- A summary and keywords are provided on page 1.

- The text of the scenario begins on page 2.

- Suggestions for questions to be asked of the participants are found on the last pages.

When handing a scenario to students, instructors may choose whether to include page 1 (the scenario summary) and the last pages (questions). Instructors may choose not to include the questions, for example, if they wish to tailor the question list to their course requirements or to separate the time when students read the case from when they access the questions (which could be useful for evaluation purposes). The easiest way to do so is for the instructor to download an entire scenario, and then "Print to PDF" only the pages the instructor wishes the students to read.

Instructors may pick and choose, from the suggested questions included with each scenario, those most relevant to their audience or course, and to the points they want to make. For some scenarios, specific questions are proposed for specific audiences, such as law students. Instructors can also generate their own questions.

We opted to not offer answers to the questions we included, since each case may be freely downloaded on DRI Press's website, and therefore widely available to students. We believe the questions are straightforward and instructors may easily build a response grid for each question, based on the content of the scenario, the learning points of their courses, and their general knowledge of the phenomena each scenario presents. If further elements are needed, instructors are invited to contact the authors of each case.

We propose several ways of using the scenarios.

1. In-class open discussion

One or several scenario(s) may be offered as readings prior to class. The instructor may send questions ahead of class, along with the scenario, to guide the students' preparation. Conversely, she may raise the questions during class. The scenario(s) may be provided in association with other readings (from the list at the end of this book, or scenario-specific readings) that may cast a specific light on the story. This combination may lead to in-class discussions, facilitated by the instructor or by students.

2. In-class presentation

One scenario is assigned to a group of students, who then present the entire scenario in class, or answer a subset of questions. In this option, several groups of students may work on the same scenario, but on different questions.

We suggest presentations of anywhere between 15 and 30 minutes. Students may take up to one hour of class time, should they also be asked to organize and lead the class discussion. Depending on their specialty, they may orient their presentations in different ways (there is no one-size-fits-all end product).

3. Evaluation mechanism (take-home test)

Students may be asked to read a specific scenario and to hand in their personal analysis, based on some of the questions provided (or other questions devised by the instructor). This is particularly useful if certain scenarios have already been used in class; then a different scenario can be used as a take-home assignment.

4. Evaluation mechanism (in-class exam)

Students may be asked to read a scenario at home, prior to the exam, or during the exam (depending on the duration of exam), and then answer some questions relating what they have learned in class to the specific scenario.

Specific instructions for scenario #11: Rare Earths Elements

This scenario is different from the others both in content and in what it asks of students: to contend with an information-poor and competitive context, to imagine future developments and to develop strategies for responding to what might happen. There are no obvious right or wrong answers, because the outcomes are not yet known.

The scenario consists of a request for proposals (RFP) from an imaginary think-tank – the Promontory Institute – looking to develop negotiation and conflict management skills and strategies to tackle a real issue: access to rare earths elements (REEs), which is, or could become fodder for hybrid warfare. This type of scenario, called *anticipatory*, is widely used in business, physical planning, space exploration, military preparedness, and other domains characterized by complexity, risk, and uncertainty, and with very serious consequences to many.

The REEs scenario also contains a valuable lesson to which we recommend that instructors devote some class time. The scenario authors began their work in 2022, when few were paying attention to REEs outside the industries seeking them for their products. Since then, however, in a surprising (but not unlikely) twist of events, the availability of REEs has become a key international issue fraught with acute conflicts. (Note that Scenario #9 – Nord Stream also has potential for a similar lesson: just as it was being finished in 2022, the oil pipeline created some serious international conflicts, and eventually it was sabotaged.)

In scenario #11, students play the role of Minerva Group consultant teams aspiring to win the Promontory Institute contract. All interested parties competing for the consulting contract must answer Promontory's questions in their response to the RFP. Some students may play the role of think-tank representatives evaluating candidates, and generating a dialog between think-tank and applicants.

The information provided to students is purposely vague. Since they are not expected to be well-versed in the geography, history and geopolitics of REEs, the scenario aims to have students reflect on what information they would need to make wise decisions under uncertainty, how they would acquire it if it exists, or how they would manage absence of information they deem important. The question of which information is necessary for making robust decisions is an old quandary worth addressing in debriefs, since students tend to want it all (especially when it appears to have no cost). They should be encouraged to ask themselves how the information they are seeking would change their strategies (by pretending they already know it). If it does not, it is a sign that they don't need it.

The duration of the exercise can be determined by instructors according to the needs of their course. At a minimum, two sessions are needed: one for presenting and discussing the tasks and organizing teams, and, at least one week later, a second session for presentations and evaluations by observers (or Promontory evaluators). If there is time, evaluators could be given time to read the proposals after their presentation, to formulate their observations, and then present and discuss them in class at a third session. The exercise could also be run over several weeks or an entire semester, with points in time when participants present their progress and get feedback to improve their proposals. Since the topic of this case – international competition to secure access to REEs – is now unfolding in real time, students could be asked to consider recent developments, and update their proposed strategies, as well as reflect upon the quick, at times dramatic, changes which can occur in complex systems. They could also ponder how decision strategies could be made robust to such events. For example, long-term goals and plans to reach them are particularly non-robust (vulnerable to failure) in the context of complex systems.

The scenario itself contains a set of questions to which the Promontory Institute (the RFP issuer) seeks answers. We suggest that instructors ask students to respond to the questions already embedded in the scenario. They might also guide the students through the process by adding the probing questions presented in the last part of the document, and even ask the students to propose more questions they believe should be answered.

Throughout, we recommend that students be asked:

- What information they need/have, and how trustworthy it is;

- Reasons behind proposed strategies – preferably up-to-date information that can be assessed by everyone, but also, for example: assumptions (which, if wrong, could lead to failure); political biases; probabilities for risky variables; and likelihoods of success.

- How they would evaluate success (criteria);

- What they would do, should their proposals fail to achieve the objectives they propose. This is called a *pre-mortem.* It is an important strategic tool with which students need to be familiar. It compensates for the widespread confirmation bias, or tendency to see only how proposed strategies could succeed, which leaves them vulnerable to failure.

Here are a few suggestions regarding the process for this exercise.

Participants should form teams of 3-4 Minerva experts (as would happen in reality), and take on roles within the team which they deem necessary for producing a strong proposal. For example, one might become an expert in rare earth elements (REEs), where they are currently mined, and where else they might be found; another could become the technology expert; another might specialize in negotiation strategies; someone might take on the task of probing international conflict risks, such as hybrid warfare tactics. The team members should agree on the nature of the expertise and describe it in relationship to the REEs issues.

Each Minerva team should produce a proposal to the Promontory Institute. At the end, each team should be asked to present its proposal, followed by questions, suggestions and answers from other teams.

A few observers (depending on the group size) could be assigned either as outsiders or to play the role of evaluators for the Promontory Institute. They should:

- Become familiar with REEs, hybrid warfare, and the challenge of negotiating REEs access among western democracies.

- Develop a set of criteria driven by the Promontory Institute's objectives as well as by the general list of questions provided in the case.

- Pose questions to each team of presenters to elicit the extent to which the team has given thought to issues. Teams should be given the opportunity to respond.

- Issue a ranking of proposals (and explain it) based on how the Minerva teams addressed the task.

- If time permits, discuss the team's internal work process.

The grading for this exercise (if necessary) should not be based exclusively on the observers' ratings, although their arguments could be considered.

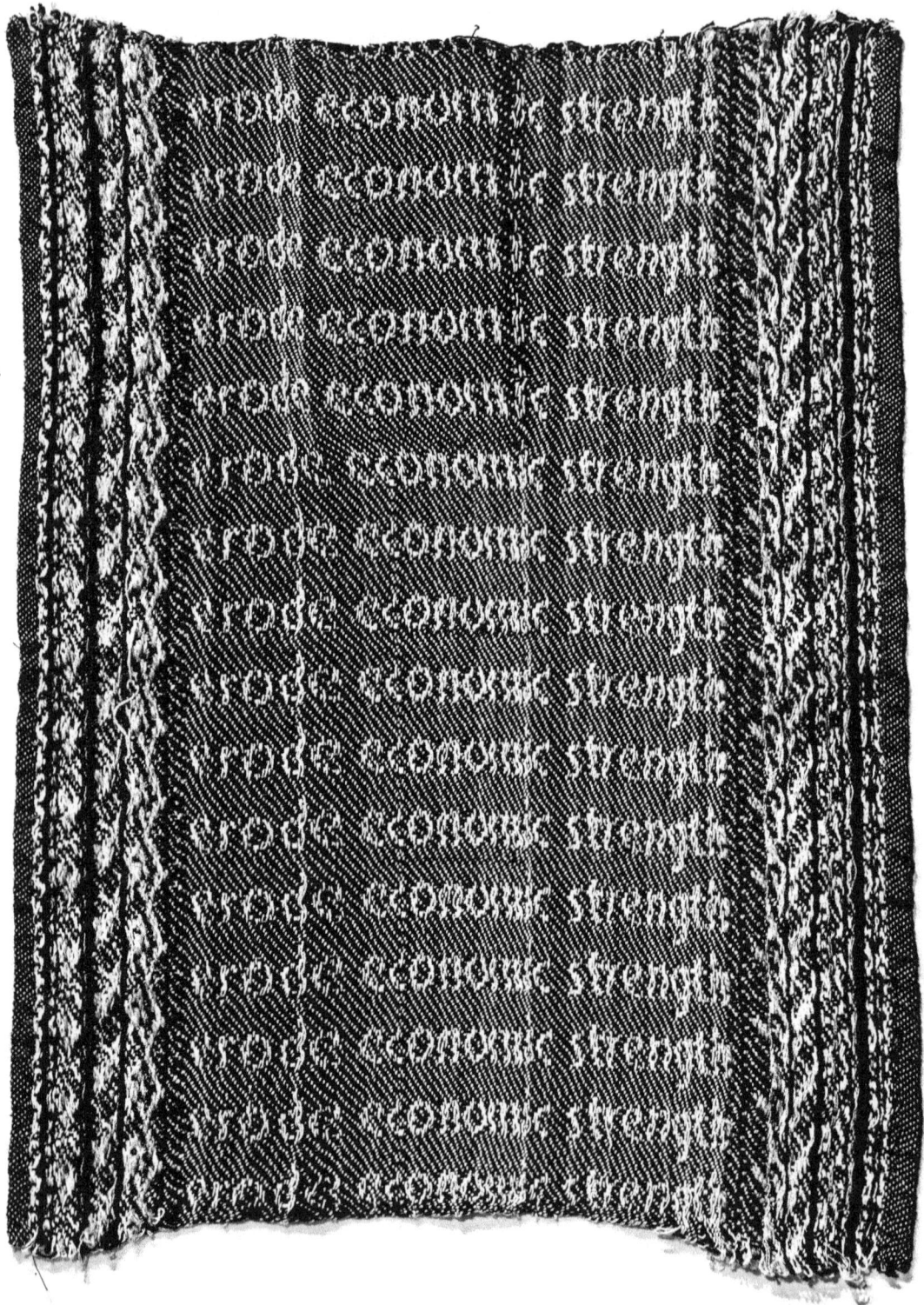

"Erode economic strength." From a series of weavings by Rachel Parish, with quotes from Qiao and Wang's *Unrestricted Warfare* (People's Liberation Army Publishing House, Beijing 1999.) In color at https://rachelparish.com/projects/gentle-and-kind-things/

Part 1:
Individuals Facing
Hybrid Warfare

1

Halkan – Brace for Impact

Christopher Corpora, Anne Leslie, Andrea K. Schneider & Jeff Senger

This case presents the scenario of a cyber ransom attack on a global company which, among other clients, serves the defense sector. It describes the events leading to the full-blown cyber-attack, over which looms the shadow of a hostile State actor. It takes the perspective of the company's Cief Information Officer, in charge of cybersecurity, who witnesses a series of security breaches, but also examines how the different professional cultures within the company hamper constructive action on the matter.

This case describes an all-too-common scenario, but with clear signals that hybrid warfare may be at play. It aims to show the complex nature of a hybrid warfare scenario, with many actors (visible or covert), a complex web of interests, and the complexity of decision-making for the target's C-Suite.

* * *

Keywords: Hybrid warfare – Cyber criminality – Ransomware – Corporate preparedness – Corporation – Defense contractor – Cybersecurity – Hostile State actor – Covert action – Organizational culture and design – Short-term vs. long-term reaction

* * *

Support readings:

- Hinshaw, A., Borbély, A. and Chrustie, C. (2022). Where Is Negotiation in Hybrid Warfare? Cardozo J. Conflict Resol., 24, 517.

- Moty Cristal's podcast on how to negotiate with cyber terrorists: https://podcasts.apple.com/us/podcast/18-expert-cybercrime-negotiations-and-strategic/id1622926747?i=1000576997035

HALKAN - BRACE FOR IMPACT

Christopher Corpora, Anne Leslie, Andrea K. Schneider & Jeff Senger[1]

Disclaimer
Although this scenario is designed to look real, it is not a true story. We believe such events may happen (or may have happened) in a different context, but the scenario as described, and especially the characters, are purely based on the authors' imagination.

John Kyle woke abruptly. It had been a fitful night's sleep. He knew that the coming days would be difficult.

Kyle is the Chief Information Officer of the Halkan Company, a public company and global player in the business software sector. Halkan is a multi-billion-dollar corporation which advises companies and public organizations about their software needs, and tailors IT systems (e.g., Customer Relations Management or Human Resource Management packages) to fit with its customers' needs. Halkan has offices all over the world and, among other clients, it holds defense contracts.

As CIO, Kyle is tasked with the strategic, operational, and budgetary responsibility for the company's Information Technology area, which includes cybersecurity and protecting the corporation's sensitive data. He now faces both historic problems and an immediate crisis.

Ten months before impact

Kyle knew when he took the job that challenges with system security were ahead. While in the past Halkan had been generous in funding cybersecurity measures, the IT team had struggled to stay within the budget to train their IT specialists, purchase software and run tests. Now, there has been talk of future money-saving measures, including staff cuts, that would make his department's job even harder.

In the past, the company had not always taken protective measures that many would consider routine. For example, three years previously, the company purchased "special" security software, but no one knew at the time whether it was effective. A year and a half later, they bought software designed specifically to help detect hacks, but, for some

---

[1] William A. Donohue and David Matz contributed to the discussions in this case's development.

reason, they never installed it. These issues were raised to Kyle's predecessor, but it was unclear how she responded. Internal auditors were unable to determine what happened.

To make matters worse, the company was generally supportive of employees across the company using a variety of coding languages to address their needs, but this diversity ended up making it more difficult for the cybersecurity unit to detect problems.

Five months before impact

More recent actions intended to be helpful ended up in controversy. When Kyle arrived, he set up a "Red Team" initiative, designed to identify security vulnerabilities. The team hacked into the cameras and identification systems that limit access to the C-Suite. While some at the company appreciated the alert of vulnerable systems, others thought this went over the line.

Shortly after the Red Team hack, Kyle approached Marlena Moreau, Halkan's CEO, to fund a security plan, but she dubbed the plan as too expensive for immediate implementation, and a "tough sell" to the Board. She decided that the team must keep working within their current budget to implement the security plan.

In Moreau's defense, Kyle recognizes that she is trying to blend cultures across the company, seeing strong leadership and collaboration as the necessary first steps to promote rigorous risk assessment and a cohesive, comprehensive defense strategy against hacks and attacks. Kyle certainly supports these efforts, realizing that when all these elements align, an organization has a greater capacity to prevent, detect, respond to, and recover from attacks of any kind.

But these good intentions are not always sufficient to resolve internal and external disputes related to such policy decision-making between management, the Board, and tech support. Technology support staff and management staff inside the organization often do not connect, due to differing priorities. The technology staff focuses on their specific concerns while management seeks to address broader performance issues in the company. They speak different languages and have different cultural perspectives.

Disputes with external suppliers persist, as well. Some question the use of outside suppliers for cybersecurity needs. How could they be helpful when an attack or breakdown occurs? How can these individuals collaborate to mitigate risk? Others are concerned that the company does not include all the stakeholders – such as insurance companies, clients, and government regulators – that can be necessary to develop an external strategy for dealing with an attack.

While trying to collaborate with leadership across the company, Kyle is also managing the IT staff, who focus on narrow technical strategies to prevent and detect attacks. He recognizes that it is the people, leadership, management, and negotiation issues that enable the technical strategies to be effective. Kyle believes competencies like "Effective Leadership," "Collaborative Climate," "Internal Integration," "Innovative Culture," "Technological Capability," etc., will be critical to the future of the company here.

Kyle recognizes that these cultural and structural issues may have left the company vulnerable to the current emergency.

One week before impact

Kyle was informed by his team that they had detected an intrusion, and the initial investigation showed that it may not be the first. Assailants had placed various bots and micro-programs throughout part of the system, and his team believes that they may have been there for months, combing through various highly sensitive files, apparently to prepare a ransom demand.

When he learned about the intrusion and its potentially devastating effects on the company and its brand, Kyle immediately called Moreau to request a meeting to inform her about the breach. During the meeting, Moreau was livid. She knew that her Board would need to be informed immediately.

The explanation about how the intrusion occurred would need to be related to Board members in lay-person's terms as these people are not technology-oriented. Many were selected to be part of the Board because of their connections in the Department of Defense rather than for specific skills. In fact, Moreau is not technically sophisticated either. She is the daughter of the former CEO of the company, but is also a former United States Senator, who gained her position because of her brash, direct, and competent management style, as well as her contacts in Washington. At the end of the meeting, Moreau charged Kyle with the task of finding out what was going on so he could prepare a report to her and the Board about their options.

To deal with the intrusion, Kyle immediately called in the third-party vendor who sold the company its "special" security software three years ago. Halkan's lawyers quickly got involved and threatened to file suit.

Unfortunately, a lawsuit will have little practical impact – after additional research, the lawyers discovered that the vendor was a shell company for a hostile State actor. This entity had surreptitiously planted a back door into the software solution Halkan had purchased. When Moreau found out that the vendor was a potential hostile State actor, she called law enforcement and the company's insurance investigators. It is standard practice for these groups to immediately take control of infected servers and allow for a counter-cyber operation.

Impact

Two days ago, intruders, who identified themselves as "The Tantalus Field", locked down the company's system. As is typical in these circumstances, the intruders asked for a payment of several million dollars in bitcoin to free the company's system. But, to add to the complexity of the situation, the Tantalus Field also demanded that the company either supply their own or purchase a cache of automatic weapons to be sent to a third country to help the resistance there. Kyle has never even heard of this kind of demand!

Kyle and Moreau are unsure that Kyle will be able to control the company's response. Law enforcement is demanding that Halkan supply complete information so that they may coordinate negotiations, suggesting that they will use psychological tactics. The insurance company argues that it can arrange the secret weapons deal.

Halkan needs a strategy to coordinate a broader response and recovery plan. As Kyle sees it, he has multiple negotiations to manage:

- With the Board to allow the executives the freedom to manage this as best they can.

- With law enforcement over who is even leading the negotiations and company decisions.

- With the insurance company to either bring them in with law enforcement or to allow them to negotiate the ransom.

- With the rest of the executive team and Moreau to ensure that going forward, the IT department has both the resources and staffing needed to prevent a future incident.

Based on demands from the Board of Directors, Moreau has just tasked Kyle to provide Halkan with broad leadership/management reforms that can prevent this kind of incident in the future. At first, the plan will need to identify the significant cultural issues between management and internal/external tech support and develop a strategy for dealing with the perpetrator of the attack, including determining the identity of that group and their motivations.

All of this plays out as Halkan must also manage its public relations in the face of this incident and must ensure that the Department of Defense is also reassured that the security of one of its primary suppliers is not permanently damaged.

Possible questions for all audiences

1) What elements make you consider this may be more than a mere cyber-attack, and rather a full-fledged hybrid warfare situation? What are the different warfare techniques at play in this scenario? How should the fact that this may be a hybrid warfare situation impact the response to the attack?

2) Draw a comprehensive stakeholder map of the case, separating internal from external stakeholders. Who are the relevant people and institutions that should be considered in this situation and how do they relate to one another? List and prioritize the interests of each of the main stakeholders of the case.

3) What would be the pros and cons of paying the ransom (and delivering the weapons)? How do you interpret the request for weapons? How should it be dealt with?

4) To resolve such an issue, actions must be taken along different timelines (short, mid, and long term). What actions belong to the short-term response? What actions are necessary, but on a longer timeframe? How do you compartmentalize different action timeframes?

5) What are the pros and cons of getting law enforcement agencies get involved? Would you recommend for or against it?

6) What Public Relations strategy would you advise? Should Halkan notify their clients of the attack? All of them or only their clients from the defense sector?

7) What in the description of the events makes you consider that Halkan is a healthy organization, or, *au contraire*, an unhealthy one? What elements in its culture and structure would you consider helped / did not help in responding to this crisis?

8) After such a crisis, what longer-term action plan would you suggest? How would you pitch it? What changes to the management and governance structure would you recommend as a long-term strategy to prevent cyberattacks?

9) All the preemptive actions mentioned were internal to the IT department. Should IT be solely responsible for cybersecurity? Or is it everyone's problem? Across a complicated organization, how can cybersecurity be made a consistent priority?

Possible specific questions for lawyers and law students

Your law firm represents Halkan, with Kyle as your primary point of contact. You have been called in to provide advice about what the company needs to do now, and what they may need to do in the future.

You are meeting with your fellow associates to consider immediate and longer-term actions. You should consider and have ready some initial conclusions/recommendations for each of the following:

1) What elements make you consider this may be more than a mere cyber-attack, and rather a full-fledged hybrid warfare situation? How should the fact that this may be a hybrid warfare situation impact the response to the attack? In particular, how do you interpret the request for weapons? How should it be dealt with?

2) Draw a comprehensive stakeholder map of the case, separating internal from external stakeholders. Who are the relevant people and institutions that should be considered in this situation and how do they relate to one another? Do include the possible regulatory authorities that you might need to contact, beyond law enforcement. List and prioritize the interests of each of the main stakeholders of the case. From these reflections, what would be the pros and cons of getting law enforcement agencies involved and would you recommend for or against it?

3) From the company's perspective, what would be the pros and cons of paying the ransom (and delivering the weapons)? As the company's lawyer, what course of action would you advise regarding the payment of the ransom – and the delivery of weapons? Why? Will the insurer's lawyers agree?

4) What public relations strategy would you advise? As the company's lawyer, would you advise full / partial / no disclosure to stockholders about the crisis? Should Halkan notify their clients of the attack? All of them or only their clients from the defense sector?

5) To resolve such an issue, actions must be taken along different timelines (short, mid, and long term). What actions belong to the short-term response? What actions would you advise on a longer timeframe? How do you compartmentalize different action timeframes?

6) As the company's lawyer, you will be thinking about possible legal liability for the company due to the crisis. Are there specific steps you will want to advise the leadership of the company to take regarding preserving information? Do you want to make sure that all conversations with the Board about the crisis are recorded? Are there other steps beyond information preservation that you will want to advise the company to take to protect itself in the event it is sued due to these

events? What does the company need to do to protect itself from any potential criminal case due to the demand to purchase arms?

7) The company would probably implement lots of changes, based on the harsh learnings of the crisis. What would be your role, as the company's lawyers, in those changes? What is best for your client in the long run to protect against future legal liability?

2

OIL DEVELOPMENT IN OGONILAND

Oluwaseun Ajaja, Michelle LeBaron, Mariam Omotosho & Stanley Omotor

This case follows Pere, a young Nigerian serving as a community relations operative for a Chinese oil company exploiting an oil field on the Ogoni River. Pere was a witness to an oil spill provoked by a rebel group's looting operations and is drafting his statement for the federal investigation commission. The oil spill rendered the area inhospitable, angering local communities and exposing the inertia of compensation and reparation mechanisms.

While preparing his statement, he reflects on the complex web of parties involved, including foreign States with possible nefarious goals, ready to use unlawful activities (corruption, data harvesting, etc.) to reach their objectives. He also wonders whether he is being surveilled and whether his life may be in danger.

This case is set in a specific time period: 2015-2022.

* * *

Keywords: Hybrid warfare – Oil spill – Foreign interference – Surveillance – Militancy group – Religious authorities – Civil unrest – Witness tampering – Death threats – Corruption – Nigeria

OIL DEVELOPMENT IN OGONILAND

Oluwaseun Ajaja, Michelle LeBaron,
Mariam Omotosho & Stanley Omotor[1]

Disclaimer

Although this scenario is designed to look real, it is not a true story. We believe such events may happen (or may have happened) in a different context but the scenario as described, and the characters, are based on the authors' imagination. Pere drops his pen after striking out the last paragraph of his written statement. At noon, he will be filing his written testimony before the Oil Spill Commission headed by the former Chief Justice of the Federation. By tapping the former Chief Justice to head the Commission, the government indicates its commitment to procedural fairness, openness, and accountability. The Commission's mandate is to investigate and prepare a report on the environmental degradation and impact of the oil spillage that destroyed a substantial area of Ogoniland. The spillage has rendered much of Ogoniland uninhabitable for the past six years. The Commission was set up in the aftermath of increasing agitation from Nigerians and pressure from the international community. Pere was both a witness to and a victim of the spill, and the Commission wants to hear his testimony. This would be Pere's first appearance before such a quasi-judicial body.

CIOC and Deity

At age 23, Pere, who played amateur football with the Warri Wolves Academy, had accepted an offer to join CIOC, a Chinese oil company operating in Ogoniland, after an injury abruptly ended his football career. Pere's employment pathway was a newly crafted corporate social responsibility initiative, which CIOC recently embarked on to express its

[1] The authors owe a great debt of gratitude to the following people who participated in the drafting of earlier versions of this scenario, namely Phyllis Bernard, Chris Corpora, Robert Dingwall, John Gilmour, Chris Honeyman and Sharon Press.

commitment to the development of Ogoniland by empowering its Indigenous[2] groups. CIOC made these special arrangements to pacify Ogoni locals, many of whom had resisted CIOC's efforts to explore for crude oil from the Ogoni riverbank. The rationale for the resistance has multiple components. However, the predominant reason was that the riverbanks are home to the traditional deity and have been so uninterruptedly for over 500 years. The deity, in turn, has long been seen as guardian of the community's well-being, especially in environmental terms.

The exploration test conducted by CIOC confirmed that the Ogoni riverbank area has the highest concentration of crude oil deposits. Having secured an oil prospecting lease from the Nigerian government, CIOC pleaded with the traditional chief priest of Ogoni to appease the deity in preparation to commencing oil prospecting and extracting from the Ogoni riverbank. Specifically, CIOC sought the chief priest's permission and assistance in relocating the deity from the riverbank to another part of the community. CIOC undertook to bear the financial burden of the move. Although the community and the chief priest initially resisted the overtures, they reluctantly gave in when the Nigerian government weighed in. Yet, the chief priest warned of impending consequences. As part of the concessions for relocating the shrine, CIOC agreed to construct a community health center, a tertiary educational institution and motorable roads to link Ogoniland with its neighboring villages.

Despite the statutory requirement of payment by the federal government of 13% of oil revenue to state and local governments, that revenue had a history of never making its way to the Ogoni and similar communities. So CIOC undertook to reserve employment quotas to Ogoni community members in furtherance of its corporate social responsibilities. Mindful of the recent oil-spill incident in the neighboring Jessi community, inhabitants of Ogoni also impressed on the CIOC to personally undertake to clean up any oil spill which may result from CIOC oil prospecting and extracting activities in Ogoniland. Subsequently, representatives of the federal government, CIOC, and Ogoniland signed a memorandum detailing these undertakings. By late 2009, CIOC officially began oil exploration in Ogoniland.

The Oil Spill

Pere took a sip from the local gin he was consuming. He rubbed his puffy eyes and tried to recall the incident that formed the subject of his proposed testimony. It happened on May 9, 2015. At the time, he had been in the employment of CIOC for almost six years. That Saturday, Pere was playing football with other young adults in the community playground constructed and managed by CIOC. Suddenly, they heard loud chants and saw six vehicles filled with militants moving fast past the community center. The militants, a local

[2] We note that various terms which have been widely used to describe groups of people who are not part of the mainstream economy are now challenged. A solution universally acknowledged as respectful has not yet been found; for example, some terms that are currently seen as acceptable in English, or even favored, may give offence when translated literally into other languages. We are using several overlapping terms here, and we mean no disrespect by any of them.

group comprising predominantly young community members, who claim to be fighting for the development of the Niger Delta, had gained notoriety within the previous three years. Although the militants had originated as an activist group, in recent years, they had engaged in "illegal oil bunkering"[3], destruction of property, kidnapping for ransom and occasionally, outright murder. Although the group claimed the focus of their anger was foreign interests operating within the oil-rich Niger Delta region, they had recently expanded their illicit acts to attacking local people whom they perceived to be sympathetic to the interests of the foreign companies prospecting and exploring oil in the region. The local community's fear and mistrust of the militants was not helped by the militants' apparent but unexplained access to Russian hardware – and not just the ubiquitous AK-47s, but some deadlier weapons as well. The militants denied any Russian assistance, but doubts persisted.

That fateful day, the focus of the militants' anger was unmistakable. They were chanting "*CIOC go hear am, dem nor won pay us our money abi.*" Almost everyone scampered for safety as they heard these words. Yet, for reasons that Pere is still unable to articulate, he chose to follow the militants at a distance. The militants' complaint was that for the past two years, COIC had failed to honor its promise to reserve employment quotas to Ogoni community members. As one of the largest employers of labor in Ogoniland, COIC's failure to honor its promise had resulted in an uptick in unemployment in Ogoniland that has further decimated their standard of living.

Pere watched from afar as the militants blew up one of the pipelines and immediately began to siphon oil to their trucks and drums. Apparently, CIOC's monitoring team was alerted to the breach and they later claimed that they immediately shut off the pipeline. By then, thousands of barrels of crude had spilled and contaminated parts of the communities' land, farms and water. Pere stayed hidden, observing as the private security company employed by CIOC to monitor and secure the pipeline responded, but it was ill-prepared for the militants' sophisticated military hardware. Within 15 minutes, the militants had outfought the security officers, killing seven and severely injuring 15 others. Pere was horrified to see the militants methodically execute the wounded, one after another.

Several other young Ogoni were closer to the action than Pere. After besting the security team, the militants ruthlessly pursued the Ogoni witnesses. Well-hidden, Pere alone successfully escaped. As such, he was the sole witness to the disaster.

Once the militants dispersed, Pere went closer to the pipeline. He did not have his mobile phone with him, but he took one from a murdered security officer. He called for medical help. Then, he surveyed the scene, making notes with paper and pen that he found in a wrecked security vehicle. He recorded the estimated time of the attack. It took over two hours for first responders to arrive. All the while, the spillage from the pipeline was not contained. Yet, in their report, COIC has alleged that the spill was contained in less than 30 minutes.

---

[3] A euphemism for "oil theft."

Aware of the cost of clean-up, CIOC denied responsibility, alleging that the spillage was *force majeure*, and therefore out of its control – and its contractual responsibility.

Chi-Net

Recalling the latest proceedings at the Oil Spill Commission, Pere doubted that Ogoniland would receive justice from the Commission. Not only had the Nigerian government and CIOC fought the local claim with reckless disregard to procedural fairness, but news outlets and media coverage also downplayed the plight of Ogoniland. With the outbreak of the Covid-19 pandemic, the prospect of meaningful justice seems to be escaping. Yet, somehow, the Nigerian government, through the influence of CIOC, was able to secure about a million vials of the Chinese manufactured Covid-19 vaccine. At that time, no other country on the African continent had received shipment of any Covid-19 vaccines. Surprisingly, the Nigerian government insisted that Ogoniland be first in line to receive the vaccines – a position that contradicted the norm in Nigeria, where the rich and powerful would have been the first to be vaccinated.

The community rejected this overture outright, as the chief priest had warned through a town crier that the Covid-19 pandemic was a "white man's disease," a consequence of the Chinese desecrating the riverbank deity by relocating it from its natural habitat to a less sacred location. The message went on to state that only by appeasing the deity – through its re-relocation to the Ogoni riverbanks – could the scourge be stopped.

Relocation was unlikely to happen anytime soon. Geologically, alternate drilling sites would require lateral drilling, which would be very expensive. CIOC had no interest in changing the site of their activities. Instead, it convinced its government backers that it could swiftly identify and eliminate militancy in the region. To achieve this, it leaned on Chi-Net, a telecommunications company affiliated with CIOC and part of a large Chinese conglomerate.

Chi-Net enjoyed widespread popularity in the region. It was a more affordable and seemingly reasonable alternative to the local provider, NgrNet. However, growing disillusionment among its subscribers had begun to surface. Unverified allegations claimed that Chi-Net had been intercepting communications and sharing data with the Nigerian federal government and the Chinese Communist Party. Though officially aimed at tracking militant communications, the scope of these activities was reportedly far broader, leading to suspicions of widespread surveillance. Legal action was already underway to challenge Chi-Net's practices. A case had been filed in the Federal High Court questioning the legality of its actions, while two additional subscribers had taken their grievances to the State High Court. These plaintiffs alleged that their privacy had been violated after Chi-Net developed a voice detection program tailored to African voices, reportedly used to monitor and track their communications.

The Chinese government reacted negatively; they had threatened to stop installing wireless connectivity broadband across the Niger Delta if the courts found against Chi-Net. As Niger Delta governments had relied on this ongoing broadband construction to stimulate foreign technology investments, such a move would be disastrous to the government's plans to wean the region off its oil dependency.

French and English companies also offered broadband connectivity, but neither of these initiatives were subsidized by their home governments, so construction would cost twice the price of Chinese infrastructure. U.S. contributions were unlikely given its withdrawal following the death of two American diplomats in the region. A series of subsequent U.S. Congressional hearings into these deaths were jeopardizing the ruling party's election prospects.

Pere was aware of these complexities and knew that his testimony could unravel the delicate balance in the Niger Delta. He had received veiled or blatant threats from apparent members of the militants, from his superiors at CIOC and even from people purporting to work for the government, each urging him to have a different recollection in his testimony. Pere looked back to his football career days and wondered how he got here.

He took another sip of his local gin, yawned, and re-read his witness statement. Satisfied that he had succinctly captured what he witnessed, he attached the draft to his email, pulled out his Chi-Net phone and called the lawyer representing Ogoni communities at the Commission. Pere was ready to "face the music." With a deep breath, he sent his attached witness statement to the lawyer, who would file it before the Commission by noon.

Possible questions for all audiences

1) What elements make you consider this may be a full-fledged hybrid warfare situation? Identify all hybrid warfare mechanisms (potentially) at play in the scenario. How might they work in conjunction with one another?

2) Draw a map of all main parties involved in the story. Who are the relevant people and institutions that should be considered in this situation, and how do they interrelate? List and prioritize the interests of each of the main parties in the case.

3) Might Russia be involved? If so, what might be their role and their motives?

4) Companies drilling on foreign soil must often invest heavily in community relations (hiring local mediators, communicating with opinion and community leaders, etc.). These stakeholder management efforts are done under the umbrella of corporate social responsibility. Could they also be used as hybrid warfare mechanisms? If so, how might they be operating in this scenario?

5) This scenario does not present a direct attack using hybrid warfare (unlike most other case studies in this book). Hybrid warfare tools can also be used to reap economic benefits or protect investments. Discuss this more subtle use of hybrid warfare.

6) Communication networks are strategic assets, especially when data theft and espionage are involved. From a public policy perspective, what limits should be placed on foreign companies setting up and operating such networks? What risks arise from granting cellular network deployment and natural resource harvesting permits to companies from the same foreign country?

7) Assuming you do not live in or come from Nigeria, could such a scenario take place in your home country? What would play out differently in your home country? Are there local activist groups like the militant group in your home country?

Possible specific questions for lawyers and law students

1) Can impartial and efficient dispute resolution mechanisms operate in a scenario like this? How do you perceive the role of the Oil Spill Commission headed by the former Nigerian Chief Justice?

2) Can local communities expect to obtain meaningful results given the structural relationships involved?

3) Should Pere look for legal counsel? If you were Pere, what questions would you ask your lawyers?

4) If you were Pere's lawyer, what would you advise him to do? How would you respond to his questions?

5) In the scenario, Chi-Net appears to be accessing data from ordinary citizens without their consent. Is the data protection legislation in your country strong enough to prevent such risks? What can and should be done to regulate access to private data on information networks?

3

A NATIONAL CRIME REPORTER

Calvin Chrustie, Sam Cooper & Scott McGregor

This scenario depicts the legal troubles met by a journalist, in conjunction with his investigative work on the Chinese Communist Party's involvement with transnational organized crime and the corruption of Western politicians.

It enables a focus on the concept of lawfare, defined as the misuse of the law and the judicial system against an opponent. In this case, Chinese operatives are suspected of using the American court system to silence critical voices: their assets sue a journalist based on frivolous defamation allegations, forcing him to invest resources to defend and protect himself. Such very public lawfare strategies also serve to deter future critics.

The case enables students to look at the weaponization of the law against one individual, but also to consider the systemic impact of loose regulations and permissive judicial institutions on creating "cover" for illegal activities by foreign actors.

* * *

Keywords: Hybrid warfare – SLAPP lawsuit – Journalist – Weaponization of the law – Lawfare – Intimidation – Doxing

* * *

Suggested references on lawfare:

- Chaudhury, D.R. (2021), View: how China misuses Interpol to settle domestic scores and stifle dissidence, the Economic times of India (https://economictimes.indiatimes.com/news/defence/view-how-china-misuses-interpol-to-settle-domestic-scores-and-stifle-dissidence/articleshow/86160172.cms?from=mdr)

- Goldenziel, J.I. (2021), Law as a battlefield: the U.S., China, and the Global Escalation of Lawfare, Cornell Law Review, 106, 1085.

A NATIONAL CRIME REPORTER

Calvin Chrustie, Sam Cooper & Scott McGregor

Disclaimer
This case is inspired by real events; however, the story, the protagonists' names, characters, and incidents portrayed in this document are fictitious. No identification with actual persons (living or deceased) and places is intended or should be inferred.

A brilliant career in investigative journalism

The main character in this story is Shane Williams, a former, highly talented officer in the US Armed Forces. Although specialized in intelligence, he was involved on various battlefields, where he incurred injuries severe enough for him to withdraw from active duty.

Upon return to civilian life, ten years ago, he was keen to apply his research, analytical and writing skills to journalism. He started his second career as a crime reporter with the San Francisco Daily newspaper. His main interest, as a journalist, was topics where he saw his fellow citizens and his country particularly vulnerable: threats from transnational organized crime networks, especially the Triads connected to China.

From eight to five years ago, Shane uncovered some concerning stories that included a network of Triads connected, through shell corporations, to several casinos in Northern California and in Las Vegas. It appeared that they had also bought large amounts of real estate in San Francisco and the Bay area.

This appears to be one of the world's most powerful transnational organized crime networks, believed to be laundering billions of dollars for the cartels, including profits from the sale of fentanyl and other drugs to mentally vulnerable people in the US and other Western democratic countries. Rumors have it that the Triads are in fact directly controlled by the Communist Party of China and have hundreds of billions of dollars of dirty money invested here and there, mostly in real estate.

What Shane uncovered, along with a network of trusted affiliate journalists are direct links between the Triads on the one hand, and California and Nevada State and local Government officials on the other. Such links take the form of campaign contributions, as well as donations in the billions, in support of schools, hospitals and other social causes. In other words, part of the money laundered is used to influence politicians, and more is used to buy a name for the Triads' unadmitted business associates in the eyes of the public.

Investigating the story led to mounting concerns relative to the relationships between local and national politicians, Triad leaders, and businesspeople suspected to be members of the Chinese Communist Party and its "United Front."

The United Front

The United Front is a Chinese Communist Party effort aimed at building a network of key individuals that are loyal and useful, to advance its interests. It was first developed domestically (the "United Front Work Department"), before being expanded overseas through various United Front organizations.

Initially, the United Front's foreign operations mostly aimed at controlling the Chinese diaspora. Some, if not most, of their activities are within the boundaries of the law. For example, it uses internet celebrities for influence campaigns on social media, or their assets to produce reports for Chinese intelligence services. It is also believed to carry outright professional espionage operations and to have strong ties with transnational organized crime structures.

This large and widespread network relies on carefully selected businesspeople, expatriates, and artists. Critics say Beijing's United Front goes as far as influencing governmental policies of other nations by cultivating business and personal relationships with elite business leaders, who are in turn influential with elected politicians.[1]

Although the association to the Chinese Communist Party is downplayed, the United Front is funded and supported by various areas of the Chinese government, including the People's Liberation Army and the Ministry of State Security.

A stream of publications

Along with other reporters who followed his lead, Shane published some hard-hitting stories and exposés on crime, corruption, money laundering, fentanyl and links to US politicians, business leaders and Chinese suspected operatives, including people assumed of being either crime figures or Chinese Intelligence representatives – maybe both. Coincidental to his reporting, the FBI, DEA, and Homeland Security began sharing press releases connected to the Triads.

Over the course of the next several years, Shane and his network of journalists wrote several books on these criminal networks and their operations in the US, highlighting direct human and financial links between criminal networks, Chinese suspected government operatives and US politicians.

At the same time, the US government began sharing intelligence reports concerning the threat of China among its national security agencies, as well as those of fellow NATO countries'. An increasing number of reports identified several grave issues, including:

- Cyberattacks attributed to China.

---

[1] See for example this BBC report: Ewe K & Bicker L. (2024), United Front: China's 'magic weapon' caught in a spy controversy (https://www.bbc.com/news/articles/c878evdp758o)

- Concerns regarding fentanyl being weaponized by China against the civilian population.

- Numerous cases of US politicians being compromised by China.

- Accusations of insufficient data protection and security compromissions at global Chinese technology companies, such as TikTok,[2] Huawei,[3] ZTE and others, leading to sanctions and restrictions of activity in various Western countries.[4]

- The unjustified detainment of Westerners, especially US citizens, on Chinese soil.

As a result of a series of national media stories from Shane and a dozen other journalists, coupled with Western Intelligence Agencies' enhanced reporting on the threats posed by China, newspapers and news channels started reporting on these issues daily. Recently, international tensions are increasing and so is the rhetoric between China and the US, including in the military and diplomatic arenas.

Social media posts regarding Shane's reporting on national security issues are either highly supportive, or highly negative. Support generally comes from concerned citizens, as well as security experts from all Western democracies. Criticisms seem to come from automated accounts that are relayed by "useful idiots", people who tend to systematically doubt the quality and ethics of mainstream journalistic work.

Shane has recently moved from San Francisco to Washington, DC, initially as the Lead Reporter for the Wall Street Times on their National Security Desk. Last week, he accepted a position at the Washington Mail as the Chief Editor for National Security and China.

Lawfare in action

In the past six months (i.e., since he started working for media with national markets), Shane has been served with several lawsuits accusing him of defamation and negligence related to a series of articles he wrote. The lawsuits focused on the following newspaper stories:

- An American-born Californian Senator (of Chinese extraction) accepting $800,000 in cash from a Beijing businessman, then distributing it to various State and local politicians running for upcoming elections.

- The then-US Vice-President advising the CIA and FBI not to disclose warnings to several US and State Congresspeople that their lives may be under threat from both Chinese and Russian operatives.

---

[2] https://en.wikipedia.org/wiki/Censorship_of_TikTok

[3] https://foreignpolicy.com/2021/04/30/huawei-china-business-risk/; https://www.bbc.com/news/world-us-canada-63764450

[4] https://www.euronews.com/next/2024/08/12/eleven-eu-countries-took-5g-security-measures-to-ban-huawei-zte

- The portrait of an LA-based businessman (and legal "green card" US resident) who, in his earlier life, was a senior Chinese military officer. Among other career highlights, he is now believed to have run the Chinese Army aerial surveillance unit from 2002 to 2012 and to have been on their National Security Board for Arctic Warfare. In his article, Shane depicted him as an operative involved in the fentanyl (and other drugs) trade and money laundering. A close acquaintance to the LA Chinese Consul General, he appeared to socialize with many Californian politicians on the one hand, and with Triad leaders on the other hand. Many of this individual's US political associates are coincidentally associated with business leaders in the Silicon Valley tech world.

Shane has recently heard rumors that his own life may be in danger.

Some details on Shane's legal issues:

Shane has now been served with three civil suits, originating from various people named in those past stories. Several of the claimants appear to have ties with the United Front or direct relationships to members of the Chinese Communist Party. An element that puzzles Shane: all civil suits target him personally, but not the news organizations he worked for – and which published his stories. The timing of such suits also appears anything but coincidental.

These lawsuits may be characterized as SLAPP: Strategic Litigation Against Public Participation. In other words, intimidation lawsuits, intended to silence critics, who must bear the human and financial costs – as well as possible reputation effects – of having to defend themselves in court. The aim of such lawsuits is for defendants to censor themselves and quit their opposition or criticism of the plaintiff. It may also serve to deter others from voicing similar criticisms. Focusing on individuals and avoiding joining large publishers in the suits may be a means of keeping the publishers, with their deep pockets, from paying to defend the writers.

SLAPP lawsuits benefit from legal systems that are both expensive and permissive of frivolous claims (such as in most of the US States); such claims are rarely convincing and seldom backed by much evidence, the objective being not to win the argument so much as to harass and if possible, bankrupt the defendant. As they are an obstacle to freedom of speech, some jurisdictions have passed anti-SLAPP laws that make it easier to kill SLAPP lawsuits quickly and at little cost. So, the suits tend to be designed such that they can be filed in jurisdictions that have not done this.

To add insult to injury, the subject of the third news story announced his judicial claim by purchasing ad space in a national newspaper, thus appearing to place more effort into publicizing his claim than into pursuing a credible legal remedy.

Furthermore, with the help of online trolls and fake accounts, the same person spread posts widely relaying these ads on social media, adding personal information about Shane (his personal address, his marital status, the age, and gender of his children). The act of publicly providing personal data about an individual without his consent is called "doxing." In this case, it is blatantly used to further intimidate Shane. Few remedies exist in the US, because of weak laws of data privacy as well as the broad Constitutional protection for free speech.

Possible questions for all audiences

1) This case shows a complex hybrid warfare situation. List all the hybrid warfare techniques depicted in the case.

2) Draw a comprehensive stakeholder map of the case. Who are the relevant people and institutions that should be considered in this situation, and how do they relate to one another? List and prioritize the interests of each of the main stakeholders of the case.

3) How much would you be concerned if you were in Shane's shoes? How would you react?

4) Shane is in a position where some of his needs could be met by negotiating "behind the table", i.e., with people on his own side. Whom should he contact (lawyers, public agencies, his bosses, former employers...)? What should he try to negotiate (protection, compensation, etc.)?

5) Are journalists protected well enough against such actions taken against them? What could be done to increase their protection? Do not hesitate to refer to the reports and website of the NGO Reporters Without Borders (https://rsf.org/en). Their Press Freedom Index may be a good starting point.

6) What international coordination would be needed to protect Western democracies from the activities uncovered by Shane's journalistic work?

7) How do you analyze the elements uncovered and published by Shane through his investigative efforts? Do you deem realistic the portrait he is drawing of the situation, especially the link between a foreign government and transnational organized crime?

8) How may a State, such as the USA in this scenario, react to such actions taken on their soil by a foreign government and its assets? Rate different types of reactions (diplomatic protest, economic retaliation, threat of military action, deportation of foreign assets, etc.) in terms of probability and political acceptability. What could be the long-term effects of such actions or inaction?

9) More and more, people's private information is being revealed on the internet, to cause harm to people and organizations, or in retaliation for otherwise unrelated actions. How should society deal with such a phenomenon? Do you feel that your country's laws on data protection are sufficient? Can anything be done by individuals to curb these practices?

Possible specific questions for lawyers and law students

As a lawyer, you are meeting with your associates to consider how best to advise your client. You should consider and prepare some initial conclusions/recommendations for each of the following:

1) If you were Shane's lawyer, what would you advise him to do in this situation?

2) If you were the lawyer for Shane's current employer, what course of action would you recommend to your client? Would you try to coordinate a response with Shane's lawyers?

3) If you were the designated judge in any of the lawsuits, how would you approach such a case? Discuss the different arguments that the legal representation for Shane (and/or his employer) may develop and how much merit they would have.

4) Would you advise negotiation or ADR mechanisms (esp. mediation) for Shane to try to solve the lawsuits he is involved in?

5) Shane's work has led to uncovering criminal activities, but also financial links between a political actor, local politicians, and a web of businesses, some legal, some clearly illegal. Are your country's laws efficient at preventing such criminal activities? Is your country's legal system well-equipped to prosecute people involved in such activities?

6) This case demonstrates the possible use of SLAPP lawsuits and doxing in hybrid warfare. Should the legislature (in your country) act against these phenomena? How?

7) The cases here are based in US law and judicial procedures. Are laws in other countries generally / your country in particular more or less protective against frivolous lawsuits and doxing? Are there any other kinds of statute that could affect these cases that might exist in your country, but not in the US?

8) The news media environment changes rapidly in the digital world. In corporate media, reporters describe a reduced capacity to undertake crucial investigations regarding hybrid warfare threats that combine illicit foreign and domestic business elites, organized crime, and hostile state actors or proxies, particularly as outsized defamation claims from these threat networks mount and have the effect of "chilling" reporting. At the same time, journalists who take advantage of modern technology to report independently describe an inability to secure legal threat coverage and insurance. Are your nation and related jurisdictions doing enough to protect the "Fourth Estate"? What legal solutions would you suggest?

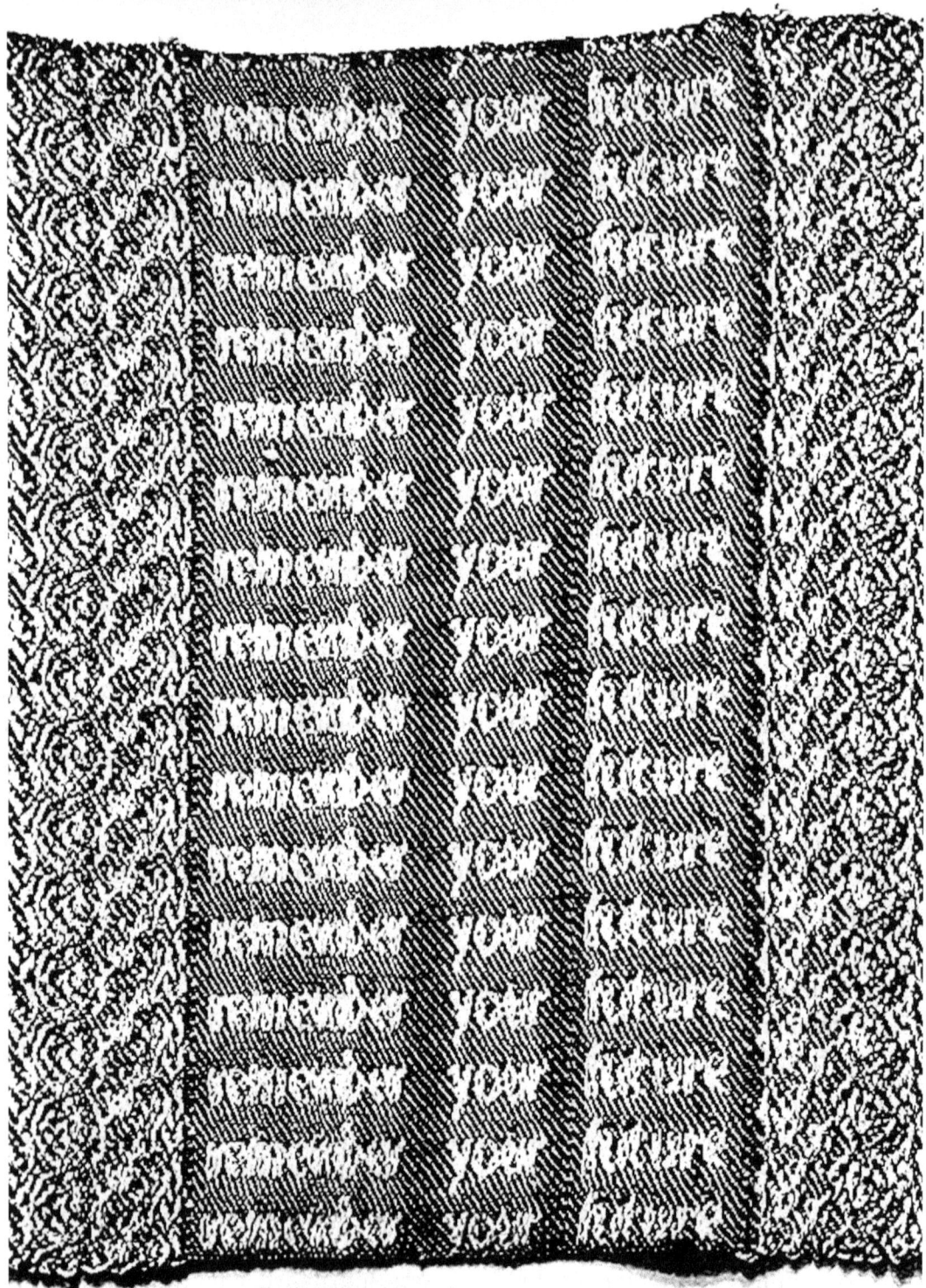

"Remember your future." From a series of weavings by Rachel Parish, with quotes from Qiao and Wang's *Unrestricted Warfare* (People's Liberation Army Publishing House, Beijing 1999.) In color at https://rachelparish.com/projects/gentle-and-kind-things/

Part 2:
Individuals Being Weaponized

4

DISINFORMATION – PART OF A BUNDLE. HOW CAN MALIGN ACTORS TARGET ANY ONE OF US?

Kamil Mikulski & Christopher A. Corpora

This case involves two civil servants, who live rather regular lives as a married couple. Jane works for the Ministry of Health, while John works for the Ministry of Energy; his job leads him to contribute to the preparation of the negotiation of a new Free Trade Agreement with a neighboring State.

Jane has suffered from drug addiction and has discussed it with strangers online. She becomes the target of a malign actor, who befriends her, before starting to feed her with information relevant for her husband's work. The flow of information quickly becomes bilateral, with Jane providing her "friend" Mark with information relating to that work.

It later becomes apparent that Jane and John have been microtargeted by malign actors from a third nation, interested in stalling current FTA negotiations and willing to use different cybercriminal methods (hacking, spread of misinformation, fake social media accounts) for influence purposes.

* * *

Keywords: Hybrid warfare – Weaponization of an individual – Useful idiot – Misinformation – Disinformation – Influence – International negotiation – Cyber hygiene

* * *

References:

- Caramancion, K. M., Li, Y., Dubois, E., & Jung, E. S. (2022). The Missing Case of Disinformation from the Cybersecurity Risk Continuum: A Comparative Assessment of Disinformation with Other Cyber Threats. Data, 7(4), 49. https://doi.org/10.3390/data7040049

- Garcia-Camargo, I. (2021). Disinformation 2.0: Trends for 2021 and beyond. Hybrid CoE Working Papers.

- Wardle, C. & Derakhshan H. (2017). Information disorder: Toward an interdisciplinary framework for research and policy making.

Disinformation – Part of A Bundle.
How Can Malign Actors Target Any One of Us?

Kamil Mikulski & Christopher A. Corpora

Preamble

Disinformation is a phenomenon that exists within an information space. For it to thrive, communication is essential, whether it is bi-directional or one-directional. There is no universally-recognized definition of disinformation, but for the purpose of this case study, it can be viewed as "the purposeful spread of false, misleading, or exaggerated content, or the use of fake online accounts or pages designed to purposefully manipulate or mislead users" (Garcia-Camargo, 2021, p. 7).

Disinformation is frequently used as a weapon against entire societies or social groups, but it can equally target smaller entities, even individuals. Malign actors use diversified strategies to reach their audience, and disseminate disinformation across multiple media: magazines, social media platforms or encrypted channels. Even though we commonly associate it with trolls, it can be spread by bots or cyborgs – accounts administered partly by human beings, partly by computers. There are also cases when it becomes professionalized and employed by whole companies of trolls, called troll farms. In any case, it is the intent of the malign actor and the existence of manipulative elements that constitute disinformation rather than mere misinformation.

Only where there is an information flow can there be an information disorder, a part of which is disinformation (Wardle & Derakhshan, 2017, p. 5). When discussing disinformation, much of the attention is centered on the phenomenon itself or on the perpetrators – malign actors who intentionally deceive and manipulate their audience. Moreover, scholars and policymakers debate how to contain this threat or how to bolster societal resilience, to mitigate its harmful societal effects.

In effect, the focus is largely on the present, with little attention given to the evolution of the threat and its future potential to influence hearts and minds. Disinformation can affect and victimize an individual outside the focus area. These spillover effects can either be targeted or unintended outcomes. The shambolic nature of these cascading effects supports the desired effect of chaos-focused disinformation operations, which aim to destabilize a target audience from within.

The future of disinformation may introduce new tactics, techniques, and procedures designed to exploit our vulnerabilities in even more sophisticated ways. Microtargeting, leveraging multiple platforms, and exploiting human weaknesses are tactics already employed by these malign actors. Additionally, disinformation rarely operates in isolation — it is typically used in tandem with other non-kinetic hybrid threats, such as cyberattacks (Caramancion et al., 2022).

Characters

This case study tells the story of Jane – not a politician, nor an employee of a security service, but an ordinary government employee – who was microtargeted by malign actors. This attack was neither instigated, nor provoked by her. However, she inadvertently contributed to her predicament through poor cyber hygiene and questionable transparency.

Jane is a citizen of Libera, married to John. She works as a technical advisor for the Liberan government at the Ministry of Health. Jane considers her working environment particularly stressful and demanding, so she has been reaching for drugs to stay up longer and perform better. Her best-kept personal secret is that she is a high-functioning drug addict.

John is also a citizen of Libera, who also works for the government, at the Ministry of Energy. He holds a senior position and must work long and odd hours. His hobby is motorcycles. He is a supportive husband and one of the only people who know of Jane's addiction.

Mark is a virtual acquaintance of Jane's. She met him in an online support group.

Libera is a Federal Republic and liberal democracy located somewhere on Earth. It is currently negotiating a Free Trade Agreement (FTA) with neighboring Agraria. It is a developed economy, has vast natural resources reserves, and its society enjoys a high standard of living. Liberans living by the Liberan-Agrarian border fear that increased trade in natural resources could damage the environment and have negative effects on their communities.

Agraria is a developing country and a liberal democracy. It looks for natural resources to support its growing industry. Through negotiation, it is looking to develop international trade with its regional partners. Agraria would rather trade with Libera than Rusovia in hope for technology transfers.

Rusovia is a Federal Republic with an authoritarian regime, which shares a border with both Libera and Agraria. It is known for aggressively pursuing its political objectives and weaponizing disinformation to weaken and polarize societies in other countries. Rusovia's population remains rather poor, even though the country is rich in natural resources. It looks for new markets and eyes Agraria.

Part 1 - Jane and John

It was a Friday evening, and the weekend was just around the corner. Jane skimmed through the local news, waiting for John to join her so they could watch a series and unwind after an intense week. John was deep in conversation about motorcycle matters with his online community. When he is not working at the Ministry, he spends as much time as he can exploring all kinds of things related to vehicles. She knows these moments are precious to him as he works hard on setting the scene for the Liberan negotiating team in Free Trade Agreement (FTA) negotiations with Agraria. Jane does not share her husband's interest, but that has never been an issue. After all, she has her own hobbies and a no-less-demanding job, and she too deserves some me-time.

Despite the fast pace of work, Jane is praised as a high-performer and an overachiever. However, few people know that there is a darker side to her productivity. She used to maintain her long working hours by regularly using illegal stimulants. At times, it was difficult to conceal her drug addiction from her boss and colleagues, but she was quite fortunate – since the pandemic, the Ministry had become more amenable to remote work. She looks out the window and wonders that if anyone were to find out, things would not go well for her. Such a revelation would undoubtedly erode trust, lead to questions about the validity of her work, and potentially cast a shadow over the Ministry. Personally, Jane feels she might be relegated to a less visible role or advised to take an extended leave, which would derail her career trajectory. Alternatively, she could simply be fired.

Her grim contemplations were suddenly interrupted with a burst of laughter from behind John's screen. "No way! You didn't!" she heard. She had no idea what was going on there, but that little distraction was enough to reroute her thoughts to something more pleasant. Sometime later John joined her on the couch, and they finally could watch their favorite series and rest a little bit after that long day.

Part 2 - Leaking data

"We are writing to let you know of a data security incident that may have involved your personal information," was the first thing Jane read the next Monday morning when she opened her office email application on her phone. It was not the first time she had seen that message in her lifetime, and it caused more irritation than terror. She thought sleepily that she would have to update her password once again, since whichever of the portals she was signed into could not keep her data safe.

When she returned from work, she found her husband at home, clearly agitated. He explained that the previous day, he had been chatting with friends from his online motorcycle club. They were reminiscing and sharing laughs over past experiences. When it was his turn, and in response to stories about the troubled youth of some club members, he half-jokingly and half-seriously shared a bit of their family history. He mentioned that someone close to him had struggles with drug addiction and had made poor choices in the past, including stealing from their own family. Now, he said, that revelation seemed to be drawing more attention than he had anticipated.

After hearing more details, Jane comforted her husband. While she considers his actions thoughtless, he has not said anything that could be directly linked to her. Everyone knows it is better to be safe than sorry, and there are plenty of people online that one should not trust. For her part, she believes this nasty moment would be lesson enough to deter him from making similar mistakes in the future. Jane then shared about her day, especially about the security breach she had discovered that morning. It turned out the hacked database belonged to the Ministry of Health and the digital footprints led to hackers associated with Rusovia.

The very next morning, Jane opened her computer to check her social media. Immediately, her eyes were drawn to a prominent advertisement banner: "Thinking of your health? Try our product!" Accustomed to aggressive and nonsensical marketing, she initially brushed off such banners. However, when she noticed that every other "suggested for you" post related to alcohol, drugs, or other medical topics, she began to suspect something was amiss with her browser. She decided to visit the usual forums where she had previously sought support during her difficult times of more intense addiction. She tried to maintain a low profile on social media and added as little information to her account as possible. This strategy had helped her feel secure enough to even exchange messages and share experiences with other users.

When Jane checked these groups, she immediately noticed a negative change. Most were now inundated with new posts: targeted articles, promotions for new "remedies," and discussions from long-time users venting about their overflowing inboxes. Apparently, many netizens had been contacted by strangers – some received spam on their emails, others on social media, and some even received phone calls or text messages from dubious companies. However, everyone seemed to tie this unnerving, targeted attention back to a recent data breach at the Ministry of Health. While Jane found it disconcerting, she figured there were worse things in life than being contacted by spammers. For her part, she only found an ordinary message from one of the forum users, named Mark.

Part 3 - Is a friend in need always a friend indeed?
Jane had been observing Mark engage in various threads for several months and remembered often agreeing with his posts. This time, he reached out to her to complain about "their" forum being spammed again, suggesting that the moderators should intervene. Jane engaged with the topic, and the ensuing conversation turned out to be witty and fun. She learned that Mark works for the Association for Cross-Border Cooperation, where he analyzes the impact of government regulation on the environment and people's lives. Ultimately, Mark expressed his fatigue with their forum being continuously raided by scammers and trolls and suggested moving to a popular messaging app with encrypted communication. Jane happily agreed, and they exchanged numbers. After all, she interacted with most of her friends – both real and virtual – through messaging apps.

As a few weeks passed, Jane found her acquaintance with Mark growing and developing. They spent a lot of time exchanging messages and recordings, discussing her work, the effects of governmental policy on ordinary people's lives, and potential solutions to assist them. She appreciated his good heart and caring nature – a contrast to some of her colleagues at the Ministry. She also spoke of her husband, whom she barely sees due to the ongoing Liberan-Agrarian negotiations over the FTA. Although the draft agreement was largely complete, some areas still required further negotiation rounds. As usual,

John's unit worked long hours to prepare the negotiating team and provide them with all the necessary data. Most recently, they strived to collect the necessary data to justify the exclusion of carbohydrate trade in the FTA.

Quite unexpectedly, Mark sent her studies containing statistics and personal accounts detailing the detrimental effects of Liberan energy policies on the environment and the way of life of people living by the Liberan-Agrarian border. Jane felt this was exactly what John needed to finalize his inputs. She shared the studies with her husband, who seemed quite pleased to receive such useful and timely resources. A statistics-based study on the issues in question was welcomed, especially as it saved some work for the already over-stretched unit and provided additional context. She did not hesitate to mention this to Mark. He was very pleased and thanked Jane for her efforts. "How about I send you some similar studies from time to time? We have a network of experts," Mark suggested. "We would need some information on what is going on in your husband's unit to better match our studies to your needs," he added.

For the next few weeks, Jane supplied Mark with information and directions about John's unit's work and she was happy, in return, to pass on the stream of useful data that Mark kept forwarding. However, it was only after the final negotiation round that she became aware that something had gotten out of hand. John's colleagues, who were personally involved in the negotiations, suspected that the Agrarian team appeared to know their red lines and arguments. The final negotiation round went terribly, and the negotiators from Agraria seemed uninterested in setting any further round for a definite time, apparently knowing that Libera was not keen to liberalize trade in carbohydrates.

The sudden stall in negotiations and the surprising behavior of the negotiators raised questions about the strategy of the negotiating team. To make matters worse, John's team ran a secondary validation process during which they discovered inconsistencies in the data they had been fed with. Jane's mind raced with questions and potential implications. Was it possible that Mark, the good comrade, had been feeding her inaccurate information? Could he have any connection with the Agrarian negotiators? She wanted to confront him as soon as possible. She sent him an angry message, questioning the quality of the data, and interrogating him about passing information outside of their private chat. He responded promptly: "I am sorry to hear that the negotiating round did not go as you expected. As for the data, this must have been due to some miscommunication – I will do my best to supply better data in the future." Still agitated, Jane responded that there would be no more exchanges and she had lost all trust in him. When she checked the app later in the evening, she was surprised to discover that the number he used had removed his messages and that he had disappeared from social media too. She tried to call him, but the number was not available.

The next day, her phone vibrated with a new notification from a messaging app, from an unknown number: "Dear Jane, it has come to our attention that for a few years, you have been consulting specialists about a certain matter and that recently you forged a peculiar friendship with a person from a support forum." Below, she saw a few screenshots

– one from her medical records and a few from her exchanges with Mark. She quickly recognized some messages where she provided insights from John's team, but there were also other, intimate messages she had never written. Jane also saw a screenshot of her discharge from a mental hospital – one to which she had never been. She felt a chill and typed nervously: "These screenshots are fake! What do you want from me?"

Soon after, she saw a response. "Fortunately for you, we understand completely that it would be best for everyone if none of these messages were revealed to others. They might not be as forgiving as we are. We only ask that you continue helping the good people, and who knows, maybe that help could be mutually beneficial?" As she pondered her next move, she saw the typing indicator signaling an incoming message: "By the way, how's your husband? We are big fans of motorcycles too! We understand he might be having a difficult period at work but surely, he would appreciate it if you took him out somewhere, maybe to a racing gig he really wanted to attend. All we need is a little gesture of goodwill on your end. We'd like you to help secure some public funding for a few friendly organizations." "I must think it over," she wrote. "Very well, we'll be contacting you soon."

Possible questions for all audiences

1) What elements seem to indicate that we are in a hybrid warfare situation? What are the different tactics at play in this scenario? How do they play in conjunction with one another?

2) Draw a stakeholder map including all involved parties, i.e., a graphic representation of all actors, with arrows between them indicating support or opposition. Identify the main interests and values of the main actors.

3) This seems to be a patiently and well-prepared plan from the nefarious actors. How to interpret this?

4) The lack of cyber hygiene of the main characters (Jane and John) may seem outrageous; however, the scenario does seem awfully realistic. Discuss.

5) What preventive measures (at societal, organizational and/or individual levels) would you advise to avoid such scenarios?

6) Organizations are vulnerable because of their staff's conduct. What tools are (or could be) used to target individuals? How should organizations work with their members to increase cybersecurity? Does the generalization of remote work make individuals better targets for hybrid warfare efforts?

7) This case seems to exemplify the butterfly effect (a small action with huge consequences). Hybrid warfare is characterized by the fact that it does not aim at military targets but may aim at large or small organizations, or public services. Specific individuals (including with limited public exposure) may also be targeted. Discuss.

8) If you were Jane at the end of the scenario, what would you do? Please list her alternatives, with pros and cons for each one, before stating your preferred course of action.

9) Should Jane be punished for her actions? Should John? More generally, should people who are being used without their consent be considered partially liable for the damage created?

Possible specific questions for lawyers and law students

1) You are an attorney and Jane hires you for advice. What would you suggest her best course of action to be? What are the risks attached to each alternative at her disposal?

2) You are an attorney and John hires you for advice. What would you suggest his best course of action to be? What are the risks attached to each alternative at his disposal?

3) Should John and Jane hire the same lawyer? Would that create a conflict of interest? If so, how would lawyers address it?

4) Imagine the Minister of Energy investigates and discovers that the data channeled by both Jane and John to Libera's negotiating team comes from shady sources. What do they risk in terms of their employment and in criminal terms? (Assume the applicable law in both areas is that of the jurisdiction where your course is based.)

5) Consider negotiation in general: how to ensure confidentiality? How to ensure that the information parties rely on is legitimate?

6) The case describes two countries competing for the natural resources of a third one. Where do you place the limit between healthy competition and unlawful conduct? Do Nation-States have legal recourse to deal with unlawful conduct emanating from another Nation-State? If this exists, would it be effective?

5

LIFE IN 2040

Peter S. Adler, Calvin Chrustie, Sam Cooper, Daniel Druckman,
Noam Ebner & Tania Sourdin

This case involves a young character, Julie, immersed in a post-modern world where tensions are high and hybrid warfare mechanisms at full play. She is offered a career opportunity in a somewhat shady, yet stable job. After accepting it, she discovers that she may find herself at the heart of a foreign nation's efforts to seize assets from her home country.

The case walks the reader through the hardship of life in the context of climate deregulation, international tensions, and economic precariousness. Julie is portrayed as a representative of the younger generation and appears torn in a dilemma between two career paths, one of which would fulfill her values, and the other which would respond to her interests (should she be inclined to close her eyes to certain aspects of her employer's activities). Once she accepts this latter job opportunity, she starts unveiling the possible hidden agenda that she will be tasked with implementing. As she reflects whether to blow the whistle, she realizes that she is under surveillance and fears for her well-being.

This case study is particularly useful to show a diversity of hybrid warfare techniques used in conjunction with one another. It also bridges the gap between global politics and the life of an individual, offering this double focus on international affairs and their effect on the life of a particular citizen.

* * *

Keywords: Weaponization of an individual – Whistleblower – Economic warfare – Covert appropriation of natural resources – Futuristic scenario

Life in 2040

Peter S. Adler, Calvin Chrustie, Sam Cooper, Daniel Druckman,
Noam Ebner, & Tania Sourdin[1]

Preamble

There is increasing division among populations and corporations as the fight to influence Western society continues to divide democratic nations. Disinformation is being created autonomously and is spread using sophisticated artificial intelligence programs across all social media platforms – sadly, the world is at war with itself. The culprits behind these big data exploits, which try to sway sentiment and incite division, come from all walks of life and may be led by powerful Big Tech influencers, and have adopted ideologies based on any number of factors. Social justice, environmental activism, financial activism, protest groups, radicalization, fanaticism, extremism, and terrorism all have a place in this conflict-prone environment.

With natural resources rapidly becoming more and more difficult to access, nations play the winner-takes-all game of supply chain domination. Conflict is everywhere and the threat of a global war becomes a sobering reality. How did things progress so subtly? What were the indicators and hidden actions that caused peaceful nations to undermine former trade partners and allies?

The multidimensional issues are rooted in the ever-changing needs of a growing global population, in historical differences and in an unwillingness to trust. Peace follows war, they say. Or perhaps the façade of a peaceful world is what most want to believe. Or as Thomas Jefferson observed, "peace is just an interlude in which everyone rearms." Unlike the movie The Matrix, there are no red and blue pills to choose. You either go along with what governments and corporate enterprise decide your world is, or you see what is going on and act.

2040 Auslandia - Part One

Julie started the day in the normal way. After checking her phone to find out where she would be working, she got ready to travel into the city for face-to-face work. It was annoying to travel for two hours on public transport, but this was a condition of the government employment scheme that she and many under 40-year-olds were subjected to. Often, the under 40's were referred to as "the precariat" and Julie thought that this descriptor was

---

[1] Tania Sourdin served as primary drafter.

appropriate. Work, food, shelter and survival were indeed precarious. Whilst some of her work was remote, there was still an insistence that regular face-to-face work be undertaken. At least there would be air conditioning.

It was hot. This was not unusual. Climate change meant that the temperature often reached 45°C / 113°F in summer. As Julie travelled in the hydrogen-powered bus, hoping that the latest wildfire crisis would not result in unbreathable air, she reflected on her current situation and the loss of what had been a promising career in the early 2030's.

Julie had started her career in the wine sector. After this "slowed down" because of the trade wars of the early 2030's, she shifted to working in the IT sector. This too "slowed down" after it became clear that most of the more advanced computer chips in the world were being stockpiled for who-knows-what, and as non-human AI workers increasingly dominated the sector. Her next shift was to the tourism sector. Unfortunately, climate change, together with restricted border movements, meant that only temporary and infrequent work was available.

How had this happened? Julie, at 30 years of age, was angry. She was particularly angry with the government of Auslandia who had, in the view of many, "poked the dragon" far too often.

The Auslandian government had worked hard to ignore climate change, but its activities in international relations had an additional and significant impact on Julie's generation.

Auslandia is a small country in the Asian Pacific region that occupies a strategic position. Over the past decade, many issues have arisen with a major trade partner (Plata) relating to a range of questions including ownership over islands, fishing rights, and incursions. These all seem to be linked to some initial criticism of Plata by Auslandia in relation to activities linked to contagion control in the latest pandemic. Some of these issues were raised in the context of Auslandia publicly supporting the stance taken by a major ally which was perceived to be critical of Plata.

In response, a trade war erupted in 2030. The characteristics of this trade war included raising tariffs, rejecting imported goods (with little notice), and threats to abandon well-established trade arrangements. In response, sanctions under international law were invoked and litigation has progressed over almost a decade.

At the same time, cyberattacks have been taking place across Auslandia for the same decade, with media reports suggesting that Plata-based entities are involved. In some instances, these have been referred to as "data wars," as major tech companies carved up assets around the world. There has also been a steady increase in the trading of insults on social media together with attempts to stir up public opinion.

As if trade quarrels and social media flame diplomacy were not enough, there has been some reference to conventional warfare with Plata, Auslandia, and its powerful ally engaging in war games and military shows of strength. There have been thinly veiled threats by Plata to take over or establish a larger footprint in neighboring countries.

Overall, the situation has no doubt been exacerbated by frequent government changes. Indeed, it seems likely that the current government of Auslandia will soon be ousted by a new political party.

Julie sighed as the bus slowed, and then came to a standstill, in the heavy city traffic. A woman about her age caught her eye, and they shared a resigned shrug. Julie felt a little better. It was not only her own career that was stalled, forcing her to put up with hours of commuting each week just to keep her position. It was just how things were, all over Auslandia.

Julie had never seen herself as being very political. However, her trip to the city today had a second purpose. After work, she would attend a rally downtown focusing on the "age wars." She, like many others, was angry about how most of Auslandia's resources were being spent on an aging population that claimed a vastly disproportionate share of those resources. Rallies had been cropping up in every city for the past few weeks, with people showing up in growing numbers. Julie had read a couple of social media posts about the early rallies and had deleted them, as she did with most political issue posts.

But yesterday, one social media post – she could not remember who posted it – showed up on her feed, announcing a rally taking place close to her workplace. The people protesting in the picture accompanying the announcement reminded her of her friends: about her age, professionally dressed, with tired, dejected faces expressing a spark of anger. Clicking "I'll attend" seemed like the most natural thing in the world to do.

2040 Auslandia - Part Two

Several days ago, Julie was quietly approached by a former university classmate named Daiyu. They had been close friends, though their career trajectories were very different. Daiyu Chong had studied international business and was now a rising executive in a well-regarded international trading company. She is one of several children of the company's co-founder who now hold management roles – and compete with each other for promotion. They met for coffee at a small coffee shop, and at a quiet corner table spent the first hour remembering antics from their university days and chit-chatting about their families. Finally, over flat whites and Turkish toast with avocado, Daiyu cautiously asked Julie if she might be interested in taking a new position with her company.

Daiyu explained her company, Smith-Chong Investments, was working with prospective partners from Plata to pursue opportunities in the tourism sector, although Smith-Chong is also interested in rare-earth mining operations near Auslandia Springs. Julie was a skilled researcher and good writer who knew about tourism. Might Julie be interested in joining Smith-Chong to help ensure government and indigenous permissions were obtained?

Julie thanked Daiyu and said she was happy to be considered, and they agreed, pending further discussions about details, to meet again in a week.

Meanwhile, things are heating up elsewhere in the world. A new report released by the World Health Organization claimed that the global temperature has increased due in part to pollution produced from coal mining industries. Julie is aware that Auslandia's contribution to this global problem is significant, and she is keen to do something about it. In her youth, she had participated in Greta Thunberg's Zoom rallies and seminars. But those efforts have not had any real impact on the practices of polluting industries. A help-wanted ad in the local newspaper struck her attention.

An alternative fuel company had positions open for a branch in her city. The salary was not competitive. Nor were they offering benefits such as sick leave, retirement fund contributions or paid vacation. And the company's offices were on the other side of the city, which would mean a substantial commute. Julie was caught in a dilemma with the push and pull of her need for secure employment and her strongly felt ideals.

Daiyu's opening presented an attractive option. That job would enable her to pay off debts. The alternative opportunity would give her life a meaning that would be missing or delayed if she pursued more lucrative options. Thinking that she had little to lose, Julie sent a letter of interest to the alternative fuel company.

A quick reply came with a telephone interview date in a few days. The interview went well, and she was offered the job, starting immediately. Before deciding, Julie called Daiyu to keep her informed of this development. Daiyu asked Julie to give her a day to consult with her company before deciding. Julie agreed and wondered why life can often be so complicated. And, so indeed it proved, when Daiyu scheduled an interview for Julie with Daiyu's boss. Julie thanked her but also asked for a favor: Could the interview take place tomorrow? That was agreed; the interview went well, and she received an attractive offer a few hours later with benefits and perks. Feeling stuck between two attractive options, Julie had to weigh the material benefits of one job against the moral benefits of the other. This was a classic "interests vs values" conflict.

2040 Auslandia - Part Three

Julie made her decision: between her comfort with Daiyu and the well-known successes of Plata businesses globally, Smith-Chong seemed not only the most lucrative but also potentially the most future-career-oriented opportunity. Julie was hired as Smith-Chong's new Client Relations Director for Auslandia. She started immediately.

The following day, Julie attended her first day at her new job and was briefed by Daiyu and several company VPs on current ongoing initiatives, including three major investment deals close to conclusion. Her first assignment was to assess and help resolve an emerging real estate transaction. The other two investment initiatives, she was advised, could be placed on hold until the first one was resolved. The three projects are

1 – A Resort Complex: This involves the purchase of a large amount of land to build a world-class spa and resort complex providing a desert retreat, with casino facilities and an array of outdoor activities leveraging the great outdoor life. In essence, the new resort is eventually intended to be the new Las Vegas of Auslandia. The land being acquired belongs to the indigenous communities nearby and the clients are expected to be global, with a heavy reliance on the Plata tourist industry. Julie's task in this situation is to assist

the investors in developing good relationships with the local indigenous communities. However, while the indigenous communities seem very keen to facilitate this land transaction, some of the required permits appear to be delayed and the transaction seems to be stalled. There is even concern that some members of the indigenous communities may no longer support the land sale. The land is an area of about 30 x 60 km located approximately 25 kilometers southwest of Auslandia Springs. Julie is asked to meet with the indigenous groups next week and needs to prepare for the meeting with her new team.

2 – The Expansion of Auslandia Springs's Airport: Along with the above initiative, Smith-Chong is tentatively planning to expand Auslandia Spring's old, outdated airport to facilitate the anticipated increase in passengers coming to visit this world-class tourist and casino destination, expected to reach 3 million visitors per year.

3 – The Derwood Cruise Ship Port Expansion: Another part of Smith-Chong's overall plan is to enhance cruise ship capacity from Plata's ports to Derwood. Smith-Chong wishes to invest in expanding the port of Derwood to accommodate cruise ships coming from Plata. From the port, tourists will have access by train to the new Auslandia Springs resort.

Julie is now attempting to familiarize herself with the planned land transactions, and to understand the issues with permits and why some in the indigenous community are wavering in their commitment. In the interim, she heads home after her first day, setting up her new laptop and phone and calling a friend in Auslandia Springs, to advise that she may visit her next week due to work travel. Her friend works for the federal government as an IT specialist and is located at Spring Gap, a secret government facility adjacent to Auslandia Springs.

Within a few weeks, Julie becomes overwhelmed with the information she is discovering. It conflicts with the world she thought she understood. One day she also finds papers in the copying machine that someone accidentally left. They seem to be detailed technical reports on certain rare earth oxides of scandium, lanthanum, and cerium found in various parts of the country, including Auslandia Springs. Julie remembers reading that these minerals are essential in some weapons technologies such as guided missile systems, as well as in advanced computer systems. Julie knows that these minerals are in high demand in many countries around the world. Julie questions the information and wants to free her mind of the complex issues that seem to meet her at every turn. Is the venture actually more about mining than tourism? Is there something else going on? The realization that not everything is as it appears frightens her. There is another dimension to all these actions that only those privy to the information can comprehend.

Julie's suspicions grow. She reads national and social media stories about increasing numbers of cyberattacks and comes to believe her own phone and computer may have been hacked since she started her new job. She plans to have them checked out by a skilled computer specialist. Perhaps someone she knows can enlighten her now that she is beginning to open her mind to the possibilities. Her father always said, "the mind is like a parachute, it only works when it is open." With his voice echoing in her mind, she sets herself the task of finding out what is happening in Auslandia in general and in her company in particular, and how her new position and tasks may relate to a broader agenda that she is only beginning to understand.

Julie has found herself caught between doing the job she is being paid for – and doing it well – and the values that motivated her to seek social change and fight against corruption. Rather than deciding between these alternatives, she continues to probe into the company's role in exploiting the environment for profit. She worries about the consequences of bringing these practices into the public domain as a whistleblower. She would no doubt lose her job, but there may be a bigger price to pay, including threats to her safety. Moving forward in time, what more will she discover?

Possible questions for all audiences

1) What elements seem to indicate that we are in a hybrid warfare situation? The case mentions different tactics being used. Can you identify all of them? How do they play in conjunction with one another?

2) Draw a comprehensive stakeholder map of the case. Who are the relevant people and institutions that should be considered in this situation, and how do they relate to one another? List and prioritize the interests of each of the main stakeholders of the case.

3) The case mentions increasingly difficult living conditions and mentions "precariat" as the plight of future generations. How could this impact life choices, identity, and the negotiation strategies of members of these generations? In your opinion, is this future plausible – or not?

4) With two offers in hand, which way should Julie go? How do you analyze the dilemma Julie faces? If you were in her shoes, what elements would make you accept the offer from the international trading firm – or the alternative from the eco-friendly fuel company? It may be useful to list all of Julie's interests and values to see how each option may contribute to fulfilling them.

5) What is whistleblowing and how does it work? Should Julie blow the whistle? If so, under which conditions? What do you know about your country's laws re: whistleblowing: are they protective enough?

6) Many people in Julie's situation, when torn between interests and values, choose to remain in place and drive positive change from the inside; in this scenario, would you consider this a viable strategy? If so, what negotiations, if any, should Julie engage in with her employer?

Possible specific questions for lawyers and law students

1) As Julie's lawyer, how would you approach counseling her regarding which job to accept? What additional information might you want to gather to better advise Julie about her choice? Are there specific contractual terms that you might want to negotiate for Julie in each job?

2) Julie has approached you as a part of Smith-Chong's company legal team. What law (using your own country's legal code) do you need to research as part of the negotiation with the indigenous communities over the resort complex?

3) How would you recommend that Julie approach this negotiation/meeting regarding the resort complex? Specifically, should you be present (as the lawyer on this project)? Should you rent a space for the meeting, have them at your offices, or someplace else? How should Julie prepare for this negotiation?

4) Julie has come to you as her personal lawyer to discuss the information she has discovered and possibly becoming a whistleblower. What do you advise her? Do you want more information? If yes, what information?

5) As Julie's lawyer, if Julie decides to be a whistleblower, would you want to involve other people in her case? What kind of experts might you consult with? Would you have concerns about confidential communications with those experts? How would you protect the privacy/confidentiality of your conversations and other communications, both with Julie and any other potential experts that you might involve in the case?

6) What if Julie, with her deliberations on becoming a whistleblower, comes to you as the company's lawyer, not as her personal lawyer? Does this change the advice you would give her? What are the differences in your duties/responsibilities as Julie's lawyer or the company's lawyer?

7) Reflect on different countries' / your country's laws regarding whistleblower protection. Are they sufficient to guarantee the efficacy of whistleblowing and the safety and well-being of the whistleblower? What changes to the laws and regulations would you advise?

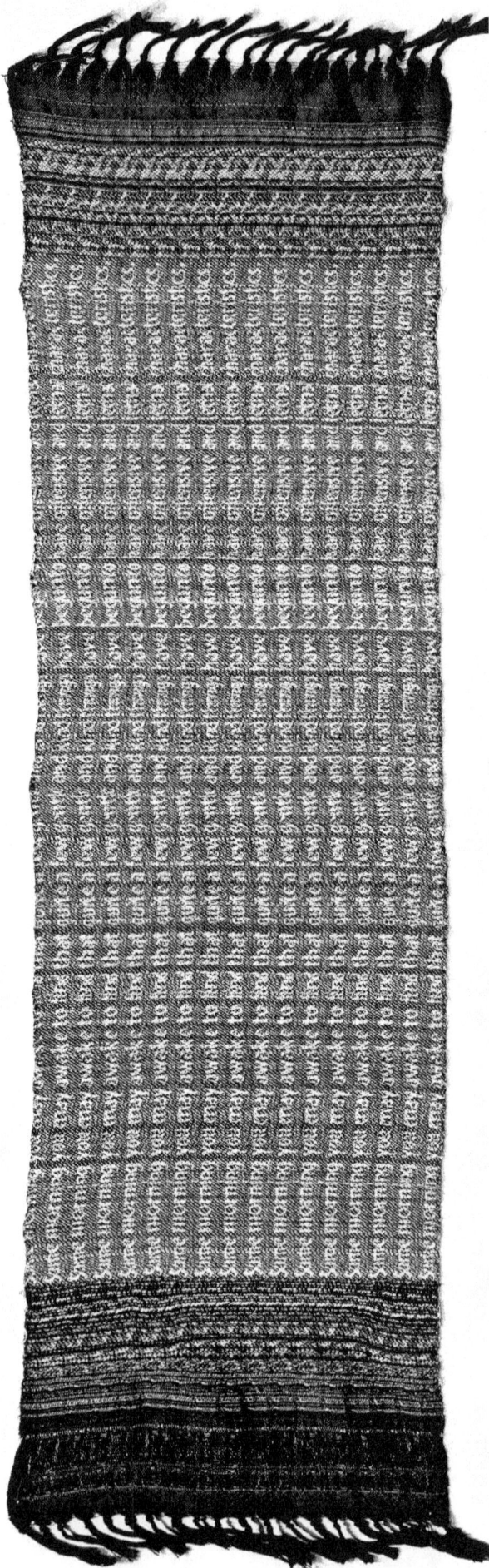

"Some morning you may awake to find that the gentle and kind things around you have begun to have offensive and lethal characteristics." From a series of weavings by Rachel Parish, with quotes from Qiao and Wang's *Unrestricted Warfare* (People's Liberation Army Publishing House, Beijing 1999.) In color at https://rachelparish. com/projects/gentle-and-kind-things/

Part 3:
Business Organizations
In Hybrid Warfare

6

NovaFeed – Modern War in the Office

Calvin Chrustie & Adrian Borbély

This case describes the plight of a news media company, based in a Western liberal democratic country (Federatio) which employs immigrants from two countries, Agraria and Voracia. When full-scale war breaks out between Agraria and Voracia, the company decides not to relay news articles from Voracia news outlets suspected of propaganda. Soon afterwards, it is hit with a ransomware attack by hackers originating from Voracia. All activities are halted, a multi-million ransom is demanded, and the staff's personnel records are compromised.

The case is particularly interesting in showing how a private enterprise may be specifically targeted because of a geopolitical crisis, i.e., how kinetic and hybrid warfare may coexist.

* * *

Keywords: Hybrid warfare – Cyber criminality – Hacking – Disinformation – Kinetic warfare – Espionage.

NOVAFEED - MODERN WAR IN THE OFFICE

Calvin Chrustie & Adrian Borbély

A few months ago, the country of Voracia has launched a major invasion of one of its neighbors, Agraria, following longstanding border disputes. Despite its relative smaller size, Agraria has been resisting, in the face of full-fledged kinetic war waged by Voracia, which is conducting bombings, airstrikes, naval operations, and army movements. Liberal democracies, such as Federatio, have pledged to support Agraria in the form of armament delivery and economic support; however, they have so far refused to get involved on the battlefield, fearing the consequences of an all-out war with Voracia.

The region has been characterized, over history, by important population movements, both before and after formal borders were drawn to demarcate Nation-States. Consequently, people who are now citizens of a particular country often have family ties in neighboring countries (e.g., Agrarian people have family in Voracia, and vice versa).

In this context, NovaFeed Inc. is a Federatian tech firm which specializes in the distribution of online news stories through a digital platform on smartphones. Wherever they are, users of the NovaFeed app may access news sources from around the world and select the articles they are interested in simply by swiping. An artificial intelligence engine then analyzes the user choices to provide more accurate suggestions in the future. The longer the user uses the app, the better the content suggestions provided to him.

While the company is incorporated in Federatio and based in its capital city, its CEO is the son of Voracian immigrants, and most of its about 600 employees are of Agrarian or Voracian descent, some of them first-generation immigrants (e.g., people who came to Federatio to attend college), others stemming from families that have been emigrating to Federatio in waves over the last century. The company has contracts with 2,500 media outlets around the world, who often report on current affairs, including the war in Agraria.

Within days of the war breaking out, the company decided that, for reputational and ethical reasons, they would terminate their contracts with half a dozen Voracian media, as it was being reported that the Voracian Government and its armed forces were using those media to spread fake news for misinformation and disinformation purposes. Such fake news included minimizing civilian casualties, attempting to rebut stories of human rights abuses, and propaganda in support of Voracia's aggressive military action.

Several days after the decision was implemented, first thing one morning the C-Suite staff and legal counsel were called to the boardroom for an urgent meeting. The CEO briefed them that the night before, they had been hit with a cyberattack that affected their entire system and forced them to interrupt their services. Their 2,500 global clients could no longer share their news stories on the platform. The system shutdown was accompanied by a ransom demand for 5 million in cryptocurrency. The cyber hackers identified themselves as belonging to an infamous Voracian cyber hacking organization, who coincidentally, just days before, had publicly said they aligned with the Voracian military.

The attack and ransom demand led to the following immediate consequences:

- By freezing all NovaFeed's systems, the hackers severed some of the world's largest national news outlets' access to their global audience. It so happened that many of these news outlets were reporting on the Voracian invasion, mostly from the perspective of liberal democratic societies. The phones in the office were ringing non-stop.

- Within 12 hours, some of these clients had terminated their contracts, making their articles no longer available to the public through the NovaFeed app.

- Users who were interested in those sources were moving to competing providers.

- It also rapidly became obvious that the hackers had accessed and hijacked the company's employees' personal data.

Since half the staff members were of Voracian descent, and the other half of Agrarian origin, often with direct family ties back in their countries of origin, tensions in the office seemed to be rapidly escalating between the two camps. The international context appeared to be imported within the once harmonious company: resentment was growing, and the personnel started voicing strong concerns.

The C-Suite agreed they needed external support, both to secure the company's IT systems and to manage the crisis. But whom to call?

- Within the first several hours, disagreements emerged regarding whether – or not – to engage with law enforcement. Although they felt they needed help from the authorities, there were risks attached to such a move, especially in terms of discretion and company reputation. Plus, the C-Suite members were not clear as to what exactly police personnel could do, without taking control over the company (and circumventing the Board itself).

- A crisis management consultant was hired to provide expertise and an independent perspective on the issue.

- Efforts were made to hire specialized legal counsel, law professionals experienced with such cyber incidents. However, many refused to get involved, fearing they would then themselves become targets of Voracian hackers.

Within the C-Suite, disagreements rapidly grew on whether to be transparent with employees regarding the fact that their personal data may be in the hands of Voracian hackers aligned with the Voracian military and intelligence services. Employees of both Voracian and Agrarian descent could be directly exposed.

The C-Suite is particularly concerned with the fact that for the previous holiday party, HR put together what was then a fun teambuilding exercise. They sent a survey to all staff members asking them where they have family roots (where their grandparents were born, where their family's favored vacation places were, etc.), so that an interactive map could be created, enabling employees to identify with whom they may be related, or share a common history. All the data used to set up this map were in the HR database that has been hacked, which now places the personnel's relatives back in the region also at risk.

The C-Suite immediately considered the option of paying the hackers. However, concerns were raised that paying the ransom to get the business up and running could be considered an illegal transaction. Indeed, such a money transfer may very well violate international sanctions against Voracia, its government and wealthy supporters. It may also violate other Federatian or international illicit finance laws.

The crisis management consultant raised the fact that intelligence suggests that, even if the company did pay the ransom, there was a high probability their systems would not be returned to functioning order, or that they will be extorted again. Furthermore, there was no guarantee that the staff's personal data would be retrieved and not sold to a third party or used by Voracian intelligence services to target individuals working for the company – or related to them.

On day 3, the CEO made the executive decision to pay the ransom. His reasoning was that this was less harmful than seeing dozens of his company's clients vanish daily, which equated to millions in lost revenue.

Possible questions for all audiences

1) What elements seem to indicate that we are in a hybrid warfare situation? What are the different warfare tactics at play in this scenario? Discuss the link between kinetic and hybrid warfare mechanisms.

2) Draw a stakeholder map of all concerned actors, with their relationships to one another. Such a map is a graphic representation of all actors, with arrows between them signifying opposition or support. Identify the interests and values of the main actors.

3) NovaFeed Inc. is a private company, not a military operation; yet it became a target due to its business and the way it is staffed. Despite these elements, it seems ill-prepared for such a scenario. How do you explain this? What could they have done to prepare?

4) Regarding the decision to exclude Voracian outlets accused of propaganda: should the Board have included the staff in the decision-making process? Should all have raised the security level in anticipation of a likely attack?

5) Should the company have been transparent with its personnel about the data theft? Discuss the pros and cons of the decision to communicate or retain information.

6) What could the hackers do with the stolen data? At first sight, this attack has to do with economic coercion or subversion (extortion and/or destruction of the NovaFeed business). But the data could also be used for transnational suppression (harassment of people that remained in the war-torn region) and/or espionage (using these people to blackmail and recruit new assets in Federatio). What other possible uses are there?

7) International conflicts are sometimes "imported" into an organization's personnel. As a business manager, what steps can you take to prevent this or deal with it?

8) Should the company pay the ransom? Please address the pros and cons of both alternatives, before justifying your decision.

Possible specific questions for lawyers and law students

1) If you were the lawyer hired by NovaFeed, what would you advise your client to do and why?

2) Imagine that NovaFeed pays the ransom, without consulting their lawyers ahead of time. In other words, lawyers discover this after the fact. What risks do the company and its CEO face?

3) An employee of NovaFeed consults you, as a lawyer, regarding personal data being stolen by a hacker group linked with an adversary nation. Is the employee entitled to compensation? What would you advise in terms of litigation and negotiation? What would be the drawbacks of such a claim?

4) Assume the company's contracts with news generators include a typical *force majeure* clause. What risks does NovaFeed face from their clients? Are we here in a *force majeure* scenario that would prevent clients from asking for compensation? More generally, apply the criteria for *force majeure* to hybrid warfare scenarios.

5) Do you understand the decision of several law firms not to get involved in the situation? Does this infringe on your jurisdiction's attorney-ethics rules? In other words, what are the reasons why a firm may refuse to advise and/or defend clients? Are ethical codes up to date regarding such international risks?

6) As a lawyer advising or defending a client who is a target of hybrid warfare, do you consider yourself at risk? Would you notify your insurer if put in such a situation?

7

MONEY DOES NOT COME FREE

Adrian Borbély & Calvin Chrustie

This case tells the tale of three childhood friends turned entrepreneurs who create a company in the field of medical prosthetics. The products they sell could have military applications. Like many start-uppers and despite little business acumen, they need funds to develop their business, and end up dealing with venture capitalists and wealthy investors.

A series of events lead to the founders' loss of control over their company and its hostile takeover by agents of a potentially hostile country. Their innovation, developed in a Western country for the purpose of helping disabled people, may end up being used in a Super Soldier program by the scientific arm of a foreign nation's armed forces.

The case study aims to trigger reflections on the fragility of the financing systems provided by capitalism, and how nefarious actors may play the capitalist game against them.

* * *

Keywords: Hybrid warfare – Capitalism – Venture capitalism – Protection of strategic industries – Naivety – Lawyers – Hacking of innovation – University partnership – Lawfare

MONEY DOES NOT COME FREE

Adrian Borbély & Calvin Chrustie[1]

Disclaimer

This case is inspired by real events; however, the story, characters, company names and incidents portrayed in this document are ficti- tious. China is cited as the nefarious State-actor, as the country and its institutions have been accused of similar activities in the past.[2]

Setting the stage

Mike, Angela, and Roberto have been friends since preschool and truly became insepara- ble after being tasked with organizing their middle school yearly charity run. Since then, they have been bound by the strongest of all friendships. All three were brilliant students, promised bright futures, and were born and raised in the same neighborhood of a posh suburb in a Western nation.

After high school, Angela studied biology as an undergraduate and then went to medi- cal school, as she always dreamt of being a healer. This is linked with her family history: she witnessed her grandmother struggle with chronic asthma while her father, who was injured at work on a construction site, lost most of the use of his left arm. Mike was a heavy video game player as a child; he naturally chose computer programming as his col- lege major. Roberto was much less certain about what to do with his life; but since he was excellent at math and interested in physics, he chose an engineering curriculum.

The three took a chance and applied to university programs in the same large urban area; fortunately, all three were accepted. Naturally, they decided to rent a flat together, to keep their friendship alive and together discover what adult life has to offer. Even so, at no point did they get romantically involved with one another. They sadly returned the keys of their apartment when the boys graduated and took jobs a few hundred kilometers away. Angela then moved into a smaller flat while finishing her medical studies.

The scene now shifts to several years later. One evening, they met to celebrate Angela's completion of her residency at a local hospital. With a few friends, they had a fancy meal, plus a few cocktails, and finally went to Angela's place for a bottle of champagne. Once their friends left, the three of them sat in the small living room and reminisced about the

[1] The authors wish to expand their gratitude to Yan Alperovych, Professor of Finance at emlyon business school, for his wise advice regarding the financial mechanisms at play in this scenario.
[2] See for example: https://www.ft.com/content/cedfc2cf-209e-4af6-97f5-56fca6ebdb56

past years. Mike and Roberto complained about their boring jobs and autocratic bosses, while teasing Angela about her passage into employed life.

When Mike jokingly suggested they find a business idea they could all get involved with, all alcohol effects seemed to disappear, and the conversation suddenly turned serious. Putting their inalienable friendship at the heart of an entrepreneurial adventure: what a great idea! They ended up brainstorming ideas much of the night, as they were too excited to consider going to bed.

Around 4 AM, Angela mentioned her dream to invent a device that would help disabled people such as her father with everyday chores. Since his accident, her father had struggled with certain tasks, unable to carry heavy loads with only one fully functioning arm, or to perform precision tasks such as sawing, drilling, or hammering nails. Sleep finally caught up with them at that time and they fell asleep, Angela barely managing to walk to her bedroom, the guys crashing where they were sitting.

The next day, over fresh coffee, Roberto started explaining how recent progresses in robotics could help with Angela's dream. He told his friends about a class he took where Professor Anna Mitchell showed early work on exoskeletons: an outside structure mimicking the structure of human joints and bones, used to build human-like robots. Could such an idea be developed specifically to support non- or malfunctioning limbs and relieve disabled people from their handicap?

Over the next weeks, the three friends spent their evenings FaceTiming to discuss what could be done and had not yet been brought to market. They all had a hard time concentrating on their daily work, turning all their brainpower toward these evening meetings. They also spent weekends together at Mike's parents' suburban house, using every flat surface to draw schematics and to place post-its with more or less realistic ideas.

After two months, they knew what they wanted to create: mechanical exo-structures for injured or malfunctioning human limbs, that would enable victims of strokes or accidents to perform regular tasks. They were confident that between them they had the key skills to achieve such goals. Angela could do needs assessments with disabled people and supervise fitting and training on new devices; Roberto could build prototypes and program 3D printers and machines to produce industry-quality parts for tailor-made prosthetics; Mike could program the computer chips that would control the devices' movements and efforts.

Solving the money equation - episode 1

Angela, Roberto, and Mike live in a Western, capitalist Nation with a strong culture promoting entrepreneurship. Much like their parents before them, they all have well-paid jobs that provide them with more than they need to live comfortably. However, achieving their business objectives will force them to quit their jobs, hire human resources (esp. computer programmers and machining experts) and invest in production capabilities. Although they could reach the proof-of-concept stage in their spare time and on their savings, going further would require a lot of funds.

So, this is what they did: they founded and registered a company named a.r.m. prosthetics[3] ("a.r.m." being a double reference to one of the human limbs and their first-name initials), of which each owned a third. They drew up detailed designs and paid lawyers to register their trademark and submit patent applications in the EU, the USA, Canada, Australia, and New Zealand. They initiated an informal collaboration with Mike's *alma mater*, Professor Mitchell being excited to offer her help in running tests and experiments – asking only for name recognition for herself, her lab, and the university. Then, the three partners started drafting loan and subsidy requests. However, getting a loan from a bank proved impossible, considering the risks associated with such a business venture at its earliest stage of development.

They decided to take their inventions on the road and presented them in various entrepreneur conventions to test the market and look for investors. Prof. Mitchell suggested they participate in the *Concours Lépine*, the most prestigious European invention competition, which takes place annually at the *Foire de Paris*. They did not win, but they met several "angel investors", some of whom seemed willing to help them secure funds.

This is how they were introduced to the glorious, yet intimidating world of early-stage (or "angel") venture capital. After a few discussions, they were offered financial support in exchange for shares of their company. More precisely, they met with a business angel from their homeland, Steve, who was looking for new opportunities to invest in innovative companies. He offered them a good deal, in their view at the time: 500,000 dollars in return for 19% of the shares (each founding partner retaining 27%), which placed the company at a 2.6-million-dollar valuation. The offer stated that Steve would provide guidance and support for the next two years, with the help of his team. From the beginning, the investor pact clearly stated that Steve would be allowed to divest in 24 months' time. To explain the deal in simple terms: in two years, Steve could expect to get at least 3 times his investment (1.5 million dollars or 19% of the valuation of the company at that time, whichever is the higher number). If the exit clause was activated, should the company or the remaining shareholders not be able to reimburse him, he could take control of the company, either to operate it as he saw fit, or to sell its assets to reimburse himself. Steve assured the partners this was a typical provision in such agreements, and somewhat optimistically, they took his word for it. The contract then had an intricate mechanism in which the exit fee follows a logarithmic curve (strong incline at first, the riskiest period, going flatter over time as failure risk decreases).

In part because of lack of funds, in part because they trusted Steve and did not feel the need, neither the three founders, nor the company as an entity, had comprehensive legal guidance, a standard practice among start-up companies. The company would purchase advice *ad hoc* when it seemed needed and pay attorneys per mission, mostly to submit applications for trademarks and patents. At that stage, the founders did not order a full due diligence but asked junior attorneys, friends from college, to confirm that the terms

---

[3] The company name is purely fictional. Several companies, worldwide, use similar names. None of them was used as a model for this case. All confusion should be considered purely accidental.

of the investor pact seemed standard. They told them that nothing stood out as out of the ordinary.

They were quick to sign the paperwork and get to work, with the support of a great team of consultants, all employed by their new partner and keen to give them "sound advice" on how to grow their business. In addition, the company used this new capital to secure an additional half-million dollars in State subsidized loans (with 0% interest rate).

With the first round of financing now secured, Angela and the boys threw themselves body and soul into the company. They quit their jobs, rented industrial space, purchased machines, and hired a dozen technicians. They relied on business school interns as their sales force, and they started to trigger interest from wealthy disabled people, who could afford these revolutionary, yet expensive prototypical prosthetics.

A civilian invention with military applications

Months after hitting the market, someone suggested contacting their homeland's Veterans Administration to see if a partnership was possible to provide prosthetics to injured soldiers returning to civilian life with crippling disabilities. Of course, they would have to sharply reduce their prices to make their products affordable to this less fortunate population, but this could be compensated, at least in part, by quantity, considering the number of wounded ex-soldiers returning from the many recent armed conflicts. Veterans could offer proof of concept for their innovations and were likely to volunteer to serve as testers for further research. Such a partnership could also give a Corporate Social Responsibility image to the company. A meeting at the Ministry of Defense was set up to present potential collaboration ideas.

Later, Angela received a phone call from a General of their homeland's armed forces, who wanted to pay the company a visit to discuss possible military applications for their products. Sitting around the company's conference table, the four partners listened to the General explain how enhanced prosthetics like those produced by a.r.m. prosthetics could be used by the armed forces for at least two purposes:

- Increase the abilities of regular soldiers: reinforced legs and arms could enable them to carry heavier loads by foot and to resist the recoil of heavy machine guns (that currently must be anchored to the ground or fixed on a heavy vehicle to be used in combat).

- Enable some injured soldiers to remain on active duty: for now, a soldier with a disabling wound is either retired or reassigned to purely administrative duty. However, most of them would return to the battlefield if given the physical ability to do so.

After the meeting, the partners pondered this opportunity. Steve wanted to sign a wide-ranging contract with the military, as it would put the company on a great trajectory and practically guarantee its success over time. The three founders were more circumspect, attached to their initial objective of helping the weak and worried they would become part of the military-industrial complex. Participating in some "super soldier" program was not in their DNA. They stood their ground, despite Steve's pressure. This was their first open disagreement: voices were raised, and doors slammed.

Angela, Mike and Roberto consulted Prof. Mitchell, now retired, who pointed out her surprise that the General did not mention robots. Is it possible that the Army's vision could be so short-sighted? Their products (granted: with 20 more years of R&D) could have potential application as military operations robots: drone weapon and supply delivery systems, perhaps eventually even drone soldiers.

Angela, Roberto and Mike estimated that the company could prosper without such a partnership. They therefore politely declined the Army's offer, while promising to continue working with veterans in the future. Steve was fuming.

At around that time, the company suffered what looked like a minor cyber incident. Apparently, one of the interns had opened an infected attachment that contaminated his mailbox and ended up paralyzing all the company's email communications. The tech support offered by the anti-virus provider whose system was installed on their computers was able to solve the issue and restore backups, but they lost some important unsaved work and emails. No one was able to identify if any of the company's data was compromised, beyond emails.

This scare led the four partners to hire a Chief Technology Officer, whose mission would be to coordinate the programming staff and, most importantly, to ensure the integrity of their information systems, especially the proprietary technical data. The best candidate for the job was a university colleague of Mike's, who accepted to work part-time for a.r.m. prosthetics while building his own cybersecurity company. Han, of Chinese descent, was born and raised locally; he would receive a smaller salary than what the sector would typically offer, but his compensation also included shares: 3% of the company. This was Steve's idea: add a minority shareowner who would sit at Board meetings, organize exchanges among partners and mediate potential disagreements among them.

Solving the money equation - episode 2

In all these adventures, the company burnt through cash too fast compared to what it could recover through sales. After two years of full-speed operation on all fronts – marketing, sales, innovation, etc. – and still reeling from the refusal to sign with the Army, Steve requested to cash out his investment.

This came somewhat as a surprise, as the founders had hoped Steve would grant them an extension; after all, together with his team, he had been working enthusiastically on their project. But Steve refused to reconsider, as he was now interested in directing his funds toward the growing field of AI.

Neither the company, nor the founders had the funds to pay for his exit from the company. Time was pressing. Should Steve not get his money back rapidly, he would be allowed to sell his share on the market (bringing in new investors that the original founders did not know, and could not oppose), or start selling the company's assets (machines and patents), therefore crippling it. In such a short period of time, they did not have time to organize a new round of equity. Either they could borrow the money (unlikely), or they needed to bring in a new investor; otherwise, they would lose control of their company.

Luckily, Han explained that he had an uncle in Singapore who is a magnate of various industries, including real estate and shipping, with companies registered in Singapore, Malaysia, and Hong Kong. Getting close to retirement age, Mr. Lim was transitioning from hands-on industrial management to a more laid-back portfolio management. Han asked whether he could test his uncle's interest in buying out Steve's shares at a price based on the current company valuation (around 9 million dollars), which would represent an investment of close to 1.7 million, netting Steve his expected profit (plus a bit more.)

The founders met with Mr. Lim and his board over Zoom and had a chance to explain their business, its perspective, and their expectations for a financial backer with global connections, hoping they would find someone with a rather hands-off approach to investment. After Steve, they wanted to retrieve part of the freedom of movement they had lost.

Lim quickly sent a team of consultants to run his due diligence. Impressed by the company's positioning and perspectives, and convinced by Han's supportive argument, he happily agreed to invest in the company. He bought Steve's shares at market value and substituted for him on the initial investor pact; as such, he took over all the rights and duties of the previous investor, including the right to divest after two years. Only the amount of presumed profit changed, to reflect the reduced risk as the company was now a going concern. Once the paperwork was signed freeing Steve from a.r.m. prosthetics (and vice-versa), the founders opened a bottle of champagne and toasted to a new, different future.

The first months of the new collaboration were uneventful. The company's accountants reported monthly to Lim's board of directors, who asked questions about sales and cashflow, but did not raise major objections as to how the company was run. In return, every week or so, Lim's teams introduced a.r.m. prosthetics to potential Asian clients or partners: new suppliers for small metal components, wealthy Brunei citizens in need of prosthetic limbs, and so on. Angela was even invited to make a presentation at a trade convention in Kuala Lumpur.

Lim's team also assisted a.r.m. prosthetics in registering their now numerous patents in Asia, especially in China. As the company grew, R&D was identifying new robotics solutions and applications for prosthetics. Lim's legal team was quick to point out the risks if those patents were not strongly protected against counterfeiting and intellectual property theft in all markets where they wished to operate.

About one year later, after a more thorough due diligence effort, and reassured by the company's growth prospects, Lim offered to increase his stake in a.r.m. prosthetics by injecting an additional 2.4-million dollars in exchange for a further 20% of equity (company valuation: 12 million dollars). Excited to get away from all cashflow issues, the founders happily agreed.

The accident

About 18 months after supplying this fresh capital to a.r.m. prosthetics, Mr. Lim, now aged 68, had a helicopter accident. He was flying his own aircraft to his countryside estate when it apparently suffered mechanical failure. He was able to crash land on a meadow but suffered head trauma as his head hit the dashboard. The injury left him paralyzed and struggling to articulate coherent thought and speech. The once brilliant businessman and industrialist was suddenly bedridden, and his wife quickly built at-home hospitalization capabilities in their Singapore penthouse apartment.

Consequently, as no family member was directly involved in the business (heirs may own shares but were having very different careers, most of them in America and in Australia), a guardian was named to conduct business operations in Lim's name. A Singaporean attorney was appointed by the Courts with the mission to protect Lim's assets and conduct business on his behalf and in his best interest.

a.r.m. prosthetics was not immediately informed of these events. Remote family members such as Han were also kept in the dark, as the family was advised to wait before communicating about Lim's health condition, mostly to protect the business from aggressive moves from competitors.

The guardian's initial analysis of Lim's business empire made him worry about a very high level of debt. He therefore started identifying risky investments, as well as participations in businesses that did not fit with the rest of his empire. a.r.m. prosthetics was one of these. His idea was to get rid of these investments to pump fresh cash into the heart of the conglomerate. This would enable a dividend distribution to all heirs of Lim's fortune, which would reassure them and keep them quiet.

The guardian is a seasoned lawyer from an important business law firm in Singapore, which belongs to a network of influential law, audit and consulting firms based all over Asia, from Korea to Indonesia, including Bangkok, Hong Kong, and mainland China.

He inserted in the network's electronic bulletin board information regarding all the investments for sale from Lim's portfolio. Soon enough, lawyers from China started asking questions and requesting contractual documents regarding a.r.m. prosthetics (company founding documents, list of patents, investor pact, etc.).

Closing the trap

Shortly thereafter, with a.r.m. prosthetics still unaware of what was happening in Singapore, the founders were contacted by an attorney from a local boutique law firm in their own home city, who stated that he represented companies interested in investing in a.r.m. prosthetics, without giving more detail. The meeting was set up as a lunch at an upscale local restaurant. Over good food and fancy wine, the conversation was very enjoyable, as the lawyer proved curious about the company, and the personal history of the partners. But in return, the attorney was less than forthcoming in details about his clients, simply stating they are based in Asia, and they are actors in markets where Mr. Lim also operates.

After that lunch, the owners were left curious as to what this was about. They contacted a.r.m. prosthetics' lawyers with many questions – and got few answers, mostly an explanation of what the investor pact permitted and forbade. They were told that no new investor could come in without permission from current partners; if someone were to sell their shares, then the remaining partners had the opportunity to preempt the sale.

The next call came from an international law firm, with offices on all five continents, requesting a meeting with the shareholders. This time, they were invited to the law firm's local offices in the business district of their nation's capital city and greeted in a formal conference room. Only now were they informed of Mr. Lim's medical situation – and that the guardian of Mr. Lim's estate had decided to activate the exit clause of the investor pact. According to the investor pact, the partners had two months to preempt the sale, before the investor was allowed to sell to a third party. In other words, to remain in control of their company, Angela, Roberto, and Mike had to find 6.25 million dollars to cover the price for 39% of the shares, based on a company valuation of 16 million dollars. 6.25 million dollars!

Left in shock, they tried to look for options. A few weeks later, they received a registered letter from Lim's guardian, stating that he had identified a buyer for Mr. Lim's shares – a Canadian company, with a Canadian CEO and a name reminiscent of a native tribe. But upon further enquiry, this "Canadian" firm appeared to be owned by a sole shareholder, a recently incorporated company named *Shoubi*, out of Shenzhen, China. *Shoubi* means "arm" in Mandarin. The company's CEO is also listed as CEO or major shareholder in companies mining diamonds, rare earth elements and lithium all over the world. Apparently, they had offered 8 million dollars for Mr. Lim's shares in a.r.m. prosthetics – a hard-to-beat offer.

Angela, Roberto and Mike will never meet their new "partner", as the sale of the shares will take place in Singapore and will be registered there. The international law firm will represent the new partner at Board meetings, based on documents fed to them – and a.r.m. prosthetics' legal counsel, when asked, says none of this contravenes anything in the corporation's governing documents or the partnership agreement. Thus, proof of ownership would pass first to the Canadian company, then to *Shoubi* directly, then the new partner would grant power of attorney and full representation to a partner in the local branch of the international law firm. Pressed by the original shareholders, this attorney appeared to have little to say and to be mostly a message carrier to and from the Board. As per the provisions of the investor pact, the attorney was given full computer access to a.r.m. prosthetics' systems.

Not long after, Han started noticing that the attorney's account was used to set up a back door to the company's computer system, and that a lot of data was accessed and transferred, including technical specifications for their products and prototypes. The data packets were bounced through various IP addresses around the world, and it was impossible to ascertain their destination. When confronted, the attorney first pled innocence, then conceded that the new shareholder had requested full access to the company's systems. He claimed to know nothing about data transfers.

Angela's phone started ringing. Some of her contacts in Asia, especially people she had met in Kuala Lumpur, started mentioning a new entrant on the market, out of China, promising to offer products looking suspiciously like a.r.m. prosthetics' products.

Angela, Roberto and Mike decided to confront their new shareholder. They requested the attorney to ask his client to come in person to the next Board meeting. Following his evasive response, they tried contacting *Shoubi* and its CEO directly, but only received promises that he would get back to them rapidly – which never materialized.

Only a few days later, their new shareholder sent an official request that the company be relocated in China and a new management team be appointed; if the company failed to do so, they threatened to cash out their investment. Angela, Roberto, and Mike considered this for what it seems to be: pure blackmail!

Angela, Roberto and Mike immediately asked their own lawyers what protective measures could be taken. The advised course of action was to file an action with the local courts to try and put a.r.m. prosthetics under protection, something that could be done rapidly – but potentially with little effect, considering their counterpart is based in a different country.

It soon became apparent that neither the company, nor its founders, could ever reimburse their mysterious shareholder. The attorney-representative of *Shoubi* therefore went to the local tribunal with a request that the company be liquidated, and that its assets be transferred to its main creditor. The equation was plain and simple: the foreign investor was using the local courts to receive full control of all company assets, both tangible (machines, prototypes, etc.) and intangible (data, patents, etc.), as payment for their exit from the company. The attorney claimed that the founders may steal their company's intellectual property, so they needed to be ordered to leave the premises, leave their computers behind and never return. The local court found in favor of this request. Soon after, Angela, Roberto and Mike were escorted out of their offices and passcodes were changed so that they could not return.

A few days later, all personnel were notified of their lay-off, with immediate effect.

This was the end of the road for a.r.m. prosthetics. All computers, patents, drawings and trademarks, together with all documentation and client files, were now in the hands of the liquidator, waiting to be transferred to some shady company and, one could only assume, heading to one of China's army's scientific labs.

A few weeks later, on his way to Prof. Mitchell's house, Roberto drove past their offices and found them locked and empty. Machines had been dismantled and loaded into containers. Over coffee with his favorite teacher, she mentioned that she was contacted, a few years back, by a company called Strider Technologies Inc[4]. They were doing research looking at how Western universities were collaborating, consciously or unconsciously,

---

[4] https://www.striderintel.com/

with Chinese military scientists[5] and, since her lab had come up in their dataset, she was asked for comment. While she acknowledged that she collaborated and coauthored papers with Chinese scientists, she did not know these people were linked with the Chinese People's Liberation Army and had never received any Governmental contact raising concerns or asking her to limit such collaborations. Upon learning about a.r.m. prosthetics' demise, she expressed her hope that these two events were unrelated.

---

[5] https://www.theglobeandmail.com/politics/article-chinese-military-scientists-canadian-universities/

Possible questions for discussion (non-exhaustive list)

1) What elements seem to indicate that this scenario is linked with hybrid warfare? What are the different, potential hybrid warfare techniques at play in this scenario?

2) How do you interpret the cyber incident mentioned half-way into the scenario? Should business C-suite members be more suspicious when such apparently benign events occur?

3) Draw a stakeholder map with all involved parties, i.e., a graphic representation of all actors, with arrows between them indicating support or opposition. List and prioritize the interests and values of the main stakeholders of the case.

4) Should Angela, Roberto and Mike have been more careful about their shareholder structures? How could they have done so?

5) From a business perspective, should States intervene to regulate and protect start-ups and other companies developing products or services with potential military applications? If so, how?

6) Are start-uppers typically sufficiently prepared to address the legal aspects of future business venture? Should you decide to become an entrepreneur, do you feel sufficiently prepared in Law?

7) The capitalist system in its 2010s version seemed to provide free flowing, widely available money to ingenious entrepreneurs. But by now, nefarious actors are known for using Western systems and institutions against Westerners. What are the different characteristics of Western capitalist systems that could be turned against Western Nations?

8) Numerous states develop mechanisms to accompany start-ups in their growth (incubators, services offered by the chamber of commerce, access to public funding, etc.). However, do they have the means to identify and protect innovators of products and/or services that could be of national interest (not limited to military or national security applications)?

9) Do you consider the hostile takeover of the company the fruit of a long-term plan or a purely opportunistic move?

Possible specific questions for lawyers and law students

1) From a legal perspective, should States intervene to regulate and protect start-ups and other companies developing products or services with potential military applications? If so, what legal instruments could be developed?

2) Imagine you are one of the founders' friends from college advising them in this scenario. You have taken a class on hybrid warfare in law school or have heard about it at a symposium. Would such prior knowledge of hybrid warfare have led you to advise them differently, maybe to direct them toward less risky financial decisions?

3) Analyze typical investor pacts used in your jurisdiction in terms of the risks of predatory behavior. Are they sufficiently protective against hybrid warfare moves? Should they be more protective? If so, at what cost (in terms of the other clauses of such contracts)?

4) "Start-up founders tend to overlook legal aspects of their business endeavor." What is your perspective, as a lawyer, on such a statement?

5) Did a.r.m. prosthetics' lawyers do their jobs appropriately? Was there anything they could have done to prevent the trap from functioning?

6) Local law firms have been used, in this scenario, to take control over a.r.m. prosthetics. What are the ethical implications of such actions? In practice, do they raise ethical concerns? Should they? Are there any ethics rules from your location of practice addressing such scenarios?

7) To close the trap, the nefarious actors are using the Western country's judiciary to pursue their own objectives. This is called "lawfare." Are your local jurisdictions well-equipped to protect citizens and companies against lawfare?

8

TROUBLE IN AGUDAMA-EPIE

Oluwaseun Ajaja, Michelle LeBaron,
Mariam Omotosho & Stanley Omotor

This case centers around Ochuko, a young Nigerian rising star in the oil sector with expertise in oil prospecting, extracting, and refining. Ochuko returned home to participate in the growth of his country's oil and gas industry. When he arrived, he encountered many complexities including espionage, covert state players, corruption, and exploitation of local communities. He began to wonder whether his employer was a front for a foreign entity with a stranglehold on the Nigerian oil sector regulators.

This case reveals the complexities of modern hybrid warfare in the context of a semi-autocratic state where there is little accountability for government policies and actions. Players with competing interests and links to shell companies and corruption vie for control over resources. Armed conflict is endemic in this high-tension atmosphere, pointing to the ways that apparently useful international collaboration and cooperation can result in terrible consequences for local industries and populations. The consequences of seeking or exposing truths that are not aligned with powerful narratives can be dire.

* * *

Keywords: Hybrid warfare – Oil – Corruption – Public opinion manipulation – Threats – Economic coercion – Seizure of natural resources – Espionage – Favoritism – Lawfare – Civil unrest

TROUBLE IN AGUDAMA-EPIE

Oluwaseun Ajaja, Michelle LeBaron,
Mariam Omotosho & Stanley Omotor[1]

Disclaimer

Although this scenario is designed to look real, it is not a true story. We believe such events may happen (or may have happened) in a different context but the scenario as described, and the characters, are based on the authors' imagination.

Authors' note:

This scenario shows how the search and quest for control of valuable natural resources can quickly yield asymmetrical conflict, where local people, with their spiritual traditions and values, may be sacrificed on the altar of profit. It illustrates labyrinthine relations between companies and multiple government entities, in which companies act as a front for governments (national and foreign). As private and national security forces get involved, collusion hurts less powerful locals and domestic companies, ultimately compromising patrimony and autonomy.

* * *

Startled by his alarm, 40-year-old Ochuko stirs and yawns. It is 5:30 AM. He risks arriving late at his new job if he does not get up right away. As a recognized rising star within the oil sector, Ochuko's expertise straddling oil prospecting, extraction, and refining had earned him respect across the industry. After recently completing his MBA at Lagos Business School, he felt a renewed sense of pride in returning home to contribute to Nigeria's oil and gas industry.

Nearly twenty years ago, Ochuko had earned his bachelor's degree in petrochemical engineering from Gubkin University, Russia. His career began then at Gazprom, Russia's largest oil company, where he worked for five years. Since leaving Gazprom, Ochuko's list of employers has included prominent players like Royal Dutch Shell PLC, Saudi Arabia Oil

[1] The authors owe a great debt of gratitude to the following people who participated in the drafting of earlier versions of this scenario, namely Phyllis Bernard, Chris Corpora, Robert Dingwall, John Gilmour, Chris Honeyman and Sharon Press.

Co., and China National Offshore Oil. His roles have given him access to leaders, regulators, government entities, investors, and other major players in the global oil sector.

After his MBA, Ochuko began consulting for local oil companies exploring and extracting oil in the oil-rich Niger Delta of Nigeria. His expertise caught the attention of SaOil Nigeria PLC – one of the largest oil and gas companies in Nigeria – which hired him to oversee crude oil extraction from Oil Mining Lease (OML) 21, situated in the oil-rich Agudama-Epie community in Bayelsa State. The SaOil Group, a Chinese oil company, owns a 49% stake in SaOil Nigeria PLC. While the process of securing OMLs from the Nigerian Department of Petroleum Resources usually takes at least two to three years, SaOil managed to obtain its OML just fifteen months after its incorporation in Nigeria. It has been rumored that this speed was related to SaOil's unusually generous campaign contributions to key politicians, among other things, but there is no evidence to substantiate this allegation.

Agudama-Epie, where SaOil Nigeria PLC is exploring and extracting oil, is a largely agrarian and fishing community with rich crude oil deposits. Given the few roads linking it to other communities and urban areas in Bayelsa State, the norms, traditions, and culture of Agudama-Epie have remained largely intact. Inhabitants of Agudama-Epie have also preserved their deep spiritual connection with the rivers and other water bodies located in the community. People from Agudama-Epie perceive water bodies in their territories as sacred, viewing them as the connecting pathway to their ancestors.

The recent discovery of large deposits of crude oil in Agudama-Epie's sacred waters elevated this little-known community to national prominence. Recently, the Minister of Petroleum, accompanied by major players in the oil industry, visited the community by the only means available – a fishing boat. During the visit, the Minister touted Agudama-Epie as the "next big thing," promising inhabitants government support to construct "urgently needed" basic infrastructure. While there, the Minister pointed to the thousands of direct and indirect jobs that the extraction and exploration of crude oil would create for the community. Though the visit took place over a year ago, no top government official has paid a follow-up visit to the community, and the promised infrastructure has yet to materialize.

Under the Land Use Act of 1978, all mineral resources in Nigeria are vested in the federal government, which can acquire land and water under the aegis of national interest to facilitate access to the minerals. Despite promising not to use the provisions of the Land Use Act to nationalize the Agudama-Epie rivers, the federal government proceeded to cultivate relationships with special interest groups, lobbyists, and religious leaders to generate support for doing exactly this. Coupled with subtle threats to community leaders (the government is well-known for draconian responses to civil opposition or disobedience), these tactics have worked: prominent sons and daughters of Agudama-Epie prevailed on the community to permit crude oil exploration and extraction. Spiritual claims related to the water were discounted.

Following nationalizing the rivers, the government invited bids from oil companies to explore for crude. As part of its bid, SaOil Nigeria PLC undertook to refine any crude oil extracted at its soon-to-be-completed refinery, strategically situated nearby in Bayelsa State. Refining nearby would sharply reduce the cost of refined crude products to local consumers, as competitors import their refined crude from foreign refineries. As well, the refining and distribution activities would create longer-term jobs than the oil exploration phase itself – so SaOil assured the government that the refinery would provide 1,000 permanent jobs and close to 10,000 indirect jobs.

SaOil Nigeria PLC had another long-term objective that it claimed would benefit Nigeria: increasing its market access to the Nigerian oil industry by gradually establishing sister entities to control downstream activities. Ultimately, the goal of SaOil Nigeria PLC was to secure a lion's share of the oil sector and thus become an irreplaceable player with increasing influence. In setting up SaOil Nigeria PLC, the parent company was careful to ensure that 51% of the stock would be in the hands of wholly-Nigerian-owned companies. The newly created stock was sold to just two private Nigerian firms (25% to one and 26% to the other) in transactions out of the public eye. These two firms were not listed on the stock market, and much of their business was obscure. A well-respected and award-winning Lagos business journalist reported that the initial stock price was set suspiciously low, and that the two firms were controlled by families closely affiliated with key Nigerian political figures. The journalist pointed to de facto Chinese control of SaOil Nigeria PLC, writing that both firms were almost entirely dependent on China. They wrote that one of them makes goods that appeal to Chinese tastes but have no ready market outside China; the other depends on China as a virtually irreplaceable source of key materials in its supply chain.

Ochuko's principal current task is to assist SaOil Nigeria PLC in navigating oil development in OML 21. His bosses have told him that if he is successful, he will be the leading candidate for the more prestigious job of running the refinery. As he drives towards SaOil's refinery, under construction on the Epie river (the most sacred of all the waters in Agudama-Epie), he notices a traffic build-up. CEC – a member of the conglomerate to which SaOil Nigeria PLC's parent company belongs – has begun constructing roads to link Agudama-Epie to urban areas. CEC is notorious for being slow to situate Nigerians in higher paying jobs; the company has fueled resentment by importing not only Chinese technicians and managers but even front-line supervisors and semi-skilled mechanics in preference to available locals. Ochuko shakes his head and mutters unhappily under his breath: "These Chinese people are taking over our country; wherever you turn, you find them constructing one thing or another."

Ochuko's frustration is not misplaced. With barely concealed subsidies from the Chinese Government, CEC had outbid local competitors for the contract to construct SaOil's refinery, and sub-contracted technical aspects of the construction to its sister companies. Given multi-layered and complex contractual relationships between them,

CEC and its sister companies had consistently outbid local competitors, even on infrastructure jobs that local competitors were well-qualified to handle.

CEC's contractual terms with the government do not permit CEC to be granted any regulatory concessions, nor any access to classified data or intelligence briefings. Yet CEC appears to be receiving both kinds of help. Rumors swirl that – in addition to turning a blind eye to a range of regulatory shortcuts, especially when they are deniable – some senior government officials (for some yet to be ascertained reasons) are providing CEC with intelligence data not available to other firms.

In turn, and pursuant to the 2017 Chinese National Intelligence Law, CEC allegedly passes on the intelligence reports it obtains from Nigerian government officials to Chinese intelligence agencies including the Ministry of State Security (MSS), which critically analyzes the reports on Nigeria's affairs. It also appears to rely on such information to identify stressors and conditions that could help CEC gain a more significant foothold in the country's political economy. CEC also apparently shares much of that information with its sister firms, giving all of them an edge over competitors across a range of commercial activities.

Recalling his experience working for other prominent oil companies, Ochuko wonders whether the Nigerian government has considered the consequences of CEC's complex relationships. He also worries about the implications of the rumored flow of sensitive state secrets to the Chinese intelligence agencies. Based on his experience at Saudi Arabia Oil, he suspects it may not even end there; he suspects that the US National Security Agency may well have the electronic capacity to piggy-back information from all these flows. This could potentially result in US allies such as the Five Eyes also having access to information kept secret from ordinary Nigerians and other Nigerian firms. Because there is no evidence of any attempt by the Five Eyes to interfere with this information flow, Ochuko suspects that they have decided simply to monitor it, with a possible future objective of feeding disinformation into the information stream. If any of this is true, the implications for Nigeria are unclear, but worrying all the same.

Ochuko has long suspected that – through such piggy-backing – the US has been able to stifle competition, creating a dwindling field of competitors (and therefore contract terms unnecessarily unfavorable to Africa) in telecommunications, infrastructure, and oil industries within resource-rich countries. A report recently released by the World Trade Organization confirmed some of his suspicions. He wonders whether China or the US (or both) have strong-armed the Nigerian government to roll back its anticompetition law and regulations within the Nigerian telecommunications and oil and gas industries. Considering China's and the US's competing ideological stances, Ochuko's curiosity is piqued.

Ochuko also questions whether Nigerians or members of the international community are aware of CEC's connection to the CCP and to Chinese firms in apparently unrelated industries. He worries about the consequences of these complex relationships for Nigeria's political economy, but feels resigned. He thinks aloud: "Nationally, no one will hear of this, not when the Broadcasting Commission keeps an intrusively probing eye on news outlets and other media not owned by the government or its cronies." Indeed, a media outlet that released an exposé on a reported oil spillage caused by NelOil (another CCP-backed company) which destroyed the environment of the neighboring Burutu community found itself invaded by a group of unidentified paramilitary personnel of mixed race, acting on "orders from above", without any further explanation. Such incursions, generally justified under the disguise of "national security", aimed to silence dissent and curtail public discourse. The same outlet had also alleged that NelOil had conducted a sham risk impact assessment which NelOil claimed had shown minimal adverse impacts for the Burutu community. They further reported that the risk assessment consulting company was a shell firm located outside Nigeria and operating under the control of NelOil. SaOil Nigeria PLC used the same company for its risk impact assessment in Agudama-Epie.

Monitoring and silencing extended beyond media firms. A social media influencer who exposed some of the complexities and distortions in the industry, and publicized the death of about two dozen Burutu inhabitants from environmental degradation, was arrested on charges of fraud and leaking state secrets. Observers view these charges as thinly veiled attempts to suppress dissent and dissuade others from speaking out.

As ever, the local populace relies more on local rumors than on the necessarily suspect national press. Locals are currently seething from the rumors, and from their growing suspicions that they will be shut out of long-term employment or other gains resulting from all this activity. This anger has generated increasing attacks on the construction, equipment, and employees of SaOil Nigeria PLC and its sister companies. Responding to these threats to its investments, SaOil tapped a Chinese security firm for help. The security firm's rank-and-file personnel are Nigerian, though not the more senior officers. Tensions within the security firm are rising, and a local journalist claims to have unearthed proof that the staff have deliberately been recruited from the northern part of Nigeria, with which there is considerable tension with the oil-rich Agudama-Epie area. The security firm claims to be providing "technical support" to the Nigerian government in battling the increasingly aggressive militancy in the Niger Delta region.

Recently, an American security firm's trucks and personnel have been observed in Agudama-Epie. This firm appears to have strong military ties and is employed by an American oil company operating a lease 200 miles from Agudama-Epie. Journalists have inquired about their presence far from their supposed area of concern but have received no explanation. Coupled with the visible presence of Nigeria's security patrols, Ochuko worries that civil unrest is about to break out in the Niger Delta. General agitation has led to increased tensions between civil society organizations and oil industry players in the area. Ochuko worries that a mishap might ignite a flame of violence that could consume the region. While foreign interests could promptly exit, any long-term impact would be felt by Nigerians who would be left with the mess.

Aware of this risk, civil society organizations and community leaders in the region have tried to influence the Nigerian government to de-escalate tensions. In a recent meeting with the Nigerian Security Council, the president promised to study their request and act accordingly. However, a recently botched counter-militancy operation that led to the death of two Chinese nationals involved in Nigerian military efforts – apparently by military hardware exclusively used by the United States military – threatened to further escalate tension in the region. Subsequent investigations revealed that the hardware was a knockoff and not US hardware. China then became the leading suspect in most local people's eyes. But would the Chinese government kill its own citizens? What would it gain from doing so? Or could this be corporate sabotage by a competitor, seeking to undermine China's investment in the region? The answers to these questions are unclear.

In addition, a case at the Federal High Court alleging the direct involvement of the Nigerian government in invading the media outlet who exposed NelOil's questionable oil extraction practices has stalled. The government has claimed that the delay relates to national security concerns. Ochuko is not surprised. In his employment in Chinese, Russian and Saudi Arabian firms, this is a familiar tactic that governments employ to protect their interests and investments. But whose interest is the Nigerian government protecting in this instance? Answering that question would be a complicated task; Ochuko feels ill-prepared to undertake it. Yet, he does know that – until that question is answered – the fate that befell Burutu could be minor compared to what awaits Agudama-Epie.

Possible questions for all audiences

1) What elements make you consider this may be a full-fledged hybrid warfare situation? Identify all hybrid warfare mechanisms at play in the scenario. How do they play in conjunction with one another? What do you notice about the nature of hybrid warfare as you apply a conflict analysis lens to this situation?

2) Draw a map of all stakeholders involved in the story. Who are the relevant people and institutions that should be considered in this situation and how do they interrelate? List and prioritize the interests of each of the main stakeholders of the case.

3) From Ochuko's perspective, what is the broader context of these issues? How can he and others find out the truth about where power levers exist, and who is pulling them?

4) Describe the conflicts and issues in this case. How do they relate to control over resources, access to sensitive information, use of militaries and private security firms to silence dissidents or other issues?

5) Who are the main parties in the emerging conflicts, and what are their interests and worldviews? Consider state actors; non-state actors including companies (foreign and domestic); press and social media; private citizens; intelligence agents/security actors; militias and militaries; members of civil society. Anyone else?

6) What obstacles prevent protection of national and community interests?

7) What part do rumours play in grey zone conflicts, as gleaned from this scenario? (For example, misinformation; whistleblowing; distraction; others?)

8) Given the labyrinthine nature of transnational dynamics, what roles do companies play in shaping foreign and domestic policies?

9) How might more powerful countries use proxies (including less powerful countries; shell and complex networks of companies; or people from local communities incentivized to champion resource extraction activities, etc.) in their relations with each other?

10) What effect might arms proliferation, under the guise of infrastructure safety, have on conflict escalation?

11) Describe the broader context within which these conflicts are unfolding. (For example, how do they relate to erosion of the rule of law and transparent governance; corruption; espionage; abuse of right to self-determination of indigenous peoples; neocolonialism and other phenomena?)

12) Which conflicts are manifest, and which are latent? How do local interests in relation to resources relate to access to sensitive and security information? What roles is the national government playing in relation to dissidents?

13) In hybrid warfare, economic, political, technical, social, intelligence and security resources may be used to influence or control sovereign states and local populations. How might these resources be implicated in this scenario?

14) With transnational transactions on the increase, what roles do companies play in countries' foreign policies? Consider, e.g., economic exploitation; political manipulation; and other actions by foreign actors that attract neither repercussions nor accountability, creating environmental and health hazards through resource exploitation activities.

"Undermine the legitimacy of key institutions." From a series of weavings by Rachel Parish, with quotes from Qiao and Wang's *Unrestricted Warfare* (People's Liberation Army Publishing House, Beijing 1999.) In color at https://rachelparish.com/projects/gentle-and-kind-things/

Part 4:
Geopolitical Cases

9

Nord Stream – A Commercial Project With Geopolitical, Environmental and Energy Security Implications

Barney Jordaan & Leonard Lira

This case sketches the background to the development of the Nord Stream pipelines. This is a controversial project: the construction of one (then a second) pipeline connecting Russia and Germany via an underwater route beneath the Baltic Sea. The project was nearly completed prior to Russia's invasion of Ukraine which began on 24 February 2022. Despite subsequent events – including the bombing of the pipeline in September 2022 – dramatically changing the scenario, it nevertheless serves as confirmation of the potential implications of situations where private commercial actors negotiate with State-owned or State-controlled counterparts.

* * *

Keywords: Hybrid warfare – Nord Stream – Natural gas – Supply disruption – Private companies – Geopolitical implications – Energy independence – Germany – Russia – Ukraine

* * *

Sources:

- Adomeit, H. (2016). Germany, the EU, and Russia: The Conflict over Nord Stream 2. Available at attach_670.pdf (europeangashub.com)

- CNBC U.S. warns companies to abandon work on Nord Stream 2 pipeline (cnbc.com)

- Goldthau, A. (2016). Assessing Nord Stream 2: Regulation, geopolitics & energy security in the EU, Central Eastern Europe & the UK. Available at *Goldthau July 2016.pdf (asktheeu.org)

- Kardaś, S. (2019). The great troublemaker: Nord Stream 2 in Russia's foreign energy policy. International Issues & Slovak Foreign Policy Affairs, Vol.28(3/4): 25–44. https://www.jstor.org/stable/26905904

- Lang, K.-O., & Westphal, K. (2017). Nord Stream 2: a political and economic contextualisation. Available at https://nbn-resolving.org/urn:nbn:de:0168-ssoar-51318-5

- Neumann, A.; Göke, L.; Holz, F.; Kemfert, C. & von Hirschhausen, C. (2018). Natural gas supply: No need for another Baltic Sea pipeline. Deutsches Institut für Wirtschaftsforschung (DIW), Berlin, Vol. 8(27): 241-248.

- Pan, L.; Wang,Y.; Sun, X.; Sadiq, M. & Dagestani. A.A. (2003). Natural resources: A determining factor of geopolitical risk in Russia? Revisiting conflict-based perspective, Resources Policy, Vol. 85, Part A. The Nord Stream 2 gas pipeline and Germany's relationship with Russia. (2021). Strategic Comments, 27(3), i–iv. https://doi.org/10.1080/13567888.2021.1929494

Nord Stream – A Commercial Project With Geopolitical, Environmental and Energy Security Implications

Barney Jordaan & Leonard Lira[1]

Authors' note

This case was drafted in 2021 and last edited in October 2024. It is based on the way the events have been depicted by Western media at the time. The fact that this version of events is used in this educational document does not mean the authors are endorsing it. The incident has been subject to misinformation and disinformation; later events may color this scenario and affect the questions for discussion we propose. While reading the scenario, we therefore invite readers to position themselves at a specific time during the events described, and to clarify their time standpoint when discussing it.

* * *

History

Gas trade between Russia and Western Europe dates to the 1970s, when the then USSR started gas deliveries to Western Europe. Russia is home to 17 percent of the world's conventional gas reserves. The energy industry is crucial for its domestic economic development, with growth being driven to a substantial degree by large infrastructure investments.

Overall, the natural resource sector contributes significantly to Russia's GDP. Oil and gas revenues account for over half of the Russian budget income and two thirds of total export revenues. They are also the source of significant opportunities for corruption, which helps to ensure the stability of the current political system and hold on power by incumbent political actors.

For most of the past 40-odd years, gas deliveries to Europe have run smoothly, despite the heyday of the Cold War, via two sets of pipelines:

[1] Primary drafters. The authors are grateful for the inputs received from our Project Seshat colleagues Anne Leslie, I. William Zartman, Sanda Kaufman and Heidi and Guy Burgess in developing this case. A special word of thanks to Adrian Borbély for his comments and suggestions. The remaining errors are our own.

- Soyuz, built in 1978 and originating in Southern Russia / Kazakhstan, and Brotherhood, constructed in 1983 and originating in Northern Russia, both passing through Ukraine.

- Yamal, constructed in the 1990s, passing through Belarus and Poland.

Multinational pipelines raise several issues regarding ownership and operation. Traditionally, even though there is a global operator of the pipeline, each country operates (or chooses the operator of) the parts of the pipeline sited on its soil. Using their "transit monopoly" status, they may also collect a fee for each unit of hydrocarbon transported by the pipeline – and negotiate to buy some for their own consumption. They may also influence the amount of product flowing through the pipeline. This raises no issue when countries are allied (such as Belarus and Russia on the one hand, or EU member States on the other hand).

On the first pipelines travelling through Ukraine and Poland (Soyuz, Brotherhood, and Yamal), between 1991 and 2005, there were no fewer than 55 incidents involving suspension or threats of suspension of Russian energy supplies. A major crisis occurred in 2009 when Russia cut off gas supplies to 16 EU member states, which particularly impacted East European countries and their economies. This followed a dispute between Russia and Ukraine over gas deliveries and prices. At the time Western observers established a causal link between the timing and intensity of these conflicts and Ukraine's so-called "Orange Revolution" and its subsequent re-orientation toward the West. Since 2014, the disputes over natural gas exports have reached a new quality with the Russian annexation of Crimea and South-eastern Ukraine as well as the subsequent sanctions by the EU and the United States against Russia.

The 2009 crisis highlighted the political links between Gazprom – the pipelines' operator – and the Russian government, and the strategic importance of Russian gas exports for the Kremlin. The general view that Gazprom is more than a mere commercial enterprise is justified also by the close interconnections between the corporation and top government officials past and present. For instance, before becoming President of Russia, Dmitry Medvedev was chairman of the board of directors of Gazprom.

In part to mitigate the risk of meddling by foreign Nations, in part to increase the amounts of natural gas flowing to Europe, another infrastructure was built more recently, this time travelling through the Baltic seabed (i.e., mostly in international waters) from Russia to Germany: the Nord Stream pipelines, Nord Stream 1 (NS1) being inaugurated in 2011 (construction started in 2005) and Nord Stream 2 (NS2), designed to double its capacity. Construction started in 2011 and was almost completed by 2021.

The operator of the Nord Stream pipelines is Nord Stream AG, a consortium incorporated in Switzerland, owned at 51% by Gazprom, the remaining 49% being shared by energy companies from Germany, France, and the Netherlands. As such, the project was funded by these different actors, under the supervision of their respective State authorities.

Studies suggest that energy and Russian foreign policy are much closer linked than commonly assumed, with oil or gas deliveries either being a cause of Russian intervention or a means thereof.

The construction of the Nord Stream pipelines

In September 2005, Gazprom and its Western European partner companies concluded an agreement to construct a first transboundary submarine gas infrastructure, NS1. The pipeline, taken into service in 2011, carries large volumes of gas from Russia's Baltic coast to Greifswald in Germany. The pipeline stretches some 1200 kilometers under the Baltic Sea, which makes it one of the world's longest undersea pipelines. Even before NS1 entered service, a decision was made to double capacity through a second pipeline (NS2) that would follow the same route under the Baltic Sea.

The Nord Stream infrastructure aimed to bypass the old Soviet-era energy transit infrastructure that traverses Ukraine, Belarus, and Poland. For these countries, this means the loss of billions of dollars in transit fees as well as these countries' transit leverage. Russia, on the other hand, was provided with an opportunity to cut off gas supplies to Ukraine and Poland without hurting major West European customers such as gas-dependent Germany, the staunchest supporter of the project in the EU.

Some experts have argued that the energy consumption forecasts on which the NS2 project is based significantly overestimate natural gas demand in Germany and Europe and that there will be no supply gap if NS2 is not completed. Different profitability studies also suggest that high losses can be expected from the project. In other words, the project might be a waste of money.

The German government's stance has been consistent that the Nord Stream project is a purely commercial project involving private investors and that the government, and the EU for that matter, therefore, should refrain from interfering. Its operators also argue that it is a profitable, private sector investment project that is necessary to secure natural gas supplies for Germany and Europe. Politically, however, the construction of the Nord Stream pipelines is strongly contested both within the EU and by the USA.

Controversies

Nord Stream is a controversial project for several reasons:

A. It is contested because of its geopolitical implications, given Russia's increasingly assertive foreign policy, especially in Eastern Europe. Because of these concerns, several newer EU member states and the USA have pushed for higher diversification of the European gas import portfolio. They view Nord Stream as potentially cementing Russia's dominant role in EU gas supply and as a political instrument to deprive Eastern European transit countries not only of their transit revenues but also of an important insurance policy against Russian meddling.

B. Three EU legislations called "energy packages" underpin the EU's drive to expand free market principles to the energy sector. The EU aims to enhance consumer choice, market transparency and competition in energy sources, including natural gas. The EU's regulatory efforts also aim at enhancing market robustness and resilience. The liberal market paradigm that informs the EU's gradual opening of energy markets can therefore also be a tool for addressing increasing insecurity over Russian supplies, transit, or other external energy challenges. The EU has declared itself in favour of Ukraine as the main transit country for Russian natural gas imports and supports Ukraine's efforts to strengthen its independence by facilitating natural gas purchases from Western Europe. However, Nord Stream runs counter to these ambitions, putting the credibility of the EU gas policy at risk.

C. While the United States also supports efforts to strengthen Ukraine as a transit country, and while the first Trump administration imposed sanctions on private actors participating in the Nord Stream project, sanctions have since been lifted by the Biden administration, effectively giving the pipeline the all-clear.[2]

D. There are concerns within the EU about its own future energy security if it becomes too dependent on Russia for its energy needs.

E. Gazprom has a history of corrupt dealings, and the fear is that such corruption may also have played a role in the Nord Stream deals, whose primary beneficiaries are Russia, Germany and the companies forming part of the consortium. Some of these private actors from the EU have also been accused in the past of not shying away from underhand dealings. Former German Chancellor Gerhard Schröder is the Chairman of the Board of Nord Stream AG. His acceptance of the job less than one month after he left the chancellor's office prompted widespread criticism in Germany. He and Russian President Vladimir Putin had worked closely on cementing German investment in the pipeline.

F. Ukraine will be particularly hard hit if it were to lose its significance as a transit country. Its gas infrastructure is likely to lose all meaning for Europe and there will be much less chance of securing external financing for the modernisation of Ukrainian gas pipelines. There will probably also be much less European interest in the integration of Ukraine's gas sector with that of the EU, especially if the current EU gas market reforms were not going to be substantially advanced and

---

[2] The decision to withdraw its objections to the pipeline was made after a 2021 meeting between President Biden and Chancellor Merkel of Germany. According to reports, the Biden administration calculated that continuing to express its disagreement with a nearly finished pipeline strained its relationship with Germany for little benefit. A face-saving alternative was found in the form of an agreement that pledges to establish a billion-dollar fund to provide energy security for Ukraine and sustainable energy initiatives across Europe. The down payment is roughly $250 million to promote Ukraine's transition to clean energy and improve energy infrastructure security. The agreement also provides that should Russia use energy as a weapon or engage in military aggression in Ukraine, Germany will "press for effective measures at the European level", including possible sanctions. This is probably cold comfort for Ukraine. For the Biden administration the vagueness of the agreement is diplomatically deliberate to suit its reluctance to acquiesce to a deal that so advantages Russia as well as Germany.

effectively implemented. Russia has an interest in ensuring that closer political, military, and economic cooperation between the EU and Ukraine, with its emphasis on free trade, will not work. Vladimir Putin's aide for Eurasian integration, Sergey Glazev, is on record stating that Ukraine will be driven into bankruptcy. Nord Stream will remove one of the few strong cards still held by Ukraine in its asymmetrical relationship with Russia.

G. Nord Stream has other drawbacks as well, including a potentially negative ecological impact on the fragile Baltic Sea basin with its unique ecosystem, which the International Maritime Organization has given the status of a particularly sensitive sea area.

H. Vast changes in the global energy markets may already have made Nord Stream obsolete. If the project does not make (or no longer makes) economic sense in terms of ongoing gas pricing, as many analysts allege, the only beneficiaries will be the companies involved in the construction consortium and Russia for its own strategic purposes. If this is the case, European unity could be severely impacted.

I. Nord Stream also raises national security and military concerns. Sweden rejected plans to use the strategically sensitive island of Gotland as a base for construction because of concerns about national security. Given increased Russian military presence in the Baltic Sea since 2014, there are fears that Russia might use the project as an excuse to extend its military presence in the area.

J. There are growing fears within the EU that Russia is deliberately trying to weaken EU cohesion and that Nord Stream will provide it with a further opportunity to do so. The project has already caused disputes between Germany, its Eastern neighbours and some of the Nordic countries. There is a fear among some Eastern European states about the possible strategic and geopolitical consequences German-Russian rapprochement will have for them.

Nord Stream, therefore, would appear to be more than simply a commercial project. It is embedded in a charged geopolitical context that enlarges Gazprom's export options, cements Russia's grip on Europe, and puts Germany in a strategically more advantageous position than its EU partners, while depriving some Eastern European countries of their insurance policy against politically motivated supply cuts by Russia.

February 24, 2022: The aftermath of Russia's invasion of Ukraine

Prior to Russia's invasion of Ukraine, on 22 February 2022, the grey zone conflict in Eastern Europe surrounding Ukraine and the Russia-to-Europe pipeline network included a series of low-intensity military, political, and economic actions taken by Russia against Ukraine and its allies in the region, in addition to Russia's 2014 invasion of Crimea.

Among other things, Russia's invasion of Crimea sparked concerns regarding Europe's dependence on Russian energy and led to pressure being brought to bear on the Nord

Stream project. From the beginning, many European countries, including Ukraine and Poland, expressed opposition to Nord Stream, emphasizing its potential negative impact on European security and energy diversification. Several countries and entities, including the United States, also imposed sanctions, and called for a halt to the Nord Stream project. In December 2021, construction activities around NS2 were suspended due to U.S. sanctions targeting companies involved in the project.

Despite the temporary suspension, efforts were made to complete the pipeline. In early 2022, Russia announced plans to finish the remaining portion of the pipeline independently, reducing reliance on external contractors. However, the United States continued to impose sanctions on entities and individuals involved in the construction and operation of NS2 which were aimed at deterring involvement and financing of the project, making it more challenging to proceed.

Germany, a key proponent of Nord Stream 2, faced criticism for its support of the project amid the geopolitical tensions. On February 22, 2022, the German Chancellor announced that his country suspended the certification process for the pipeline in reaction to Russia's recognition of the self-proclaimed republics in Luhansk and Donetsk in East Ukraine.[3] This meant that the pipeline, though virtually completed by then, could not go into operation.

In his announcement, the Chancellor said that Russia's recognition of the Russian-controlled territories constituted a "grave breach of international law that broke with decades of agreements between Russia and the West."

The decision drew condemnation and threats from Moscow, where the former Russian President and Deputy Chair of Russia's security council Dmitry Medvedev tweeted: "Welcome to the brave new world where Europeans are very soon going to pay €2.000 for 1.000 cubic metres of natural gas!"

At the same time, Germany kept arguing that the pipeline was a commercial project that would enhance energy security and contribute to stable gas supplies. In July 2021, the United States and Germany had reached a political agreement regarding Nord Stream 2. As part of the agreement, Germany committed to support Ukraine's energy transition and security and promote European energy diversification. Germany also committed to utilize all available leverage to facilitate an extension of up to 10 years to Ukraine's gas Transit Agreement with Russia. It also committed to establish and administer a Green Fund for Ukraine to support Ukraine's energy transition, energy efficiency, and energy security, with both Germany and the US promoting and supporting investments in the Fund.

September 26, 2022: the sabotage of the Nord Stream pipelines

In September 2022, both pipelines were filled with gas, but none was delivered to Germany, for the following reasons:

---

[3] https://www.reuters.com/business/energy/germanys-scholz-halts-nord-stream-2-certification-2022-02-22/

- Operations had not officially started on NS2.

- Operations were halted on NS1. The official reason given was maintenance: an oil leak was found on the main turbine on the Russian side. It was not rapidly repaired, Gazprom claiming operations were slowed down due to the EU sanctions against Russia (a claim that was disputed at the time).

On September 26, sudden pressure drops were detected on both NS1 and NS2. A rapid enquiry led to discovering multiple ruptures on two separate sites, both close to the Danish Island of Bornholm, linked to a series of underwater explosions that were picked up by seismic sensors. The gas contained in the pipes leaked to the water surface. Both pipelines were rendered unusable, probably permanently.

Both Russia and the US were quick to claim acts of sabotage and soon, investigations both by European Nations and by Russia drew similar conclusions. However, it is not entirely clear who was to blame for what Russia was quick to call "an act of international terrorism." Fingers were pointed at Russia, Ukraine, the USA, and other NATO members. Russia's military warships were observed in the zone of the explosions days prior to the bombing; but the USA had warned in early February 2022 that should Russia invade Ukraine, it would halt NS2.[4] And a suspicious sailboat, rented by a Polish company owned by two Ukrainian men, was observed in the area. The UK's Royal Navy was also pointed at. While many had a potential interest in the permanent halting of Nord Stream, and while only slim evidence could be gathered to identify the real culprits, a report in the Washington Post of November 11, 2023, pointed to the involvement of a senior officer in the Ukrainian special operations forces.[5]

Putin's dilemma

Meanwhile, President Putin is facing a wicked problem: his framing of the problem as a dispute between Russia and Ukraine is now widely perceived as having been insufficient to predict the sudden unity among Western (and many Eastern) European nations, let alone the lengths to which they have been prepared to go in sanctions and weapons delivery. The inability of Russia to control the conflict externally, contrary to its predictions, has resulted in incidences of Russian State security forces implementing more grey zone tactics internally, to control the narrative and sustain the Russian population's support for the ongoing military operations in Ukraine, as well as externally.

---

[4] https://www.reuters.com/business/energy/if-russia-invades-ukraine-there-will-be-no-nord-stream-2-biden-says-2022-02-07/

[5] Ukrainian military officer coordinated Nord Stream pipeline attack: https://www.washingtonpost.com/national-security/2023/11/11/nordstream-bombing-ukraine-chervinsky/

Relevant actors' positions (prior to February 2022)

The positions of potential players related to the Nord Stream project prior to February 2022 are listed below. The lines become blurred as parties to the contract expand to include "invisible hands" controlling the outcome of the transaction with considerations that transcend mere maximisation of profits.

Students are invited to review these positions and then use the questions posted below to reflect on the complexity of this case.

More recent events have shown who are the real players above the commercial level. They have demonstrated, for example, how quickly the project could be terminated by political actors who, just weeks before, nobody thought had the stomach for the resulting pain, especially Germany. However, *any* hybrid warfare case must be examined in the context of the time in which it is set: change is the most likely future condition,[6] and 20/20 hindsight tends to obscure the real choices available to real participants at the time. So, despite subsequent events having dramatically affected this scenario, it nevertheless serves as confirmation of the potential implications of situations where private commercial actors negotiate with state-owned or state-controlled counterparts. Accordingly, the key postures of key players are given here as of late 2021:

The European Union

There is disagreement within the EU-28 over future relations with Russia, including energy relations. While Brussels officially proclaims solidarity with Ukraine, concrete political measures are dictated by short-term crisis management. Moreover, a degree of disillusionment is detectable within the members of the Union.

Southern & Eastern European Governments

Firstly, Southern & Eastern European governments are concerned that Gazprom could target its market power significantly more precisely by ensuring adequate supplies only to the Northwest European markets (via Nord Stream), while manipulating the volumes flowing via the Ukrainian corridor to central Eastern and South-East European markets and Ukraine itself.

Second and more importantly, Eastern European countries also fear that loss of transit status will weaken their position in talks with Russia. Although these concerns cannot be rejected out of hand, their situation appears rather different from the perspective of the North-Western European markets; they perceive a danger of becoming drawn into political quarrels between transit states and Russia (regardless of who is to blame).

Northern & Western European Governments

Countries such as Italy and Austria are questioning the legitimacy of continued EU sanctions and policies against Nord Stream. Many of the Northern and Western European countries feel that the EU is overemphasizing Russia's aggression against Ukraine (an

---

[6] The phrase "A week is a long time in politics" is attributed to former British Prime Minister Harold Wilson, ca. 1964 – but more recently often upgraded to "a lifetime."

Eastern regional issue) in comparison to the benefits of the Nord Stream deal, and that this is to the detriment of the Western European countries' economic development.

Northern & Western European Corporations

The Western European firms (especially those who participate in Nord Stream AG) would like to see their partnership with Gazprom expanded through the pipeline construction, especially given that their supply contracts with the Russian energy giant extend for decades to come. In view of the complex current market situation, characterised by declining production within the EU, depressed gas prices and a difficult business environment in Russia, they are interested in strengthening their market positions as suppliers, energy traders and/or gas producers, and safeguarding their investments in Russia. This strategy also reflects a very pragmatic attitude towards economic realities: in the short and medium term (until the end of the 2020s), Gazprom can supply gas to the EU in flexible quantities at competitive prices.

The United States

The Biden Administration has called Nord Stream a "bad deal" and said that U.S. opposition to the pipeline is "unwavering." Nevertheless, U.S. officials have suggested the Administration's ability to prevent the pipeline from becoming operational is limited, even with additional sanctions. They at times also have expressed concern that additional U.S. sanctions could jeopardize U.S. – German and U.S. – European cooperation in other areas, including countering Russian aggression. Accordingly, the Administration's diplomatic efforts increasingly appear to be aimed at helping Ukraine maintain its leverage as a gas transit country even if the pipeline becomes operational. The US asserts that Moscow is building pipelines in the Baltic for geopolitical motives, specifically that they aim at weakening Ukraine by bypassing it as a gas transit country.

The Russian Government

Expanding into external energy markets is one of Moscow's key political goals. It is an important instrument for achieving the State's political goals, as they use the energy sector as an important domestic and foreign policy tool. Strengthening the State's position on international energy markets serves to increase Moscow's geopolitical influence. On the one hand, the project allows Russia to cease using Ukraine as a transit country. On the other hand, it increases Russia's political leverage toward the European Union, by driving a potential political wedge between central European countries such as Poland and Slovakia, and Western European countries like France, the Netherlands, and Germany. Since oil and gas are Russia's main exports, any contract its State-owned enterprise, Gazprom, enters almost always has political (and security) undertones. Therefore, in Russia, Nord Stream is both a commercial deal and a matter of national interest.

Gazprom

New export pipelines are also important to Gazprom's attempts to achieve its own economic goals. The construction of new gas pipelines is intended to maintain and, in the long term, even strengthen Gazprom's position on the European market (in recent years, its share has regularly exceeded 30 per cent, and in 2018 has reached 36.7 per cent). The Baltic connection will allow Gazprom to directly supply its largest market, Germany, to expand deliveries, and to reduce the transit risks to other major customers (including France). However, since 2014, Russia has made it abundantly clear that it is seeking alternative export routes, to avoid or minimise gas transport through Ukraine, which it now regards as an unacceptable risk. For the Russians, this was the main reason to build Nord Stream. At the height of the crisis over Ukraine in 2014, the Kremlin and Gazprom headquarters both called for a complete end to Ukrainian transit. During the following year, 2015, the position was somewhat relativised, with Gazprom now intimating that it had been told to negotiate post-2019 transit terms with Ukraine.

The German Government

The German Government is determined to strengthen economic cooperation with Russia despite EU sanctions on Moscow. Furthermore, Germany has taken actions to reduce EU legal sanctions that would affect future negotiations. Economically, this is important for Germany as it seeks to secure a major gas distribution centre within its own territory. The dilemma for Germany is to stay aligned with critics of the pipeline and sustain a strong Western stance against Russia, while securing its own economic aspirations that the pipeline offers.

German Corporations

Like the German government, German corporations believe Nord Stream to be a purely commercial transaction with important long-term benefits for the German economy and company profits. Additionally, it is a bonus for European energy security. However, they consider controversies as an indication that the project has possible unforeseen risks.

Possible questions for discussion

The following questions do not have an immediate, clear answer, and can apply to any State or corporate actor in this case study. Questions are divided into two parts, depending on the time position respondents are required to adopt.

Questions focusing on part 1 (prior to Russia's 2022 invasion of mainland Ukraine):

1) What, if anything, makes Nord Stream a simple business transaction, and what makes it seem different from other business-to-business transactions?

2) The case outlines several levels of interactions: between companies, between the States directly involved (Russia and Germany, maybe the EU), or at a broader international level (including Ukraine and the USA). Taking the perspective of interest-based negotiation as popularized by Fisher and Ury: what are the interests at play at these different levels (common, compatible, and competing)? Would it be possible to find an agreement that satisfies all actors? If so, what would it look like?

3) Gazprom appears to be both a capitalist company (aiming for shareholder value maximization) and a tool of the Kremlin's political agenda. How does one negotiate with such a double-role actor?

4) What are the asymmetrical issues present in this case? In other words, what aspects of this case seem clouded or hidden? For example, who was really negotiating with whom? Who had the most leverage and what did that consist of? What were the respective no deal alternatives of the parties to the deal at the time?

Questions focusing on part 2 (after Russia's invasion of Ukraine):

1) Given the violent conflict present in the region, can the parties continue commercial negotiations in good faith?

2) From the perspective of general negotiation theory, are interest-based negotiation models capable of delivering mutual gains appropriate to resolve the current conflict given all the players involved and the broader economic, environmental, and geopolitical implications of such deals? If not, how should those interest-based negotiation models be augmented?

3) Develop a map indicating who the stakeholders are that are directly or indirectly connected to the Nord Stream case.

4) Assume that you have been asked by one of the commercial players involved in the original transaction (e.g., Shell) prior to the deal being negotiated with Gazprom to provide advice about the potential pitfalls of the proposed transaction. Knowing what you know now from the information provided in the case study:

   a. Which potential pitfalls can you identify?

   b. What would your advice to your client be about how to deal with those?

   c. Based on the stakeholder map referred to above, whom would you advise your client (a) to engage with, (b) about what and (c) in what order?

   d. What would your advice to your client be about the most appropriate dispute resolution processes in the event of disputes arising from the agreement or a party's non-compliance?

5) What are the long-term implications of these shifts in relationships for regional stability and security, what are the possible outcomes of the conflict, and what can be done to prevent a further escalation? How would you advise companies and governments that you may be consulting about the next steps forward?

10

NO GOOD DEED UNPUNISHED

Mark Galeotti & Chris Honeyman

This hypothetical scenario presents a multiplayer situation, around the proposal of the European Union to site a nuclear power plant in Bosnia and Herzegovina. Rivalry over where it should be located, and what prime contractor is to be dominant, and therefore what country since all the possible contractors are closely associated with major powers, has resulted already in a possible shift of location and a three-way contest over the relative influence of the US, Europe, and Russia in the project – with China never far away as a further influencer. Tensions are further inflamed by the apparent murder (though a simple accident cannot be ruled out) of the European Commission official assigned to investigate the merits of the competing locations and make a final recommendation.

Rather than having obvious individual protagonists with whom the reader is invited to identify, this case presents a variety of institutional or national players, any of which might be the focus for a given reader.

This case study serves to present the classic hybrid warfare problem of attribution, in which it is distinctly unclear who is responsible – if indeed a murder has occurred. That lack of clarity allows multiple parties to construct and promulgate narratives claiming each in turn is victim rather than perpetrator. It also situates the immediate conflict within a known history of extreme and longstanding conflict which has frequently been exacerbated by the ambitions of individual politicians. Finally, this scenario presents a clear example of a real-world problem for all such cases, in which events may rapidly overtake a case designed even recently. This case study deals with that situation by asking readers to mentally place themselves within a specific time in history (circa 2019), as well as within a particular place.

* * *

Keywords: EU cooperation – Nuclear powerplant siting and funding – Bosnia and Herzegovina – Commercial competition – Murder – Transnational crime activities – Political tensions – Russia – France – China – USA.

No Good Deed Unpunished

Mark Galeotti & Chris Honeyman[1]

Disclaimer

Although this scenario is designed to look real, it is not a true story. We believe similar events could happen (or may have happened) in a different context, but the scenario as described, and especially the local characters, are based on the authors' imagination. The dynamic between the main players (EU, Russia, and China) is believed to be realistic.

In reading this scenario, please assume the year is 2019.

The European Union's plan to underwrite the construction of a nuclear power station in the divided state of Bosnia and Herzegovina (BiH) was meant to be a significant act of economic uplift and political solidarity. It has instead become a nightmare.

Some background information on Bosnia and Herzegovina

BiH is a recent country situated in the Balkan peninsula in South-East Europe. It was part of Yugoslavia until the country exploded in the early 1990s with the independence proclamations of Croatia and Slovenia. In 1992, BiH proclaimed its own independence from a Yugoslavia now mostly populated by Serbs. The Serbs who remained on BiH soil then took up arms to try and retake the country from ethnic Bosnians, leading to a 4-year long deadly war including a blockade of the capital city Sarajevo. In 1995, NATO intervened to try to stop ethnic cleansing. The Dayton Accords of December 1995 confirmed the country's existence and borders and established two regional administrations: the "BiH Federation" and the "Republika Srpska." Multiple political and military leaders of the time have since been convicted of war crimes and heavily sentenced by the International Criminal Tribunal for the former Yugoslavia in the Hague. In 2016, the country applied for EU membership; its application remains pending.

BiH, like most Balkan countries, is keen to join the EU – keener, to be honest, than most EU countries are to welcome new members with serious economic and governance challenges and histories of inter-ethnic rivalry. In the past, this has often meant supporting "stabilocrat" regimes that may be corrupt but at least will not rock the boat. This

[1] The authors owe a great debt of gratitude to the following people who participated in the drafting of earlier versions of this scenario: Veronique Fraser, Howard Gadlin, Art Hinshaw, Roy Lewicki, Leonard Lira and Scott McGregor.

time, Brussels was adopting a more positive stance, proposing some major development projects that would seem to offer all kinds of advantages, and not least signal a commitment to the Balkans. The policy could be summed up as: "we will help you with economic growth such that you will be less of a needy candidate in the future."

In BiH, the key plan was to build a nuclear reactor, both to provide cheaper power for economic diversification and to allow decommissioning of some of the dangerously polluting older units of the coal-fired Tuzla thermal powerplant. An investment that would also bring public health and environmental benefits.

An initial study strongly recommended siting the new plant near Prijedor in Northern BiH, notably as it would also support the expansion of the local manufacturing and food processing industries. Prijedor is in the predominantly Serb *Republika Srpska* part of BiH, but from Brussels' point of view, that was simply another plus: helping reconcile to a European future a region more prone to look to Moscow for support.

Brussels is simply underwriting, not directly building the plant, and so a joint venture, UNE (for *Ujedinjena Nuklearna Energija*, United Nuclear Energy), was founded between the European Investment Bank (EIB), the BiH Government, and the local *Republika Srpska* Government. The contract went out to tender and three consortia emerged as the frontrunners: one headed by the US Westinghouse Electric Company, one headed by Russia's Rosatom, and one headed by China General Nuclear Power Group. Although the last of these operated with numerous local partners and intermediaries to try to bypass previous US sanctions, eventually UNE decided this posed too great a risk. The contract looks like it is going to be awarded to the Rosatom-led consortium, not least thanks to heavy lobbying in Banja Luka, the de facto administrative capital of the *Republika Srpska*.

At this point, the US government began to raise the alarm, claiming not only that this would give Moscow long-term influence in *Republika Srpska*, but also that this would leave the country potentially dependent on power coming from a region which could conceivably break away. INTCEN, the EU's intelligence fusion unit, belatedly began echoing these concerns.

A group of BiH parliamentarians began circulating a proposal instead to site the plant in Tuzla, to compensate for the closures at the coal-powered plant there, an idea which quickly found favor in Brussels, which was eager to resolve the issue. Tuzla, after all, is in the majority Bosniak part of BiH and already at the center of power distribution networks. There was even brownfield land available for development.

The *Republika Srpska* government was understandably furious, as was Moscow, especially when Brussels implied that Rosatom's bid was implicitly also off the table. Well-funded Russian cultural centers and local politicians began angrily drawing attention to the way that US pressure had also, in effect, handed the contract to the last competitor in the race – headed by a US corporation. A case was also brought in Brussels claiming that this move would violate EU anti-monopoly law.

As tensions rose, Moscow suggested that it might be willing to contribute towards the cost of a reactor in Prijedor, Bosnia, ideally with (but, if necessary, without) EU participation. Russian and Russian-influenced media began presenting this issue as an existential test of European political will: is it more than just a puppet of the USA? Politicians considered close to Moscow, especially in France, joined the fray.

Coincidentally enough, at this point, a "compromise" was announced: a new joint venture between Rosatom and the French corporation Framatome, itself majority owned by EDF (France's historical national public electricity provider), itself largely held by the French State. The Government in Paris, keen to assert European "strategic autonomy" from Washington, and desperate to underwrite its ailing domestic nuclear industry, started asserting that its role will ensure there could be no malign abuse of this contract, if the Prijedor contract goes ahead.

A crucial role in deciding this will be played by a European Commission official attached to the EIB, tasked with making a final assessment. Krzysztof Mielczewski, a Pole known both for his meticulous investigations and his deep skepticism of Russian intentions, is a controversial figure, but despite a campaign to present him as "Russophobe", he is the man on point. He travels to BiH, and has conversations with stakeholders, engineers, analysts, and politicians. He is being driven to Sarajevo airport for the flight home when his car suffers an unexpected and catastrophic brake failure and ploughs into a truck. He is killed instantly.

Immediately, the rumor mills begin grinding. He was killed by Russian assassins because he was going to rule against Prijedor. He was murdered by the Americans precisely because even this Russo-sceptic had come to realize that the Prijedor option was the right one. He was murdered by local business interests. Even more conspiratorially, he was murdered by the Olga Cell of the Informal Anarchist Federation International Revolutionary Front (a group linked to previous violent attacks on nuclear scientists and engineers). The information leading to this last conclusion, however – even more than the evidence supporting the other theories – cannot be substantiated and may have been proffered to throw investigators off the trail.

What survives of Mielczewski's notes does not conclusively prove which way he was inclined, but does reveal that he had received, from anonymous sources, a pack of copied company registration and cadastral documents. Not only was the extension of Tuzla's coal-powered plant – which would never be built if the nuclear project goes ahead – to be funded by a loan from Exim Bank of China, but the proposed brownfield site for a nuclear reactor there is registered to a Bosnian company that, in turn, is owned by "PSLP", a Chinese corporation whose owner was a former Ministry of State Security General – in other words, a spymaster. There is no specific reason to suspect that this would give Beijing any special leverage, but it would be a lucrative deal for PSLP, and it comes at a time when European governments are especially conscious of the risks attached to Beijing's economic tradecraft.

Several intemperate public statements from Members of the European Parliament and other figures follow, to which Beijing reacts with evident fury. The new Chinese ambassador to BiH, a high-flying young "wolf warrior," calls Brussels a "den of spiteful xenophobes forcing the people of the Balkans to be their anti-Chinese conscripts." A cyberattack hits EIB systems. Beijing denies any responsibility, and when forensic analysis of the malware points to a Chinese connection, it claims this was a provocation launched by "malcontents" from "Taiwan Region" (in its own formal terms, the Republic of China, but known to most outside China simply as Taiwan).

In this furor, the revelation by the citizen journalism outfit Bellingcat that several officers of Unit 29155, Russian military intelligence's notorious "wet work" (murder) team, had travelled through Sarajevo just days before Mielczewski's death is almost lost. Almost, but not quite, as an unlikely alliance of anti-Russian US and European sources and Chinese "patriotic influencers" on social media hype this as "proof" that Moscow had him killed.

Although Moscow seems reluctant to challenge Beijing so directly, local politicians in *Republika Srpska* have no such qualms, and instead start conjuring all kinds of lurid conspiracy theories. When a crowd picketing the Chinese embassy in Sarajevo turns ugly and starts throwing stones, the Russian Serbian-language outlet that covers the region, Sputnik Srbija, fails even to report it. However, several ultra-nationalist contenders, vying to replace multi-term *Republika Srpska* president Milorad Dodik, fasten on this as a wedge issue and sign an open letter in the main daily newspaper, Dnevni Avaz, calling on Sarajevo to "stop our country being sold to China."

At this stage, the EU is tempted to pull the plug on the whole affair, and a memo to this effect leaks to a Brussels newspaper, suggesting that the European Commission wishes it had never entertained this idea. But...

If the EU backs away, it will simply consolidate the impression in the Balkans that it is clueless and spineless, forever making promises that it never will fulfil or even intends to fulfil. Countries looking to consolidate their interest in the region – Russia, China, Turkey – will only gain.

Paris has a specific desire to get at least part of the contract for the Prijedor reactor; it frankly does not regard Moscow as a long-term threat.

Moscow is angry, and if it cannot get the contract, will use this to stir up resentment in *Republika Srpska* – and across the Balkans more broadly.

Beijing is furious at yet another example of "panda bashing" – even if it is not clear whether PSLP was a Trojan horse for the Ministry of State Security or not.

America is annoyed that Europe once again seems naïve and inconsistent.

Rumors persist that the Russians and Chinese are using their criminal networks to leverage the Bosnian mafia. Trade-based money laundering, weapons trafficking, human smuggling and political influence are all threat streams that are exploited by Transnational Organized Crime groups. The Tito and Deano cartel, one of the main players in Europe and based out of Dubai, is often tapped to assist State-sponsored criminal groups or agents sent to conduct illicit activity in the country. Many question how the narcos gain so much power, but these people are not aware of the interconnectivity between those that hire the cartels to do the dirty deeds – "wet work", sabotage, extortion, kidnapping

– and Nation-States that utilize their services, allowing for plausible deniability by their agencies. The criminal elements can silence dissenters, influence decision-makers and use fear as a tool that anyone can purchase, for the right price.

And BiH is up in arms that it is being used as a proxy battlefield, with the Serbs pitted against the Bosniaks. If no reactor is built at either Prijedor or Tuzla, then it will continue to develop its coal-fired power stations, with all the consequent costs to local people's health and the global climate.

Glossary

Bellingcat: an independent international group of researchers, investigators and citizen journalists using open source and social media investigation to probe a variety of subjects. It is active in more than 20 countries.

BiH: Bosnia and Herzegovina, a country of 3.3 million and locus of an intense war (1992-95) which included a long list of atrocities, the effects of which continue.

China General Nuclear Power Group is a large electricity supplier based in Guangdong Province, and is heavily engaged in nuclear projects, although as of 2014 more than half of its capacity came from wind, hydro, and solar plants. It has also pursued large projects abroad, including in the UK and Malaysia. As of 2018, it is under US sanctions resulting from a finding that it had stolen advanced US nuclear technology and supplied it for Chinese military use.

The European Investment Bank (EIB) is the lending arm of the European Union and asserts that it is the largest multilateral lender in the world as well as one of the main financiers of climate action worldwide.

Exim (Export-Import) Bank of China is one of three institutional banks in China chartered to implement State policies in industry, foreign trade, economy, and foreign aid to developing countries, and to provide policy financial support to promote the export of Chinese products and services.

Framatome is a French nuclear power company with 14,000 employees and concurrent projects in Finland, China, and the UK as well as in France. It is 75% owned by the French EDF Group; Japan's Mitsubishi Heavy Industries owns about 20%.

INTCEN (EU Intelligence and Situation Centre) is a relatively small (70 staff as of 2013) European Union intelligence unit. Following the 2001 Al Qaeda attacks on the US, it developed first into a forum for the exchange of sensitive information among the main national European intelligence services, and later added a counterterrorism cell. More recently it has been responsible for strategic analysis and research based on input from member States' intelligence services.

Milorad Dodik is a *Republika Srpska* politician. Originally seen as relatively moderate and reformist, he has more recently been characterized as a Serb nationalist and an authoritarian. Since 2019, he has served as the Serb member of the three-member presidency of Bosnia and Herzegovina; previously he was president of *Republika Srpska* from 2010-2018.

The Ministry of State Security, or "Guoanbu", is the civilian intelligence, security and secret police agency of the People's Republic of China, responsible for counterintelligence, foreign intelligence and political security.

Republika Srpska is part of Bosnia and Herzegovina (BiH) and is the home of the 1.2 million Serbs within the country. Its main city is Banja Luka.

Rosatom State Atomic Energy Corporation is the largest electricity producer in Russia, supplying 20% of the country's power and employing 275,000 people in 400 business units. It is also heavily engaged in nuclear power development abroad and claims to have the world's largest portfolio of such projects (35 current, in 12 countries.)

Tuzla Thermal Power Plant is the largest power plant in BiH and consumes over 3 million tons of coal a year. The city of Tuzla was ranked by the World Health Organization in 2017 as having the second worst pollution in Europe.

Unit 29155 is a Russian military intelligence (GRU) organization tasked with foreign assassinations and other activities aimed at destabilizing European countries.

Westinghouse Electric Company, based in Pittsburgh, originated the alternating current method of electricity distribution in the late 19th century. In more recent years it has concentrated on nuclear reactor development, and its technology is used in 430 reactors around the world. From 2006 to 2018, it was essentially owned by Japan's Toshiba, but after Japan cooled on nuclear power following the Fukushima disaster, Toshiba unwound its position, and since 2018, Westinghouse has been owned by a consortium headed by Brookfield Business Partners.

Wolf warrior: Taken from the title of a 2015 movie, this term is now used to describe a subset of Chinese diplomats who engage in a highly aggressive style of diplomacy, which includes loudly denouncing any criticism of China.

Possible questions for discussion

1) What are the different hybrid warfare techniques at play in this scenario? How do they play in conjunction with one another?

2) Draw a stakeholder map including all involved parties, i.e., a graphic representation of all actors, with arrows between them indicating support or opposition. Beyond national governments and international organizations, include private, NGO and criminal groups. Identify the interests and values of each actor.

3) For each non-governmental organization you identified in question 2, explain whether the role of this organization appears to be something that could have been done by a unit of a government directly.

4) What mental shifts are needed to make it possible to consider the case in contemporary terms, as if you had arrived on site a week later as the replacement for the late EU official, rather than with months or years of hindsight? Is anything comparable as a mental shift needed for studying hybrid warfare cases generally?

5) Is it useful in analyzing this case to apply the classic concepts of evidence, burden of proof and of innocent-until-proven-guilty, taught in detail to lawyers (and to everyone else, via movies and books)? If so, why? If not, what might be an alternative basis for analysis?

6) Setting aside the fact that the Russian 2022 invasion of Ukraine immediately obsoleted any possibility of commercial tie-ins involving Russia: as of its assigned date, does the exercise appear plausible to you? If so, why? If not, why not?

7) Is there a role in this scenario for any convening or mediating entity? If so, what could it be?

8) In this scenario, what negotiations would you expect each of the following to be engaged in, publicly or secretly: European Union; Paris; Moscow; Beijing; Washington?

9) After considering different scenarios, what do you consider the most likely outcome as to construction of the power plant? Why?

11

RARE-EARTH ELEMENTS MINING AND MILLING CONFLICTS

Guy Burgess & Sanda Kaufman

This case study uses the technique of developing "anticipatory" scenarios. It offers students the realistic situation of a think-tank seeking to acquire negotiation and conflict management skills from outside partners, in the context of a project on global strategies regarding the mining and acquisition of rare-earth elements (REEs).

REEs (mostly metals) are key to modern consumer electronics, electric transportation, and military systems. They are not really rare, though known reserves are limited. Current sources are in China (largest), Vietnam, Russia, India, Brazil, and in southern Africa, a place rife with conflicts and international meddling. Considering the stakes, hybrid warfare tactics may be at play to skew the market in favor of certain actors, and against others. Such a possibility presents numerous opportunities for negotiation and conflict prevention.

This case study encourages students to focus on thinking, strategizing and decision skills, as well as imagining an uncertain future using anticipatory scenarios for developing responses to emerging hybrid warfare threats.

* * *

Keywords: Hybrid warfare – Rare-earth elements – Uncertainty – Anticipatory scenarios - Strategic conflict management framework –Simulation – Consultancy – Think-tank

* * *

Some additional elements about how to administer this case are presented in the General Teaching Note on p. 41, particularly starting on p. 47.

Rᴀʀᴇ-Eᴀʀᴛʜ Eʟᴇᴍᴇɴᴛs Mɪɴɪɴɢ ᴀɴᴅ Mɪʟʟɪɴɢ Cᴏɴғʟɪᴄᴛs

Guy Burgess & Sanda Kaufman[1]

Introduction

This case study is about an ongoing, real-world challenge: the vulnerability of developed democracies to the disruption of supply of raw materials critically important to their economies. It uses anticipatory scenarios as tools for developing response strategies. As such, this case requires participants to imagine, and deal with, situations that might occur in the future, rather than analyze situations which have already happened and therefore typically have plenty of information available about them.

Anticipatory scenarios are used here to develop necessary skills that complement analytic skills used in traditional case studies. Unlike predictions, anticipatory scenarios require imagining various futures and strategizing about how to obtain favorable outcomes. This is especially useful in dealing with complex situations that are difficult to predict because they are novel in some key respects, change all the time, and/or are plagued by high levels of uncertainty. The anticipatory scenario approach, increasingly used in business, urban planning, medicine, finance, and military contexts, allows exploration of possible developments and preparation of responses to them. This approach helps uncover vulnerabilities in strategies and actions which might not be apparent otherwise. At the very least, it can reveal some of what we do not even know that we do not know.

The rare-earth elements (REEs) pose "wicked" (read "complex") challenges, meaning that any action in pursuit of objectives may have unexpected negative consequences to be considered and weighed against the expected benefits. One characteristic of wicked problems is the fact that information about them is often missing, incomplete, or hard to obtain, and what there is obsolesces rapidly. Therefore, students addressing such problems need creativity and flexibility. They will have to imagine unfamiliar contexts, contingencies, and (intended and unintended) consequences for a changing number of stakeholders. In the process, students will also be called on to identify and consider some moral dilemmas, and to confront parties whose intentions are not what they seem or are outright inimical to democratic values. They will have to surface their assumptions, test them against reality, reject those which do not match, and adopt new ones. Chiefly, students will be asked to produce strategies (expressed in "if-then" statements contin-

---

[1] Rishi Batra, Heidi Burgess, Calvin Chrustie, Barney Jordaan, Anne Leslie, Leonard Lira, Scott McGregor and I. William Zartman contributed to the discussions that led to this case.

gent on current and new geopolitical and technological considerations)[2] rather than fixed steps toward a solution.

Background information

Rare earths elements (REEs), mostly metals, are key to modern consumer electronics, electric transportation, and military systems. Access to REEs is highly prized by high-tech, industrial powers worldwide. As geopolitical tensions have intensified in recent years, so has competition for access to these minerals. They are not really rare, though known reserves are limited. Current ones[3] are in China (largest deposits known so far), Vietnam, Russia, India, Brazil, and in southern Africa.[4] Considering the stakes, hybrid warfare tactics may be at play to skew the market in favor of certain actors, and against others.

Let's develop an example of an anticipatory scenario regarding southern Africa (SA). This region has potential for increased REE mining above current levels, which could improve the economic situation of its inhabitants and could alleviate the dependence on current sources. However, SA has also seen some of the world's most dangerous and deadly conflicts. We might expect that increasing pressure to secure access to REEs in SA might lead to a global crisis, resulting from a simultaneous increase in social and political tensions in Africa's mineral-rich areas and rapidly accelerating global demand for the region's mineral resources.

To a largely unknown degree, this crisis is likely already occurring. Global powers and giant resource corporations commonly resort to "hardball" strategies as they struggle to build and maintain social and political support for their mineral extraction efforts, while undermining support for their rivals' extraction efforts. A country (e.g., China, home to extensive REE deposits) might acquire lands in SA to block other countries' access, to preserve their own position as the largest supplier and to control global REE flows.

In the many cases where ethical competitive strategies do not produce the desired results, it is not uncommon for competitors to resort to "dirty tricks." These range, for example, from various types of espionage, blackmail, or threats against individual decision-makers who are not adequately compliant, to disinformation campaigns, sabotage, and even acts of violence (generally staying just under the threshold that might provoke large-scale, violent countermeasures). Such strategies fall under the umbrella of hybrid warfare (HW).

---

[2] For example: REEs are necessary for electric vehicles. We can assume this will continue. However, demand is already slackening for such vehicles, which currently have battery and other problems and lack infrastructure. While in the future all these challenges may be resolved and electric vehicles will be in high demand, there is also the possibility of new technologies coming online for non-fossil-fuel-powered vehicles, which will diminish to an extent the demand for REEs and the race to secure them.

[3] Rare earth elements: where in the world are they? https://www.mining.com/web/rare-earth-elements-where-in-the-world-are-they/

[4] Particularly in five countries: Mozambique, Angola, South Africa, Namibia, and Malawi. Bekoe et al, Rare Earth Elements in Africa: Implications for U.S. National and Economic Security (Institute for Defense Analysis, 2022), at https://apps.dtic.mil/sti/trecms/pdf/AD1204908.pdf

What might happen if this HW-backed competition for REEs in SA were to get out of hand and result in large-scale acts of violence targeting mining, processing, and shipping facilities, as well as the area's civilian population? Triggers could be, for example, a few spectacular acts of sabotage (such as, elsewhere, the attack that destroyed the Nord Stream pipeline in 2022 – see scenario #9). There are also well-founded chronic worries about more predictable attacks to global trade, e.g. on shipping in the Strait of Hormuz, already happening as of 2023, and causing expensive rerouting of shipping traffic around the Horn of Africa.

Under this confluence of circumstances, we can expect interruptions of the steady supply of the strategically important REEs on which so much of the global economy depends. The disruptions could escalate into a kind of superpower conflict by proxy which will make it impossible to assure general commercial access to SA minerals. Is there anything REE users can do in this scenario?

While we could focus on efforts to defuse the crises in SA, this case study seeks to explore a secondary crisis – one that would arise within the resource-rich, developed democracies as they embark on an urgent effort to develop more secure (domestic wherever possible) alternative sources of REEs. These democracies are not above acting unilaterally to protect their own REE supply even at the expense of allies, giving rise to fierce conflicts among "friends." This is a space requiring negotiations and conflict management to develop effective strategies against hybrid warfare by unfriendly actors and for sharing the risks and benefits associated with securing access to REEs.

This exercise asks participants to think through how they would navigate this complex environment in the quest for circumventing the obstacles arising in any region with REE deposits, such as southern Africa. A first step is developing a scenario – anticipating what problems might crop up at any selected location, and then globally. The next step is offering a robust[5] strategy that identifies risks and mitigates them to the extent possible. The case is built on publicly available information about ongoing efforts to develop alternative, stable sources for the key REE minerals.

---

[5] A robust strategy offers steps which are contingent on various possible events and threats and does not depend critically on any condition materializing. One definition by McInerney, D., Lempert, R. & Keller, K. (What are robust strategies in the face of uncertain climate threshold responses? *Climatic Change*, 547–568 (2012). https://doi.org/10.1007/s10584-011-0377-1) is: "trading a small decrease in a strategy's expected performance for a significant increase in a strategy's performance in the worst cases." The wider the range of contingencies for which a strategy is still wise, the more robust it is to surprises. A simple example is taking an umbrella on a walk in the Fall is more *robust* than relying on the weather forecast of low-probability rain.

A crisis is brewing in the developed democracies

Seventeen metallic elements are included in the rare-earth elements group (REEs). They are key components in the production of military equipment, wind turbines, and electric vehicles. They are also essential in the production and functioning of numerous widely used consumer electronics which have become critical to our daily lives. These include cellular phones, computers, and flat screens.[6] The use of such devices is rising rapidly, increasing the demand for REEs around the globe.

Access to REEs is highly prized by high-tech, industrial powers worldwide. Countries with access to REEs have a considerable leg up in developing and/or taking advantage of novel technologies. This access translates into economic benefits as well as enhanced defense capability.

REEs are neither very rare, nor earths. Like other vital resources such as water, they are not equitably located around the world. Moreover, detection of deposits and extraction of REEs are both difficult and environmentally damaging. This gives rise to a serious international competition by fair and unfair means to find, mine, and process REEs, with various degrees of regard (or lack thereof) for environmental and social consequences.

A crisis is looming within wealthy, developed democracies. They are embarking on an urgent effort to develop a steady flow of REEs from secure sources, as an alternative to competing for them in the current places where these minerals are being extracted.[7] This is largely because there are numerous downsides to reliance on REEs found at some of these locations. Chief among these downsides is the potential for unexpected disruptions in supply, which could trigger a worldwide chain reaction in several industries, some of them critical to communications and defense. For example, China or Russia (and countries in their sphere of influence) might cut the flow of supplies to obtain political or economic advantages. One region where mining opportunities might be explored is the southern part of the African continent. However, that region is frequently buffeted by violent ethnic and political conflicts, which also poses risks to the flow of REEs. Other downsides include competition from unfriendly countries which do not shrink from using covert methods to establish their dominance in the REE markets.

In some of the developed democracies – the United States or Australia, for example – attempts to negotiate the agreements necessary to develop major new mineral facilities would need to overcome obstacles such as:

- The negotiation of government subsidies (to make the development of lower quality mineral resources economically feasible).

---

[6] See *What are rare earth elements, and why are they important?* https://www.americangeosciences.org/critical-issues/faq/what-are-rare-earth-elements-and-why-are-they-important

[7] Top 10 Largest Rare Earth Elements Producing Countries: https://www.geeksforgeeks.org/top-10-largest-rare-earth-elements-producing-countries/

- Opposition from strong environmental movements which seek to block (or at least attach strong environmental safeguards to) any development.

- Widespread public hostility toward multinational mineral extraction companies.

- General distrust of the national security establishment.

- And geopolitical rivals' clandestine efforts to stir up local opposition to projects they think would weaken their strategic position.

These obstacles are likely to be counterbalanced, to a degree, by strong support from those who would benefit economically from proposed projects, and from those working in industries dependent upon the REEs. There is also likely to be intense competition between projects vying for government support.

All these pressures will make it difficult for even the most altruistically motivated negotiators to come up with agreements that wisely and equitably balance the competing interests of the various stakeholders. The focus of this project is on how exactly to do this kind of balancing, while also resisting the efforts of bad-faith actors to undermine this process by using the full array of hybrid warfare tactics.

Two entities searching for solutions to the REEs conflicts

You will play the role of members of the Minerva Group.

The Minerva Group (named after the Greek goddess of wisdom and defensive war) is a consulting consortium made up of professionals and organizations offering to assist in negotiation and conflict management in a broad range of political and security issues. The group provides consulting and conflict management services to clients seeking wise and equitable ways of handling the complexity of today's large-scale problem-solving collaborative efforts.

Minerva's members are individuals whose background and expertise are quite diverse. They specialize in helping clients navigate hostile negotiation environments where a wide range of "bad faith" actors employ a variety of sinister and deceptive tactics, in attempts to subvert negotiation processes in ways that advance their own and/or their employers' (organizations and countries) interests. Of particular concern in this context are some aggressive foreign powers employing modern hybrid warfare tactics. In the United States, recent examples include cyberattacks on critical infrastructure and food supply sources, and use of sophisticated methods (such as balloons and drones, and disruptions of communication means) to test responses to hostile moves, as well as targeted theft of intellectual property in specific areas such as REEs.

Minerva's members seek to encourage others to think strategically about how to apply the ideas which they are developing, should they be given the opportunity to do so.

The Promontory Institute is a low-key, well-funded and well-connected international initiative of leaders of major defense and technology companies, politicians and academics specializing in security and governance issues, as well as a few environmentalists and social justice advocates. Its members come from the major developed democracies and are united in the belief that the destructive politics that has taken over too many liberal democracies is making it impossible for these societies to successfully respond to the many challenges of the early- and mid-21st century including, especially, China's new brand of assertive high-tech authoritarianism. Promontory aims to show that the sophisticated application of state-of-the-art negotiation and conflict management strategies can generate wise, equitable, and politically realistic strategies for meeting these challenges. Since Promontory lacks specific expertise, it commissions, through requests for proposals (RFPs), consultants who bring the necessary skills to the problems Promontory intends to tackle.

The Promontory Institute is currently concerned about the on-ongoing vulnerability of developed democracies to the disruption of supply of critically important rare-earth elements (REEs). In pursuit of strategies to deal with this challenge, the Institute has issued a request for proposals (RFP), which the Minerva Group and its competitors have received, to generate advice. Promontory will fund only a select number of proposals-those which will persuade them of a considerable likelihood of successfully contributing to the securing of a steady supply of REEs to developed democracies.

The rare-earth elements initiative

Rare-earth elements are essential building blocks of modern, high-tech societies. Among the many challenges Promontory is committed to address with respect to REEs is the need to secure a reliable supply of competitively priced rare-earth elements to effectively counterbalance China's near monopoly on these. In pursuing this goal, the Promontory Institute is taking an international approach that seeks to strengthen and bind together developed democracies, rather than dividing them along nationalistic lines and unnecessarily creating a competition among them despite shared interests.

The Institute is calling on leading negotiation and conflict management organizations (including Minerva) to submit proposals detailing how they would structure a broad-based (and possibly ongoing) negotiation effort capable of achieving these desired objectives. Cost is not a major consideration. In soliciting these proposals, the Institute emphasizes that it seeks robust strategies likely to be successful not only in the current international climate but also in the near and even mid-term future. The Institute is also committed to using its considerable influence to help secure any needed cooperation from both public and private sector organizations which the consultants might identify as necessary.

The complex international environment is shifting rapidly. Therefore, an effort such as Promontory is contemplating is unlikely to be one-time. Rather, successful strategies will have to incorporate recurring reevaluations and negotiations[8] that would respond to new events and technologies – especially those which opponents might deploy to circumvent obstacles to their objectives.

More specifically, the Promontory Institute is looking for an organization capable of managing a comprehensive effort to negotiate approval for a series of rare-earth elements mining, milling, and refining projects that would, in a timely manner, provide a secure, competitively priced supply of these minerals which would be socially responsible and sensitive to environmental concerns.

Overall proposal process

The Institute is asking potential contractors (including Minerva) how they would structure a process that identifies and evaluates proposed projects and then secures the approvals needed to go ahead and implement some combination of projects to provide the secure sources of sought rare earth elements supply.

Part I – Selecting projects for implementation

The first set of questions that the Institute would like to see addressed by those bidding on the contract pertains to the mechanics of the process for selecting the projects to be negotiated. Included are the following:

1) How would you distill the large list of proposed domestic and international projects into a much shorter list of projects worth detailed consideration? Criteria might include, for example, the potential of projects to produce REEs; the likelihood of agreement among stakeholders; risks to the projects at different time horizons; political and economic implementability; and vulnerability to hybrid warfare tactics. How would you organize in-depth technical analyses of the shortlisted projects? The analyses will have to assess economic feasibility (perhaps with government subsidies, price guarantees and other devices requiring international cooperation) and any adverse social and environmental impacts (as well as the feasibility of impact mitigation strategies). Such analyses ought to seriously consider whether expanded rare-earth elements production is, in fact, essential and/or whether alternative technologies and sources might be preferable and expected to come online in the near to middle time range, thereby impacting demand for REEs. Worth considering: the sources, risks, and impacts of possible supply disruptions (through hybrid warfare and other tactics) and the amount of money that is worth spending to reduce the risk of such disruptions.

2) How would you verify that these analyses are drawing on sound, available information, and that they are trustworthy and trusted by key stakeholder groups?

---

[8] Recurring evaluations and tweaking are standard recommended components of negotiated agreements especially in international, environmental and planning areas, whose effects materialize over years and decades during which much can change.

3) What kind of political assessment / stakeholder analysis would you conduct to identify those likely to support or oppose potential projects and assess their ability to influence the decision? In addition, an assessment is necessary regarding how politically vulnerable these projects are likely to be. For example, are they in the category of activities that might find favor during one administration only to be overturned by the next? Can such risk be mitigated?

4) How would you structure a series of negotiations (and with whom) capable of finding mutually acceptable ways of overcoming sources of "own camp" opposition?

Part II – Responding to Hybrid Warfare Tactics

The focus of a second set of questions the Promontory Institute wants to see addressed in proposals regards how the recommended process above will be defended from "bad faith" actors. These individuals, organizations or even inimical government entities might use clandestine and deceptive hybrid warfare tactics, either to prevent the process from reaching a successful conclusion or to distort the process in ways that result in undermining rather than advancing the interests of the Promontory Institute and other stakeholders.

This will require conducting a broad "threat assessment" that looks beyond traditional negotiation and litigation arenas at the many ways in which public and private sector actors from both open and closed societies might try to undermine the ability of the Institute to achieve its primary objectives. In other words, the Institute wants potential contractors to think about all that could go wrong with a proposed project ("premortem")[9] besides everything that could go right.

More specifically, the Institute seeks to know which of the following tactics potential contractors are prepared to identify and counter, and which tactics they believe fall outside of their ability to reasonably defend against. Applicants should avoid generalities and, to the extent possible, be very specific regarding the situations to which their proposed remedies should apply, as well as where they might not be relevant.

1) Deliberate distortions of the technical assessment process: Given the role that the various technical assessments play in determining which REE projects are going to be pursued, there will be considerable incentives for parties to oversell their projects and downplay (or even sabotage) competitors. What strategies might preempt or correct these assessments?

2) The influence of corrupt officials: There is a real danger that key decision makers will attempt to capitalize on their position by demanding some type of "payoff"

---

[9] See Kahneman, Daniel. 2011. Thinking Fast and Slow. New York: Farrar, Straus, and Giroux. A pre-mortem entails imagining what could go wrong and embedding mitigation in the proposed strategies. This will not prevent something going wrong anyway. It will, however, diminish the ways in which we can be surprised by unintended side-effects of decisions (bound to occur in complex systems), and for some surprises we will be prepared, leaving time and resources to be devoted to other, unanticipated surprises.

which, while legally prohibited, can be hard to resist. A bigger threat, however, is likely to come from officials who take advantage of clever legal maneuverings to achieve the same basic result. These and other threats also derive from the space some decision makers might discover, within which they can promote agendas and pursue individual or group interests at the expense of those sought by the Institute and by other stakeholders. What measures might prevent such corrupt moves?

3) Anti-competitive business practices: Some countries might try to undermine the financial viability of a project by dumping REEs on the market at extremely low prices or by threatening near-term access to REES to businesses considering a longer-term switch to Promontory-affiliated sources. For example, in the past, China improved its economic position in various markets by such tactics and may try to do so again by cornering the REEs market. How can REE projects be protected from such actions?

4) Sensationalistic media: As part of a broad effort to attract an audience, media outlets have been known to inflate and distort modest disagreements, framing them as major social controversies that undermine a prudent consideration of the issues. What strategies might counteract such tendencies?

5) The project becoming a pawn in larger political struggles: Inevitable conflicts surrounding REE projects could easily be amplified as part of routine, "hardball" politics, or as part of a clandestine campaign in which provocateurs would seek to drive, and then benefit from, increased political polarization. This could include "mobilize the base" hate-mongering politicians across the political spectrum from left to right, and foreign powers who seek to destabilize Western democracies. Here, the concern goes far beyond legitimate substantive issues that deserve serious consideration. Flashpoints could erupt around the rights of indigenous peoples, environmental risks, jobs and wages, unionization, increased use of advanced technologies (such as AI and robotics), etc. and be exploited for their own ends by nefarious actors. What steps might lessen the impacts of such activities?

6) Information security breaches and espionage: What steps would you propose to take to prevent unauthorized and inappropriate disclosure of information as well as clandestine efforts to obtain confidential information? This will require ability to navigate today's increasingly dangerous cybersecurity environment, where hybrid warfare tactics are often used.

7) Disinformation warfare: What steps would you propose to take to anticipate, identify, and counter sophisticated disinformation strategies designed to influence decision-makers and the general public by generating and amplifying deceptive and inflammatory narratives through marketing, social media, and other strategies?

8) Delaying tactics: Competing suppliers and, especially, competing geopolitical actors are likely to take advantage of the many opportunities that democratic systems offer to anyone who wants to prevent a new project from going forward (the effect is sometimes called "sticky status quo[10]"). The large number of permits that all major projects require, along with extensive opportunities for public participation and the opportunity to appeal adverse decisions, can allow some interest groups to cause indefinite postponement of decisions that, based on the merits of their arguments, would almost certainly go against them. Here the issue is the bad-faith perversion of otherwise reasonable decision-making processes. What means do you propose for diminishing the effect of the sticky status quo?

9) Threats and intimidation: The stakes involved in this issue are high enough that it is not impossible to imagine parties willing to resort to violence and intimidation to advance their interests. It is, for example, quite possible that those involved in the negotiations envisioned above will be at risk of being kidnapped (especially in violence-prone areas). How can such actions be anticipated/prevented?

10) Other tactics: The 9 items above are but an incomplete list of tactics to be used to defeat REE projects. What other impediments can you imagine/anticipate that should be added to this list, and how would you propose to deal with them?

Potential contractors should also outline the legal and ethical obligations and constraints that will guide their efforts (especially in cases where difficult trade-offs between competing priorities are required).

Part III – Social System-Level Recommendations

In addition to measures that the Minerva Group is seeking to recommend in the context of specific REE project negotiations, the Institute would also like to know what larger, more systemic steps Minerva might propose to help society as a whole address the hybrid warfare problem. These steps might include, for example, possible changes to international laws and trade agreements, legislative or regulatory steps which could be taken by national governments, changes to the formal standards of practice which could be promoted by professional associations, education campaigns for helping the public understand the nature of the hybrid warfare problem, and public disclosure of the actions of those who chronically violate generally accepted norms. Beyond this, the Institute would like to know what training programs Minerva (and its competitors) might recommend for informing participants in negotiation efforts about possible threats to the integrity of their work, and about the best currently available options for limiting those threats. Besides skills directly related to securing the REEs supply, such training could include, for example, robust decision making, risk assessment, negotiations, consensus building, communicating across cultures and languages and others.

---

[10] This is the effect of being "stuck" with the status quo because of lack of consensus on change. The status quo is considered to have inertia.

Conclusion

The Institute considers the above to be just a preliminary list of questions that deserve consideration. They invite potential contractors to suggest other topics that they ought to consider, both regarding REEs and, more generally, ways to counteract hybrid warfare.

The Institute also recognizes that the success of this overall effort will require involving organizations with expertise in several areas including, for example, mineral engineering, market analysis, environmental impact assessment and remediation, social impact assessment and remediation, media relations, security, and permitting (and other legal issues). Potential contractors are asked to highlight areas of expertise that they think Promontory should be sure to include and specify how that expertise would interface with their conflict management strategy.

The bottom line is that the Institute recognizes that business-as-usual approaches to complex negotiations – such as those involved with expanding access to REEs – are ill-suited for today's complex and quite hostile negotiating environments. The Institute is looking for a novel approach to negotiation – one that begins with a solid grounding in negotiation theory and practice, which then adapts and extends these ideas to meet contemporary challenges.

Background readings[11]

This is an initial collection of background readings on the Rare-Earth Elements problem and decision-making in complex contexts. Note that in the complex environment of competition over an increasingly valuable resource, information changes and obsolesces rapidly, requiring constant updates and quality verification.

About rare earth elements:

- What are rare-earth elements, and why are they important? https://www.americangeosciences.org/critical-issues/faq/what-are-rare-earth-elements-and-why-are-they-important

- What are Rare Earth Elements (REEs), where are they found and how are they mined? https://etech-resources.com/what-are-rare-earth-elements-rees-where-are-they-found-and-how-are-they-mined/

- We Don't Mine Enough Rare-Earth Metals to Replace Fossil Fuels With Renewable Energy – https://www.vice.com/en/article/a3mavb/we-don't-mine-enough-rare-earth-metals-to-replace-fossil-fuels-with-renewable-energy

- The collapse of American rare earth mining - and lessons learned –

---

[11] These are some suggestions. A comprehensive literature and data search will eventually be needed for the project. Contractors are advised to propose ways to collect necessary information without getting bogged down in the vast literature available.

https://www.defensenews.com/opinion/commentary/2019/11/12/
the-collapse-of-american-rare-earth-mining-and-lessons-learned/

- Mapping rare earths projects outside China – https://www.mining-technology.com/features/mapping-rare-earths-projects-outside-china/

- Factbox: Miners gear up global rare earth projects as prices surge – https://www.reuters.com/article/us-rareearths-mining-factbox/factbox-miners-gear-up-global-rare-earth-projects-as-prices-surge-idUSKBN2AU0FX

- Factbox: Rare earths projects under development in U.S. – https://www.reuters.com/article/us-usa-rareearths-projects-factbox-idUSKCN2241L6

- Northeast Wyoming Rare Earth Resources – https://www.wyoming-mining.org/minerals/rare-earths/

- Mountain Pass California - Mining Company Determined to Restore U.S. Rare Earth Supply Chain (Updated) – https://www.nationaldefensemagazine.org/articles/2020/11/20/mining-company-determined-to-restore-us-rare-earth-supply-chain

- The Top 5 Rare Earths Companies for 2021 - https://investorintel.com/markets/technology-metals/technology-metals-intel/kozaks-top-5-rare-earths-companies-for-2021/

- Lynas Assessment Report, looking at conflicts surrounding the Lynas Advanced Materials Project (LAMP)   - https://lynasrareearths.com/wp-content/uploads/2024/04/2024-Lynas-Kalgoorlie-Compliance-Assessment-Report.pdf

About decision making and negotiations in complex contexts:

- Alkon, C. & Kaufman, S. (2023). A Theory of Interests in the Context of Hybrid Warfare: It's Complex. *Cardozo Journal of Conflict Resolution*, Special Melnick Symposium Issue, *24*(3) 101-135. Listed on SSRN's Top Ten download list, LSN: Dispute Resolution (Oct. 2023).

- Bazerman, M. & Watkins M. (2004). *Predictable Surprises: The Disasters You Should Have Seen Coming and How to Prevent Them.* Harvard Business School Press.

- Brunner, R. D. et al. (2005). *Adaptive Governance: Integrating Science, Policy, and Decision Making.* Columbia U. Press.

- Burgess, G. & Burgess, H. Intractable Conflict Challenge https://beyondintractability.org/moos

- Diamond, J. (2004). Collapse: How societies fail or succeed. Viking.

- Diep, H.T., Kaufman, M. & Kaufman, S. 2023. An Agent-based Statistical Physics Model for Political Polarization: A Monte Carlo Study *Entropy.* Special issue: Statistical Physics of Opinion Formation and Social Phenomena. *Entropy 2:* 981

- Dörner, D. (1996). *The logic of failure: Recognizing and avoiding error in complex situations* (Perseus Books)

- Kahneman, D. (2011). *Thinking, fast and slow.* Macmillan.

- Kaufman, S. 2023. How Should the Whole-of-Society Respond to Hybrid Warfare? *On track, Canada's global defence and security e-magazine* 30:43-51. https://cdainstitute.ca/hybrid-warfare-fighting-back-with-whole-of-society-tactics/

- Kaufman, S., Ozawa, C. & Shmueli, D. 2018. Negotiations in the public sector: Applying negotiation theory to multiparty conflicts. Special issue, *Négociations* 29/1: 59-73.

- Kaufman, S. The interpreter as intervener. In Honeyman, C. and Schneider, A. K. (2017). *The Negotiator's Desk Reference.* St. Paul, MN: DRI Press. Vol. 2, Ch. 100, 725-742.

- Kaufman, S. 2012. Complex systems, anticipation, and collaborative planning for resilience. In B Goldstein (ed) *Resilient Organizations: Social Learning for Hazard Mitigation and Adaptation* MIT Press: 61-98.

- Probst, G. & Bassi, A. 2014. *Tackling Complexity: A Systemic Approach for Decision Makers.* Greenleaf.

- Sunstein, C. (2007). *Worst-case scenarios.* Harvard University Press.

Possible topics for discussion (non-exhaustive list)

Complex systems constantly shift over time. Therefore, instead of plans – with objectives and sequences of actions to attain them – complexity requires strategies that also shift over time, to adapt to swiftly changing circumstances. Given the situation described, the Rare Earth Elements (REEs) challenge asks students who should respond, when, how, and what they would advise responders to do strategically.

For example:

- How to recognize hybrid warfare actions.

- How to gather and evaluate information with respect to a specific situation.

- How to debias/depoliticize response strategies and preemptive ones.

- How to imagine (anticipate) what else might happen and what responders should do, including who needs to negotiate with whom, how to evaluate the reliability of agreements, how to build in periodic reviews to change course when necessary, and how to build in recourse measures for breech of agreements.

- How time, scale, and context affect the layers of hybrid warfare, and the information needed to counter it.

- Who needs to do what when some form of hybrid warfare hits (emergency situations).

- How to test proposed responses and strategies for robustness at different time horizons (short-, middle- and long-run); how to explore possibilities that strategies might fail, not just succeed ("pre-mortem") – and how to prevent failures discovered, or negative side effects identified which might diminish the value of proposals.

- Obstacles to acting to defend own interests, structures, etc.

Possible additional questions for discussion (non-exhaustive list)

Questions about the proposal process

1) Can you formulate objectives based on the Promontory Institute initial information? What are they?

2) What additional clarifications, if any, might you ask of the Institute?

Questions focusing on REEs:

1) What types of information do you need to begin work on the proposal?

2) What criteria do you propose for evaluating information sources and their trustworthiness?

3) How to tell when you know enough about REEs?[12] What are some aspects which might be key for the proposal? What information might be shifting over time?[13]

4) What information is missing, if any? Can you proceed without it? If not, what can you do?

5) How sensitive is the proposal to errors in (specific classes of) information?

Questions focusing on stakeholders in the case:

1) The proposal requires a careful assessment of stakeholders – those who may affect or be affected by decisions to secure the supply of REEs – and their stakes.

   • What are the main categories of stakeholders currently?

   • Might the list change in the future?

   • Can their stakes be identified with associated degrees of confidence?

   • Are some stakeholders likely to subvert decision processes to take advantage of current political and economic winds?

---

[12] Hint: one way to test that is for students to pretend to already know some information they are seeking, and then ask themselves whether, now that they know, they would do anything differently. If the answer is "no," the information may not be necessary.

[13] Since we began working on the case, some of the references may have aged. For example, new sources of REEs are being discovered, and new regulatory action makes it possible for them to be mined at those locations.

Questions focusing on hybrid warfare and negotiations:

1) What kinds of hybrid warfare might be operative in the REEs case?

2) What kinds of mitigation have already been used in other contexts? Are they applicable to the REEs situation?

3) Which types of hybrid warfare activities have opportunities to be countered by negotiating joint strategies with partners? By other means (e.g., technology)?

4) Who should be involved in negotiations? (Public/private entities? At what level?)

Beyond these suggestions, discussions with participants should proceed based on their ideas, encouraging broad participation and challenges.

12

STATE COLLAPSE AND DOMESTIC DEVOLUTION – WICKED HYBRID CONFLICTS

I. William Zartman

This case study presents the tumultuous history of four States (namely the Central African Republic, Libya, Yemen, and Afghanistan) which, despite clear differences, exhibit similar traits: a power vacuum created by the inefficiency of the State leads to power struggles among local figures, fueled by corruption, looting of natural resources, interethnic or intertribal fights, all the above being aroused by kinetic or non-kinetic actions by foreign actors.

The case study demonstrates what happens when the State level is removed as a society governance mechanism. It casts a grim picture of what could happen if hybrid warfare techniques lead to the undermining of a whole State.

The case is not a structured demonstration of coordinated hybrid warfare actions. Rather, it lists a series of events that may have been fueled by hybrid warfare techniques (corruption, disinformation or misinformation, cyber activities, etc.). It serves as a reflection on what happens when the State level of governance is removed, and how chaos may be created and perpetuated by internal and external forces.

* * *

Keywords: Hybrid warfare – State Collapse – Power vacuum – Central African Republic – Libya – Yemen – Afghanistan

* * *

This case may be complemented by reading Corpora, Christopher (2023), How to undermine a Nation-State in 120 days: mediation and negotiation in a hybrid warfare world, Cardozo Journal of Conflict Resolution, 24-3, 503 (available here: https://www.cardozo-jcr.com/volume-243-symposium-2022).

STATE COLLAPSE AND DOMESTIC DEVOLUTION – WICKED HYBRID CONFLICTS

I. William Zartman

Introduction

We may think of politics – and economics and society as well, *pace* Weber – in an international context as operating at four levels: local, national, regional, and international. "All politics is local", it has been said: the State is the national level, the region several small and weak States sharing some sort of co-identification, and the international community has dominant and smaller members.

However, when the State is unable to perform its functions of security, justice, and welfare, these tend to fall to the lowest level of socio-political organization, the local community, which in many societies is the tribal level (in more developed societies, it can be the small town or neighborhood, as in the Old Wild West). That is a catastrophic development: on the one hand because the tribe cannot handle political interaction at the higher level, and on the other hand, for that reason, the situation produces a national power vacuum that sucks in the upper two levels – to promote their own local interests and to prevent others from doing the same.

This produces a *wicked situation – "pervasive, complex, and ill-structured problems"* (Lira 2010) that *"contain an interconnected web of sub-problems; every proposed solution to part or the whole of the wicked problem will affect other problems in the web"* (Docherty & Lira 2013). And because it occurs in the contemporary era, it involves *hybrid warfare* (also known as Gray Zone Conflict – Hicks & Friends 2019): *"coercion below the level of direct warfare [that] includes information operations, political coercion, economic coercion, cyber operations, proxy support, and provocation by State-controlled Forces."*[1] These definitions deserve a special note, for they generally are used for the conduct of top-level international conflicts, with the lower levels getting only the drippings; here, they are used for lowest level conflicts whose context in a political vacuum draws in the upper levels, a reversal of the usual process. The situation then is open to fishing by external forces who enter sovereign territory, either by invitation from the weak Government floating on the top of the vacuum, or without it, and providing arms to the lower-level fragments, often to complement local traditional weapons and methods. Finally, the vacuum impinges

---

[1] Center for Strategic and International Studies (https://www.csis.org/programs/gray-zone-project)

on individuals, who then are impelled to seek meaning and order in extremist religious movements.

The purpose of this case study is to provide a basis for understanding what happens when the State – the overarching unit of national life throughout the world, and the components of international order – implodes and disappears. Without getting lost in the nature(s) of the State where it exists, this case study will look at examples where it has collapsed and where hybrid warfare replaces State order as a predominant dynamic of domestic relations.

The four States considered – the Central African Republic, Libya, Yemen, and Afghanistan – are similar in their basic assignment to this category, although they differ in the idiosyncratic details, a concise summary of which follows.

The Central African Republic[2]

The Central African Republic (CAR) had never been a State before French colonial implantation in 1906 and was given independence with a State-like suit of clothes in 1960 but with nobody inside. The suit fit its second president after its first coup, after six years of independence, who declared himself Emperor a decade later; Emperor Bokassa and his Empire were removed in 1979 by a coup supported by the former colonial power. Even though it had only three presidents and one party and despite its independence in 1960, CAR remained in neo-colonial dependency with French military, economic, and administrative control. In the African Spring of the early 1990s, little noticed forerunner of the Arab Spring two decades later, CAR produced a leadership change in a free and fair multiparty election in August 1993, but it was then overthrown in a military coup. The French dominance began to weaken, and UN Development Program (UNDP) actions, the UN Mission in the Central African Republic (MINUCRA) and a peacekeeping force from the Central African Monetary and Economic Community (CEMAC) were established. After less than a decade, in 1999, MINUCRA was declared a success as a UN pilot project and was replaced by a UN Peacebuilding Support Office (BONUCA). But the Government was overthrown – again – and the coup was legitimized by a rigged constitutional referendum in 2004 and confirming elections in 2005. Its legitimacy was paper thin and the attempt at a popular mandate opened the "CAR Bush War," lasting until 2012 and compounded after 2008 by civil servants' demonstrations for interrupted pay. The central Government ruled itself for itself.

Government was left to the neighborhoods, not even cohesive regions. "Local order was weakly institutionalized." (Magnuson 2018, 263). Sultanates, chieftainships, local notables all held a weak sway and undercut each other. Governance was especially weak in the Northeastern quadrant of the country, underpopulated, underrepresented, and under-governed, speaking a local Arabic dialect instead of the lingua franca, Sango. The population is more broadly divided into sedentary farmers, mainly in the South, and no-

---

[2] I owe much to the excellent dissertation and fieldwork of Salamah Magnuson, Non-State Armed Groups: Social Contracts in Fragile States, Johns Hopkins University 2018, for this account.

madic herders in the North, the age-old conflict over land use and ownership typical of the whole Sahelian area of Africa. This division replicated religious (Muslim / Christian) and ethnic (Sahelian / Sudanese) identities, reinforced after 2004 as the looting, reprisals and suppression intensified. The State became not only absent but repulsive. There was therefore no attempt to take over the State but rather an effort to replace its functions at the local level (Magnuson 2018).

As the local saying goes: "The State stops at PK [*point kilométrique*] 12" (Bierschenk & de Sardan 1997, 441). This means that the President is "the Mayor of Bangui", the capital city, and controls only 12km out of town. He is easy to keep in power and easy to overthrow. Local administrators are posted in other cities, with little actual exercise of State functions, making the issue of neglect even more apparent. As much as anything, identity is fragmented. Tribal belonging matters, Northeastern identity is loosely meaningful although it is not clear who represents it, *Central African* identity is a point to be hidden and fought over, and religious and broad ethnic identity demands assertions and reprisals. But no one – person or organization – represents any of these, in action or allegiance. Religious cleansing, interethnic violence, personal and tribal retaliation, land disputes, cattle raids, and absence of judicial institutions drive continuing civil conflict, and any of these gives a reason for killing (ICG 2014). Out of a population of about 5 million, there are about a million Internally Displaced People (IDP) in CAR and half a million refugees (mainly in Cameroon).

By the turn of the century, local self-defense groups began to be formed here and there throughout the Northern part of the country but particularly in the sparsely populated Northeast, where they were directed against herders and raiders from neighboring Darfur in Western Sudan, where Northern CAR groups were also operating. The current and previous Presidents, François Bozizé and Ange-Félix Patassé, financed small local groups for self-defense. A more focused self-defense project was the antipoaching park rangers or "local management committees," also funded by the UNDP and directed against Sudanese intruders (Lombard & Botiveau 2012). Sheikh Yaya Ramadan, a village chief, former Mayor, and spiritual leader, was the leader of one of the groups. When he was assassinated in May 2002 by a tribal group from Sudan, the groups of Northeast CAR came together to pursue a retributive conflict with the Darfur and Chadian border tribes. After the fourth coup by François Bozizé, the following year, he began attacking the local groups in the region in April-May 2006, galvanizing them and a few movements to form the Union for Democratic Forces for the Republic (UFDR) in September 2006 (ICG 2007).

A competition with the Government for beatings, killings, village burnings and reprisals was launched, with the Government coming out far ahead. The UFDR served as a roving militia, based in the Bongo massif central to the North-East region and attacking Government forces in the towns while repelling raids from Chad and Darfur. It lived off local supplies, gained by begging or looting, and by the diamond trade from mines in the region. As the rebellion continued, Government employees in the region fled and the

Government responded with scorched-earth tactics, exacerbating the impression of ne-glect, and reinforcing the UFDR's protest.

The UFDR did not have a governing structure of its own, or even a political structure; it was as decentralized as the regions themselves; its one identifiable leader, Demane, was the military but not political official. Two early political leaders – Michel An-Nondokoro Djotodia and Abubakar Sabone – were jailed and then released to inactive UFDR units, which lived in symbiosis with rare local chiefs, tribal leaders, and sultans, but short of their open support or structure. So, they performed minimal Government functions as best they could, including health, police, and adjudication, "a collective of vigilantes and activists" (interview, Magnuson 2018, 301). But even this activity was to emphasize the neglect by Government rather than to replace it. It constituted a cooperation of tribal so-cieties of the region, with a protective armed force and alarm bells for attention.

These characteristics left the UFDR with the need either to come to terms with the Government or to raise the level of protest and organization. It signed an Agreement with the Government in April 2007, and immediately began to fall apart. Internal dissidence over the decision to sign, plus Government efforts to coopt and buy off component tribal groups, brought out the weaknesses of the movement, compounded by military defeat in a combat with the French army, but also by personal rivalries, where each aspiring leader had his own group of followers in the fractioned population. A ceasefire agreement was signed in October 2011 with the Government, further splitting the movement over the signature, and the Government did not follow through on its promises. The rigged re-election of Bozizé in 2011 showed the Northeast that no change was likely, no answer to their feelings of neglect. Bozizé was later indicted by the International Court of Justice for inciting genocide and crimes against humanity.

The year after the election, one of the absent UFDR political leaders, Djotodia, returned from exile to reunite the opposition from the Northeast. The higher goal and the common enemy formed the basis of a new alliance. The resulting primarily Muslim Seleka ("coali-tion" in Sango) found success in combat, ironically with the help of Chadian and Sudanese mercenaries. A power-sharing agreement with the Government was signed in Libreville in January 2013 through the mediation of ECCAS (the Economic Community of Central African States). Government again defected and the Coalition launched a major attack in the Northeast, and then occupied Bangui and overthrew the Government 3 months later, the fifth coup. Djotodia was installed as President in May, disbanded the Coalition in September, formed a regional force of his own, the Popular Force for the Rebirth of CAR (FPRC) in 2014, and resigned in February. But the now leaderless troops took off on a rampage against the Christian and Black African South, responding to the claims that Northern Muslims were not "Centrafricans." The Southerners responded in turn with an Anti-Balaka ("anti-balles" or charms against AK-47s) movement. In ceasefire negotia-tions in Brazzaville in July 2014, the Seleka delegation called for a division of the country in a Muslim North and a Christian South, but then dropped the demand. The FPRC raised the level of its goals, calling in August for secession with the new Northeast independent State called Dar al-Kouti after a local sultanate, to be established in December. In response, the movement broke apart again, with some fragments clinging to the original goal of attracting Government attention and others aiming to assume State functions for all of CAR, in addition to the FPRC's goal of secession.

The common demand of the rebellion was not assertive but appellant. The population called for the attention that was due to it from Government; it was an appeal from neglect that recognized the role and responsibility of Government. It did not leave the substantive phase to enter into the procedural demand to take over Government until a much later phase, when not only its hopes but also its ability to fulfill them itself had worn out; the demand for secession was vapid. Since the appeal for attention referred to universal conditions in CAR, not just the Northeast, it could have united a mass movement behind a responding Government, but internal divisions of identity kept that from happening. And were such a move to have been launched, a Government would have lacked the skills and resources to meet the demand, despite significant amounts of international aid that has flowed into CAR. So those who were installed in Bangui used the available resources for themselves (Arnson & Zartman 2005).

The conflict has been the occasion of almost annual peace negotiations and ceasefire projects. Although each usually ended in an agreement, it was in turn the cause for rejection and return to combat by fractions of the parties, claiming the agreement was unfair, the signing parties unrepresentative, the needs unmet, or the rewards insufficient. Not only the UN missions, the French support group, and the regional organizations African Union (which suspended CAR in 2013) and ECCAS served as mediators, but also international NGOs such as the Red Cross and local and often ad hoc NGOs such as interfaith pastor and imam groups have served as mediators. Although fatigue has occasionally set in among combating groups, notions of reprisal and continuing provocations have kept the pot bubbling. France, the colonial peacekeeper – in the absence of State builder – wound down its presence in 2012 out of frustration and lack of interest, leaving an opening for a newcomer. On invitation from President Faustin-Archange Touadera in 2017, Russia sent security units of the Wagner Group, provided military training and equipment, and a competing peace effort hosted by Sudan, with an interest in diamonds and neighboring uranium (Searcey 2019). The peace agreement in 2019 left large parts of the country in the hands of the rebellions and was not observed.

The "Mayor of Bangui" has little relation to the rest of the country except to send out a predative army and local administrators who were either ignored or became part of the local traditional structures. These structures are where very limited power lies, holding a social contract with the surrounding populations in the absence of one with any national authorities. But Government is not just a local traditional function; security is handled by coalitions of rebels, rising to nearly capture the capital after the reelection of its "Mayor" in 2019, repulsed with gruesome efficacy only by the Russian Wagner Group, with Syrian and Libyan mercenaries, and Rwandan soldiers.

Libya

Libya achieved independence from Italy in 1951 with a weak monarchy that was overthrown in 1969 by Moammar Qadhafi, an unusual messianic dictator who destroyed the State and replaced it with personalized rule and a corrupt and dysfunctional organization. When Qadhafi tried to return the Government to the people, he found them returning to local tribal structures; when he tried to modernize traditional politics, they reverted to "revolutionary" councils and militias that imposed centralized rule. In place of a social contract, he rewrote the Muslim religion into a Green Book of his own. In place of a national economy, he offered every citizen a guaranteed income drawn from the country's enormous oil revenues.

When this structure was destroyed in the Arab Spring revolt, politics dropped into the hands of tribal militias (Lacher 2020). Under the impetus of the Arab Spring in neighboring Tunisia and Egypt, local protests against the Qadhafi regime arose in February 2011 and were met with violence from security forces. As the revolt spread across the country in many local outbursts, Qadhafi was killed in October and the resistance broke into factions competing for leadership (Mezran & Alunni 2015). A National Transition Council quarreled over representation from the three regions of the country (Tripolitania, Cyrenaica, Fezzan), then hastily drew up elections in July 2012; the turnout was good at over 60% but the result produced a large majority of independents, and the ensuing Government was "entirely cut up by factions large and small" (Lacher 2020, 29).

In addition to the revolutionary fighters, former Government figures, and the exiled opponents, the local representatives of the tribes, villages, and militias made governing impossible. Retired Gen. Khalifa Haftar suspended the General National Council (Parliament) and the Constitution in February 2013 in the name of the General Leadership of the Libyan Army, which did not exist, and in May the GNC, which continued to meet, produced two Governments. Haftar then gathered an army in the East (Benghazi), but was opposed even in his own region by scattered groups; groups in the West (Tripolitania) broke into their own warring factions. New elections in June 2014 brought out low participation and further fractionalization. But the forces were not just regional expressions, but continually shifting alliances among fragmented groups based on local allegiances and interests and competing behavior during the Qadhafi regime and the Arab Spring. The civil war that lasted until mid-2015 was suspended out of fatigue in a temporary ceasefire, with the help of a United Nations Support Mission in Libya (UNSMIL).

A UN-backed coalition was formed in Tripoli as a Government of National Accord (GNA) in opposition to Haftar's forces backed by the members of the House of Representatives (HoR) who remained in Tobruk, but the bipolarity was only an illusion, as coalitions frittered and elements moved from one side to the other. An Islamic State in Libya (ISIL) was established in early 2014 in Derna in the East and then moved to Sirte and pledged allegiance to IS at the end of the year; when it moved to take Tripoli, forces in the region reacted and overcame it by the end of 2016 (Warner et. al., 2021). In the East, Haftar controlled, with contestation, the oil refineries in Tobruk, then quietly brought the African populations of the South into his coalition. A sharp offensive to Tripoli in April 2019 opened the third round of the civil war; even though he was soon rebuffed as his forces came apart, the war continued desultorily as a hot, unstable, self-serving stalemate (Vidaurri 2023).

Foreign "fishing" in the contest began with a bang at the very start, when NATO air strikes responded to the Government's use of violence in 2011 (Theiss 2015); direct involvement was then terminated once Qadhafi was killed, although US forces were involved in clearing ISIL out of Sirte. France, Egypt, the United Arab Emirates (UAE), Turkey, and Russia (largely through the Wagner Group) all provided armament and/or forces to various parties in efforts to buttress parties in the struggle to dominate politics; the contest was above all for political influence since Libyan oil was readily available to whoever would buy (even after the boycott over the aggression in Ukraine was instituted). Often foreign fishing was in competition with another rival, as in the case of France vs Italy or Turkey vs Egypt, undercutting efforts for cooperation. The most active force for building a Government coalition to fill the vacuum was led by the UN Special Representatives Tarek Mitra, Bernadino Leon, Martin Kobler, and Ghassane Salame who successively played active and effective roles in shaping evolving politics, but never succeeded in overcoming competing external interference and drawing together a stable coalition.

To the external world, it seemed there were a lot of top-level leading figures, and representative spokesmen. But in fact, national politics drifted on the upper surface of political interaction, without firm ties to the local base and without firm ties to a local clientele. They represented no one and lower-level groups were unstable and fragmented. In a situation that elsewhere might have called for a strongman on a white horse, not even potential candidates for national leadership appeared, and even Haftar, who would have liked to be the exception, could not consolidate his regional coalition, nor extend it to the West. There was a revulsion against looking for a new Qadhafi. The local factions, militias, village councils, and tribal structures overlapped, competed, changed allies, and had no interest in taking over Government, only in defending their own local positions and concerns. Observers' consensus is that this situation is likely to last for a long time. If foreign meddlers might be able to coordinate their interests, they might be able to impose a political structure on the top, but the gap between top and bottom layers would remain.

Yemen

In 1962, with the help of Nasser's Egyptian armed forces, *Yemen* became a Republic with the overthrow of the Zaydi monarchy; however, it was never a State. At best, it was a congeries of tribes, factions, even parties, overlaid but not dominated by sectarian groups, all handled by a central figure with his own interests in remaining in power and acting as a puppeteer of autonomous actors with interests, identities, and followers of their own. Southern Yemen (Aden) became independent from Britain in 1967 as the People's Democratic Republic of Yemen. A war broke out between a moderate and a communist faction, the latter of which, having won, launched attacks and by 1972 was in open warfare against the North. A truce that year gave way to infiltration of Sunni Salafists into the Zaydi (Shi'i) North along with an attempted coup against the President in 1979, and then armed conflict along the border with Saudi Arabia at the end of the decade. When two years of intense and unstable negotiations ended in 1990 in the unification of the two halves of Yemen, it was challenged by a secessionist rebellion again in 1994. A political party led by a leading family, al-Islah, was met in 1990 by the competing existence of the President's own party, the General People's Congress (GPC). Yemeni *mujahidin* from Afghanistan filled the ranks of the leading army commander, Yemen's second most powerful figure, but they also formed a militia of their own against the leading (socialist) party of the South, crushed in Operation Scorched Earth in 1998. A well-entrenched franchise of al-Qaeda in the Arabian Peninsula (AQAP) was established in parts of central Yemen after 2009, followed by a separate Islamic State branch in 2014.

Ali Abdallah Saleh was President and manager of the Yemeni political system in the Northern part, the Yemen Arab Republic, and unifier of the two halves of the country from 1978 until the Arab Spring of 2011. As a remarkable manipulator, he managed continually shifting alliances, juggled tribal leadership, playing off sectarian factions continually to maintain – by politics and by repression – the union of the factions of two socially and ideologically different regions. "The chaos in Yemen is actually what the Saleh regime wants." (Blumi 2011, 6).

But the most concentrated challenge to the regime came out of the arrest of a local family-sectarian official by a State agent in 2004. Husayn al-Huthi was a local activist and member of Parliament, who felt that Yemen was next after the US invasion of Iraq and Afghanistan and that the predominant religion of Northern Yemen, the Zaydi form of Shi'i Islam, needed to be awakened from its lethargy and reformed. He roused support from his own clan and from the poor, young (mostly under 18), unemployed, ignored in Saleh's coalition politics, wielding the slogan: "Death to America, Death to Israel, Victory to Islam." (Hamidaddin 2015, 125). His family, the Huthis, are an insignificant segment of a larger clan in Yemen, the Hashemi, considered the social elite under the monarchy and (by themselves) the legitimate rulers of Yemen; thus, with lower class and former upper-class associations, they are in a critical symbolic position in the maelstrom of Yemeni socio-politics. Husayn's arrest in 2004 triggered a deadly uprising, followed at the end of the year by a second war upon the attempt to arrest his father, aged 80, and third and fourth wars in 2005-2006 and 2007. In the interim, the wars attracted the attention of the neighboring Saudis and Qataris and the shadow of Iran. The fifth war, in May 2008, ran across the whole North to the gates of the capital; it was halted by order of the President, but skirmishes continued until the sixth war that began mid-August 2009 for 6 months, involving the air force and presidential guards and spillover into Saudi Arabia for another two months. The family revolt for a social cause had become an international war. Both sides had garnered some losses and gains. Militarily, Saleh had gotten stronger, although his elite allies were weakened by their inability to prevail or at least mediate; the Huthis had gathered military strength and social allies but alienated the neighborhood. All the elements of war, from media spread to mechanized arms and air forces, rolled out over Northern Yemen. But more was to come.

As the leading figures of the Government began to squabble over the handling of the wars, a coalition of the opposition, the Joint Meeting of Parties, finally including Islah as well, began negotiating with Saleh to reduce tensions, but collapsed into a full confrontation in September 2010. Now heartened by the Arab Spring in Tunis and Cairo, growing mass protests demanded Saleh's resignation in preparation for elections in April 2012. Deaths among the protesters, internal schism in Saleh's major tribal backers, splits in the army, an Al-Qaeda in the Arabic Peninsula (AQAP) attack on an army base, threatened breakup of the regional unification, and general warnings against fratricidal vacuum if Saleh disappeared brought an offer from him to prepare a transition after the elections. The street rejected it and the various forces could not unite to accept it. An extraordinary drama of acceptances and re-rejections by Saleh to a transition plan submitted by the countries on the Arabian peninsula, accompanied by military advances of AQAP militants, culminated in assassination attempts on the President, the last one nearly successful, leading to his hospitalization in Saudi Arabia. Upon returning to Yemen, Saleh brought new negotiation maneuvers, but also stalemate between his former allies and the opposition parties and clashes between tribal militias and parts of the army. After almost a year of protest and contentious rivalries, under pressure from Saudi Arabia, the US, and the UN Security Council, an agreement was signed in November 2011; foreign mediation had to turn to foreign coercion, leaving local forces, tribes and factions fragmented and weakened and the resigning President retaining a good deal of the manipulative power he had exercised while in office. But even more was to come.

With the help of a UN mediator, the parties turned to a series of sessions termed "dialogues" to set up a new system under Saleh's former vice-president. Although the results were seemingly successful, the Huthis considered that their share in government was not sufficient, and in April 2014 the seventh Huthi war broke out. As it proceeded, it took on an international dimension, with direct intervention of Saudi Arabia and the Arab Emirates as the principal opponents of the Huthis; Huthis' conquest of most of Northern Yemen including the capital, Sana'a; Huthis' use of drones to bomb the Saudi capital across the peninsula and then to join the Israeli-Hamas conflict and to interdict commercial traffic in the Red Sea; the supply of arms to the Huthis from Iran and Russia; and disease and starvation among the population in the occupied area. Saleh joined the Huthis in 2014, made a formal alliance in 2016, broke it in 2017 and was assassinated by them that year. A decade after it broke out, the seventh war has drifted into a stalemate for the parties, a horror for the inhabitants, and an unmanageable complication for the international conflict of the Middle East.

Although it purports to be a State, the Government has fled to the South, which threatened to revert to its own secessionist independence but with no strong Government of its own. The Huthis are unclear of their purposes and have become a full proxy of Iran. Under the war, the tribal groups maintained their identity but in major cases with splintered leadership, shifting alliances, bitter rivalries, and conflict conducted using the whole range of armaments from tribal militias to drones and planes and heavy materiel. Power lies in the mobilization of both traditional formations and social forces responding to the degradations of a failing modern economy.

Afghanistan

Afghanistan became a Republic with the overthrow of King Zahir Shah in 1973, but the revolution was not completed until the bloody coup of Noor Mohammed Taraki and the People's Democratic Party in 1978, who in turn was overthrown at the year's end by a Soviet incursion to install Babrak Karmal. The reaction was a broad public revulsion against foreign ideas and interference, a mass emigration into neighboring countries, and the rise of the Islamist *mujahidin* resistance throughout the country, divided by geography, ideology, ethnicity, and personalities. Afghanistan was a society of autonomous tribes, where loyalty was given to the ethnic group and its chief, operating through a committee of elders (Bokhari 1995). United only in their religious and social rejection, these groups refused negotiations with the Soviet-backed regime until the mid-1980s. Tireless efforts of the UN Secretary General's Personal Envoy Diego Cordovez produced indirect and then finally direct talks with the Soviet Union, and agreement in 1988 for withdrawal of Soviet troops the following year, leaving behind its former proxy Government, just as the Soviet Union was about to collapse.

To provide a stable successor Government acceptable to the various international and domestic forces that brought it to power, both politics and Government in Afghanistan broke down into competing parties, militias, and States, each with its tribal base. Tajik and Uzbek warlords in the North fought for domination against forces in Kabul associated with Iran, to the exclusion of the Pashtun forces in the South, as Pakistan connived to maintain its dominance. A breakdown of order and governance was the scenario, with the government's incapacity exacerbated after the mid-1990s by a devastating drought. Finally, in 1995, a protest movement arose from the neglected and impoverished agricultural Pashtun South, led by a union of Islamic students (*Taliban*) following the fundamentalist Deobandi doctrine, and swept across the country. In a country deeply impregnated with religious conviction, the movement was above all a protest against corruption, impiety, infighting, neglect, and breakdown of order, as had occurred in many places such as Algeria, Sudan, Iran, Somalia, and, earlier, Libya. However, it was itself not focused on governing but simply on restoring piety and order, and it housed al-Qaeda and its charismatic leader, Osama bin Laden, in its war against the West. As the regime pursued its imposition of religious law, attacks by the Tadjik and Uzbek Northern Alliance continued, but the turning point was the al-Qaeda attack on the World Trade Center in New York and the Pentagon on September 11, 2001, which galvanized Western military attention.

The US and NATO invaded, expanding into the International Security Assistance Force (ISAF) and by the end of the year, the Taliban were evicted; bin Laden fled with his supporters to neighboring Pakistan. The operation was successful, but the patient was still infected in its Pashtun area including Pakistan border regions in the South and East, ensuring the long war that bin Laden had promised. The Taliban organized politically in their regions, establishing a *shura* (assembly) of tribal figures, centered on Taliban leader Mullah Omar, and in 2003 began an intensified guerrilla campaign, with kidnappings and assassinations of Government and collaborating local elders, destruction of schools and clinics, and terrorizing villages. ISAF's response was difficult to make effective, unable to provide local protection, unprepared to counter anti-foreign resentment, and often counterproductive in its efforts to identify Taliban sympathizers. A surge between 2010 and 2013 brought US troops to 90,000, plus 40,000 other ISAF troops, Taliban forces being estimated at about a quarter of that figure.

An interim Government under Hamid Karzai was chosen in a conference in Bonn in December 2001, where the Taliban were not invited, confirmed the next year in a Loya Jirga (assembly of leaders that make decisions by consensus), and elected in 2004. Its police forces were understaffed and its military untrained and unprepared for guerrilla warfare. Nonetheless, the new army acquitted itself well in many engagements, but the Taliban continued to expand their territorial control. Karzai, reelected in 2009, was succeeded in 2014 by Ashraf Ghani, who had written a book on nation-building (2008). The election was hotly contested, and the Government was split by rivalries and charges of corruption – rated by Transparency (2013) among the world's most corrupt countries – over the following decade. As a result, it was more concerned with politics in the capital than with grassroots relations, the level on which the Taliban made its progress.

Popular protest movements throughout the country beginning in 2015 produced a joint holiday ceasefire in 2018, then not renewed; but secret contacts were made between the US and the Taliban at the same time, although the Taliban refused to include the Afghan Government, leading the Government to denounce the talks, including the agreement produced in February 2020. The US bargaining position was essentially: "negotiate an agreement for us to withdraw or else we will withdraw." The Taliban resumed violence after signing the agreement, launching an offensive in March that produced "the bloodiest week in 19 years" (Tanzeem, 2020). At the same time, negotiation with the Afghan Government took place off and on over the next year. The Taliban began its last major offensive in May 2021 and by mid-August entered Kabul as Ghani fled to Tajikistan and the US ordered immediate withdrawal, leaving equipment, allies, and civilians behind.

The war in its various phases since 1990 involved every military method and armament, and the gamut from individual terrorist attacks to guerrilla warfare including threats and violence against civilians to full scale air war and heavy armament. It was characterized at every phase by a Government that lost contact and empathy with the population – from the fundamentalist Taliban to the corrupt Kabul bubble – who in turn were in closest contact and identification with local traditional authorities at the village level, with whom they maintained a social contract in the absence of one higher up. In its broadest form, it was a tribal war, a war of the Pashtun return that even in its time of victory and after was contested by tribal rebels. Perhaps the State had not collapsed, but its arteries had repeatedly hardened, and it lost control of its members.

Common elements in these four cases

These four cases, on passing glance, exhibit a difference that needs no emphasis. But an analytical look shows striking similarities. None has a State: no institution with a monopoly, legitimate or not, of the use of force, no partner of a social contract, no agent of demand aggregation and conflict management. Where there was someone in the capital city capable of sending a representative (of himself) to the UN General Assembly, he had no organic ties with his population, downward as a purveyor of security and welfare or upward as a source of accountability. The contending forces and figures led a lively political existence, interacting with foreign Governments and UN Special Envoys as if they represented something; they even held elections, but were unable to provide Government services once elected (or put in place by a coup). In all, governance including dispute settlement, allocation of goods and services, and focus of identity, is located at the lowest institutional level, in the village, community, or tribe. Larger identities such as religious or ethnic are fractioned and internally contested, as they look for new leaders and authenticities: there is nothing more divisive than religious unity. Rebel forces generally follow their own local interests, independent of local governing authorities but interacting with them. They tend to function for two, often contradictory reasons: to assert and protect local autonomy and interests against competing forces, both central and local, and to put pressure on central Government to overcome its policy of neglect and grant Government services, both welfare and security. Rebellion came most frequently from marginal, disinherited, neglected regions and layers of the population.

Warfare involved a full gamut of operations. At the lowest level, it began with urban protest movements and rural kidnappings and assassinations. It moved into guerrilla uprisings, targeting rival or collaborating groups and individuals, as well as operating installations and combatting police operations. It expanded into territorial control and pitched battles with forces of order, eventually calling for governance over areas of its own. Full military engagement involving air forces and heavy materiel, but also long-range drones and missiles placed it in the contemporary military scene. The ulterior form involved foreign military forces, as individual mercenaries, militias like Wagner, and even foreign army units, in all cases except Yemen, and also missions organized by the UN.

Mediation has little purchase on conflicts of this kind, whether by countries involved (as former colonial powers) or external peacemakers (e.g., UN missions). The groups are hard to contact, inexperienced in conceding and bargaining, uncertain of their own aims, unconsolidated around their spokesmen, and not in control of implementing the results. Meeting to negotiate is often refused as implicit recognition, and signing an agreement often produces a schism. Agreements, when reached, are temporary and unstable. In all the cases, great national dialogs have been held, with UN sponsorship but insufficient results; in all cases, UN missions, including skilled Special Representatives of the Secretary-General, have been mandated, with more insufficient results...

Fishing from outside is characteristic of such internal conflicts. Foreign involvement makes them proxy wars; rather than being launched as an external State's pawn, internal conflicts provide the occasion for international involvement, sometimes unrelated to the parties themselves, and it is the power vacuum of the conflict itself rather than any party that allows external engagement. Such involvement is often preemptive, occasioned by the possibility of another's engagement. Usually, there is some element of past glory for the intervenor that is open to be retrieved out of the current vacuum – Ottoman in Libya, Wahabi in Yemen, the complex pitch of the Great Game involving Russia, Britain, India, and Pakistan in Afghanistan. But fishing can also occur when a field of raw materials, formerly in another's area of influence, becomes open for exploitation, and when a rebel unit or Government becomes open for influence and control.

These are all characteristics of *Gray Zone Conflict,* and they are amply illustrated in the four cases, among others. In all, the population is the grass under the elephants trampling them in their own name, producing famines and epidemics for those who stick it out (often dislocated as Internally Displaced People) and refugee outflows for those who cannot. Regarding all four countries, external States on the first level have been torn – as is customary – between the values and the interests of their foreign policy, called to respond to the raging humanitarian crisis with aid that often goes to the opposing side, yet risking castigation for ignoring their own values if they do not.

In such foreign involvement, the methods used have reached deeply into the unconventional. On the military side, drones are active (to save combatants' lives); mercenaries are in the frontlines; blockage of food and medical supplies and prevention of humanitarian International NGOs are weapons of war, and attacks on civilian targets (defined as terrorism by the US and UN) are characteristic. Social media and diaspora support, among the modern methods of war, seem to play a minor role in these cases. In all four countries, the conflict is one of supporting one tribal group against another, but with little attention to reaching the tribes themselves on their own terms.

The wickedness of the conflicts is underscored by the fact that international efforts such as conferences and Special Representatives of the UN Secretary General's working from the top down do not put a State back together, as the experience of Cambodia, Bosnia, and Congo, in addition to the four countries themselves, illustrate. States are built from the bottom up, with foreign help selectively and judiciously applied. What it is that starts the bottom-up process is unknown, partly because there are so few examples. The top level of politics is simply too far from the bottom to be helpful, and yet the top acts as somewhat of a lid on the disruption that the second level of regional competition would produce unrestrained. Leaving Afghanistan would leave the pitch open to a six-team rugby match; leaving Yemen would leave a significant upset in the trans-Gulf rivalry; leaving Libya would simply transfer the conflict to a match between the Russian and Ottoman Empire without bringing Turkey any closer to a return to a mutually comfortable role within NATO; leaving the Central African Republic by the French left the door and room open to Russia. And in all cases, for foreign nations to wash their hands of the situation would simply bring more bad governance and neglect of marginalized populations.

References:

- Arnson, Cynthia & Zartman, I. William 2005. Rethinking the economics of war: the intersection of Need. Creed, and Greed, Washington, DC, Woodrow Wilson International Center for Scholars.

- Bierschenk, Thomas & de Sardan, Olivier, 1997. "Local powers and a distant State in rural Central African Republic", The Journal of Modern African Studies, 35, 3, pp. 441 – 468.

- Blumi, Isa, 2011. *Chaos in Yemen: Societal Collapse and the New Authoritarianism.* New York, Routledge.

- Bokhari, Imtiaz, 1995. "Internal Negotiations among Many Actors: Afghanistan," in I William Zartman, ed., *Elusive Peace: Negotiating an End to Civil Wars.* Brookings.

- Docherty Jayne S. & Lira Leonard 2013. Adapting to the Adaptive: How Can We Teach Negotiation for Wicked Problems? In Christopher Honeyman, James Coben & Andrew Wei-Min Lee, *Educating negotiators for a connected world* – Vol. 4 in the Rethinking Negotiation Teaching Series, DRI Press.

- Ghani, Ashraf with Lockhart, Claire 2008. *Fixing Failed States: A Framework for Rebuilding a Fractured World* (Oxford University Press)

- Hamidaddin, Abdullah 2015. "Yemen: Negotiating with Tribes, States, and Memories," in I William Zartman, ed., *Arab Spring: Negotiating in the Shadow of the Intifada.* University of Georgia Press.

- Hicks, Kathleen & Friends Alice 2019. By other means – campaigning in the grey zone. CSIS (Center for Strategic and International Studies), Rowman & Littlefield.

- ICG (International Crisis Group) 2007, Central African Republic: Anatomy of a Phantom State, available at https://www.crisisgroup.org/africa/central-africa/central-african-republic/central-african-republic-anatomy-phantom-state.

- ICG 2014, The Central African Republic's Hidden Conflict, available at: https://www.crisisgroup.org/africa/central-africa/central-african-republic/central-african-republic-s-hidden-conflict.

- Lacher, Wolfram 2020. *Libya's Fragmentation.* I B Tauris.

- Lira, Leonard 2010. Design: The U.S. Army's Approach to Negotiating Wicked Problems, in Christopher Honeyman, James Coben & Giuseppe de Palo, Venturing beyond the classroom – Vol. 2 in the Rethinking Negotiation Teaching Series, DRI Press.

- Lombard, Louisa & Botiveau, Raphaël 2015. Rébellion et limites de la consolidation de la paix en République centrafricaine, Politique Africaine, 2012 / 1, pp. 189 – 208.

- Magnuson, Salameh 2018, *Non-State Armed Groups: Social Contracts in Fragile States*, Johns Hopkins University Dissertation.

- Mezran, Karim & Alunni, Alice 2015. "Libya: Negotiations for Transition," in I William Zartman, ed., *Arab Spring: Negotiating in the Shadow of the Intifada.* University of Georgia Press.

- Searcey Dionne 2019. « Gems, Warlors and Mercenaries: Russia's Playbook in Central African Republic », The New York Times (30 september).

- Tanzeem, Ayesha, 2020. "Afghan Security Forces Suffer Bloodiest Week in 19 Years." *VOA News, available at* https://www.voanews.com/a/usa_afghan-security-forces-suffer-bloodiest-week-19-years/6191522.html.

- Theiss, Johannes 2015. "NATO: The Process of Negotiating Military Intervention in Syria," in I William Zartman, ed., *Arab Spring: Negotiating in the Shadow of the Intifada.* University of Georgia Press.

- Transparency International 2013. Corruption Perception Index, available at https://www.transparency.org/en/cpi/2013.

- Vidaurri, Marian 2023. *Hard, Unstable, Self-Serving Stalemates (HUSSS) and Negotiation Collapse: The Venezuelan Experience (2014-2021).* Johns Hopkins University Dissertation.

- Warner, Jason, O'Farrell, Ryan, Nsaibia, Heni, and Cummings, Ryan, 2021. *The Islamic State in Africa.* Hurst.

Possible questions for all audiences

1) The case provides a definition of a wicked problem: a pervasive, complex, and ill-structured problem that contains an interconnected web of sub-problems so that every proposed solution to part or the whole of the wicked problem will affect other problems in the web. Apply this definition to one or several of the countries presented.

2) What steps would you propose to reconstruct a broken State, such as those described in the case study? (If you think the steps would vary widely among such situations, choose one of the four.) What roles could neighbor countries or regional organizations play in such reconstruction efforts?

3) How do you analyze the responsibilities of the past colonial powers in the current situations of their former colonies (France for the CAR, Italy for Libya, etc.)?

4) What the case does not say is that the notion of a State may be culture dependent. We tend to pin our Western democratic ideal of a State to countries which do not share our history and culture of public representation. Is the Western vision of a State even applicable to each / all countries described in this case study?

5) Max Weber stated that States have the monopoly on the legitimate use of force. Reflect on what constitutes the sources of such legitimacy. In the absence of a State, who could it be transferred to, if anyone?

6) Taking a hybrid warfare perspective, imagine you act for a State that wishes to weaken or destroy another State without direct involvement of their armed forces. For this purpose, choose any State as the aggressor, and any other State as the victim (those cited in the scenario – or others). Which tools are at your disposal to reach your objective? What game plan would you suggest?

7) The case study does not directly mention hybrid warfare techniques. Which of such methods do you think were at play in the different scenarios (taking into consideration the chronology and availability of different methods at different points in time)?

8) Is every Western, liberal democracy at risk of following the path of the States described in this case study? What makes them immune and/or at risk? You may focus the question on your home country, or another one.

9) Can you think of other States in similar situations (e.g., Lebanon)? Taking the existing cases as references, write the story of one of these other States, and discuss how it resembles and/or differs from the countries presented here.

Selected Readings on Hybrid Warfare

Leonard L. Lira & Joshua L. Levine[1]

With the humility that our immense subject requires, we aim to provide a list of valuable academic references.[2] We do not, however, seek here to conduct a full-scale review of the literature on hybrid warfare. A comprehensive literature review on hybrid warfare would be a Sisyphean task, not only because perceptions are constantly shifting in various professions regarding what is relevant, but also because, at present, the literature (not to mention its vocabulary) is evolving so quickly that there is no practical way to keep it up to date. The reader may notice that some of the recommended readings may not seem directly related to the subject. We would suggest that in these cases, the recommended readings are supplementary for understanding the complex nature of hybrid conflict. Therefore, we invite the reader to view this list as merely a suggested reading list, as offered by many contributors to this book up until its publication. However, this reading should be paired with a lookout for related new material that will undoubtedly emerge after this book's publication.

Hybrid warfare and gray zone conflict are interdisciplinary topics that intersect various academic fields. The further reading list below is organized alphabetically by the primary academic disciplines that address these concepts and their perspectives, though we must again emphasize that it is not exhaustive.

Selected readings will be classified as follows:

- Generalist publications on Hybrid Warfare by Project Seshat Collaborators

- Cybersecurity and Information Sciences

- Economics and Business

- Environmental Studies

- History and Generalities about Hybrid Warfare

---

[1] This list draws in part from contributions by other Project Seshat members, including Chris Honeyman, Steven Desjardins and Christopher Corpora, not to forget Bryan Reyes. May all of them be thanked for their contribution.

[2] Listing academic production is already a Herculean task; listing non-academic publications (news reports, etc.) would be impossible, for many reasons, not the least of which is the fact that new publications appear daily.

- Legal Studies

- Media and Communication Studies

- Military and Strategy Studies

- Political Science, International Relations and Security Studies

- Public Health

- Psychology

- Sociology and Anthropology

- Technology and Engineering

Generalist publications on Hybrid Warfare by Project Seshat Collaborators

Focus: hybrid warfare as a multifaceted phenomenon

Topics: hybrid warfare in its entirety, links with negotiation and conflict management theories

- Alkon, C., & Kaufman, S. (2022). A Theory of Interests in the Context of Hybrid Warfare: It's Complex. *Cardozo J. Conflict Resol.*, *24*, 581.

- Chrustie, C. (2023). Mind the Hybrid Warfare Gap. In *Hybrid Warfare: Fighting Back with Whole-of-Society Tactics, On Track* Vol. 30, Winter 2023.

- Corpora, C. A. (2022). How to Undermine a Nation-State in 120 Days: Mediation and Negotiation in a Hybrid Warfare World. *Cardozo J. Conflict Resol.*, *24*, 503.

- Desjardins, S. (2023). Hybrid Warfare – Is it New, is it Real, and What are the Threats, Vulnerabilities, and Implications for Defence and the Military? In *Hybrid Warfare: Fighting Back with Whole-of-Society Tactics, On Track* Vol. 30, Winter 2023.

- Galeotti, M. (2019). The Vory: Russia's Super Mafia. New Haven: Yale.

- Galeotti, M. (2022). The Weaponization of Everything: A Field Guide to the New Way of War. New Haven: Yale.

- Galeotti, M. (2024). Putin's Wars: From Chechnya to Ukraine. Oxford: Osprey.

- Hinshaw, A., Borbely, A., & Chrustie, C. (2022). Where Is Negotiation in Hybrid Warfare? *Cardozo J. Conflict Resol.*, *24*, 517.

- Honeyman, C. and Tan, R.X. (2025) A New Management System, for a New Type of Conflict? Singapore's Possible Role in Managing Grey Zone Conflict in International Commerce, *Dispute Resolution Review* (Australia) Vol 4/2:99-119.

- Honeyman, C., Chrustie, C., Schneider, A.K., Fraser, V. and Jordaan, B. 2020. Hybrid Warfare, International Negotiation, and an Experiment in 'Remote Convening'. *Negotiation Journal*, Vol. 36, #4: 573–584

- Honeyman, C., & Schneider, A.K. (2023). Hybrid Warfare: Fighting Back with Whole-of-Society Tactics, *On Track* Vol. 30, Winter 2023.

- Honeyman, C. & Schneider, A.K. (2023). Introduction: Negotiation Strategies for War by Other Means, *Cardozo J. Conflict Resol.*, *24*, 487

- Honeyman, C. and Tan, R.X. (2025) A New Management System, for a New Type of Conflict? Singapore's Possible Role in Managing Grey Zone Conflict in International Commerce. *Dispute Resolution Review* (Australia) Vol 4/2:99-119.

- Kaufman, S. (2023). How Should the Whole-of-Society Respond to Hybrid Warfare? In *Hybrid Warfare: Fighting Back with Whole-of-Society Tactics, On Track* Vol. 30, Winter 2023.

- Leslie, A. (2023). 'Redefining Contours of "Business as Usual" and the Potential Role of the Military.' In Hybrid Warfare: Fighting Back with Whole-of-Society Tactics, On Track Vol.30, Winter 2023.

- Leslie, A. (2023). Know Thyself—Embracing the Ambiguity of War by Other Means. *Cardozo J. Conflict Resol.*, *24*, 495.

- Welsh, N.A., Press, S., & Schneider, A.K. (2023). Negotiation Theories Engage Hybrid Warfare. *Cardozo J. Conflict Resol.*, *24*, 543.

Cybersecurity and Information Sciences

Focus: Role of cyber and information warfare in hybrid conflicts.
Topics: Cyber-espionage, digital propaganda, and disinformation campaigns.
Methods: Network analysis, cybersecurity threat assessment, and digital communication strategies.

- Azinheira, B., Antunes, M., Maximiano, M., & Gomes, R. (2023). A Methodology For Mapping Cybersecurity Standards Into Governance Guidelines For SME's In Portugal. *Procedia Computer Science, 219*, 121–128. https://doi.org/10.1016/j.procs.2023.01.272.

- Azzani, M. (2024). Enhancing awareness of cyber-crime: A crucial element in confronting the challenges of hybrid warfare in Indonesia. *Defense and Security Studies*, 5(1), 1–9. https://doi.org/10.37868/dss.v5.id255

- Bashir, A., Zarish, W., & Malik, R. (2024). The role of AI in hybrid warfare: A case study of Pakistan's cybersecurity landscape. *Global Strategic and Security Review*, 9(1), 86-93. https://doi.org/10.31703/gsssr.2024(ix-i).08

- Beregi, A., & Babos, A. (2021). Security and military relevancies of digitisation, globalisation and cyberspace. *Academic and Applied Research in Military and Public Management Science*, 20(1), 81-93. https://doi.org/10.32565/aarms.2021.1.6

- Caramancion, K. M., Li, Y., Dubois, E., & Jung, E. S. (2022). The Missing Case of Disinformation from the Cybersecurity Risk Continuum: A Comparative Assessment of Disinformation with Other Cyber Threats. *Data*, 7(4), 49. https://doi.org/10.3390/data7040049

- Dolan, M. (2022). Hybrid warfare in the Western Balkans: How structural vulnerability attracts maligned powers and hostile influence. *SEEU Review*, 17(1), 3-25. https://doi.org/10.2478/seeur-2022-0018

- Dos, O., Karakoca, Y. E., Camadan, E., & Baykali, F. (2023). Hybrid Cyber Security of Unmanned Aerial Vehicles. *International Journal of Advanced Mechanical Engineering and Computing*, 11(4), 179-185. https://doi.org/10.58190/ijamec.2023.65

- Humeniuk, I., Basaraba, M., & Nekrilov, O. (2021). Methods Of Ensuring Cyber Security of Critical Components networks of Information And Telecommunication Systems. *Problems of Construction, Testing, Application and Operation of Complex Information Systems*, (18), 101–110. https://doi.org/10.46972/2076-1546.2020.18.10

- Hugyik, A. (2020). Best Practices in the Application of the Concept of Resilience: Building Hybrid Warfare and Cybersecurity Capabilities in the Hungarian Defense Forces. *Connections: The Quarterly Journal*. 19(4), 25-38. https://doi.org/10.11610/connections.19.4.02

- Iancu, N. (2024). A National Security Perspective on Strengthening E.U. Civilian-Defence Cybersecurity Synergy: A Systemic Approach. *International Conference on Cybersecurity and Cybercrime*, 11, 22–34. https://doi.org/10.19107/CYBERCON.2024.03

- Kaliakin, S. V., Onishchenko, Y. M., & Nosov, V. V. (2023). Cybersecurity of the Municipal Infrastructure. *Law and Safety*, 88(1), 190-201. https://doi.org/10.32631/pb.2023.1.17

- Kelemen, R. (2023). The Impact of the Russian-Ukrainian Hybrid War on the European Union's Cybersecurity Policies and Regulations. *Connections: The Quarterly Journal.* 22(2), 75-90. https://doi.org/10.11610/connections.22.2.55

- Napetvaridze, V. & Chochia, A. Cybersecurity in the Making – Policy and Law: A Case Study of Georgia. *International and Comparative Law Review*, 2019, Sciendo, vol. 19 no. 2, pp. 155-180. https://doi.org/10.2478/iclr-2019-0019

- Nussipova, A., Khussainova, G., Kabilova, R., Aliyarov, E., & Nuralina, B. (2023). Information security communications strategy as a prerequisite to counteracting hybrid warfare: world experience. *Revista Latina De Comunicación Social*, (82). https://doi.org/10.4185/rlcs-2024-2134

- Odarchenko, R., Iavich, M., Iashvili, G., Fedushko, S., & Syerov, Y. (2023). Assessment of Security KPIs for 5G Network Slices for Special Groups of Subscribers. *Big Data and Cognitive Computing*, 7(4), 169. https://doi.org/10.3390/bdcc7040169

- Pedro-Gonçalves, C. (2020). Cyberspace and Artificial Intelligence: The new face of cyber-enhanced hybrid threats. In *IntechOpen*. https://doi.org/10.5772/intechopen.88648

- Shandler, R., & Canetti, D. (2024). Introduction: Cyber-conflict – Moving from speculation to investigation. *Journal of Peace Research*, 61(1), 3-9. https://doi.org/10.1177/00223433231219441

- Štitilis, A. (2024). Navigating the cyber front: Belarus› state control and emerging cyber threats. In *Proceedings of the European Conference on Cyber Warfare and Security.* 23(1) https://doi.org/10.34190/eccws.23.1.2518

- van de Poel, I. (2020). Core Values and Value Conflicts in Cybersecurity: Beyond Privacy Versus Security. In: Christen, M., Gordijn, B., Loi, M. (eds) *The Ethics of Cybersecurity. The International Library of Ethics, Law and Technology*, vol 21. Springer, Cham. https://doi.org/10.1007/978-3-030-29053-5_3

- Wróblewski, W., & Wiśniewski, M. (2023). Cybersecurity in the context of hybrid warfare in Ukraine: Analysis of its impact on the public sector and society in Poland. *Central European Journal of Security Studies*, 1(1), 48-60. https://doi.org/10.15804/cejss.2023105

- Zaporozhets, O., Syvak, O., Romaniuk, S. N., & Manjikian, M. (2021). In the Line of Russian Aggression: Ukraine, hybrid warfare, and cybersecurity defense. In *Routledge Companion to Global Cyber-Security Strategy* (1st ed., pp. 185–190). Routledge. https://doi.org/10.4324/9780429399718-18

Economics and Business

Focus: Economic tools used in grey zone conflicts, including sanctions, trade wars, and economic coercion.

Topics: Economic statecraft, resource competition, and fiscal impact of hybrid activities.

- Alawida, M., Omolara, A. E., Abiodun, O. I., & Al-Rajab, M. (2022). A deeper look into cybersecurity issues in the wake of COVID-19: A survey. *Journal of King Saud University - Computer and Information Sciences, 34*(10), 8176–8206. https://doi.org/10.1016/j.jksuci.2022.08.003

- Bidayani, A., Mardyani, Y., Kurniawan, Aisya, S., & Setiawan, F. (2022). Small-Scale Fisheries Management Strategy On The Eastern Coast Of The Bangka Regency, Indonesia. In *Proceedings of the International Conference on Sustainable Development* (pp. 594-606). Atlantis Press. https://doi.org/10.2991/978-94-6463-086-2_80

- Bogomoletc, E., & Lee, N. M. (2021). Frozen Meat Against COVID-19 Misinformation: An Analysis of Steak-Umm and Positive Expectancy Violations. Journal of Business and Technical Communication, 35(1), 118-125. https://doi.org/10.1177/1050651920959187

- Bruggemann, R., Koppatz, P., Scholl, M., & Schuktomow, R. (2022). Global Cybersecurity Index (GCI) and the Role of its 5 Pillars. *Social Indicators Research*, *159*(1), 125–143. https://doi.org/10.1007/s11205-021-02739-y

- Dwyer, T. (2019). Special Issue: Media Manipulation, Fake News, and Misinformation in the Asia-Pacific Region. *Journal of Contemporary Eastern Asia, 18*(2), 9–15. https://doi.org/10.17477/jcea.2019.18.2.009

- Fezzey, T., Batchelor, J., Burch, G., & Reid, R. (2023). Cybersecurity Continuity Risks: Lessons Learned from the COVID-19 Pandemic. *Journal of Cybersecurity Education, Research & Practice*, *2022*(2). https://doi. org/10.32727/8.2023.3

- Gallo, P. J., Sosa, S., & Velez-Calle, A. (2023). Business for peace: How entrepreneuring contributes to Sustainable Development Goal 16. *Business Research Quarterly*, *26*(1), 62–78. https://doi. org/10.1177/23409444221118097

- Getz, K. A., & Oetzel, J. (2009). MNE Strategic Intervention in Violent Conflict: Variations Based on Conflict Characteristics. *Journal of Business Ethics*, *89*(Suppl 4), 375–386. https://doi.org/10.1007/s10551-010-0412-6

- Govindankutty, S., & Gopalan, S. P. (2023). From Fake Reviews to Fake News: A Novel Pandemic Model of Misinformation in Digital Networks. *Journal of Theoretical and Applied Electronic Commerce Research*, *18*(2), 1069–1085. https://doi.org/10.3390/jtaer18020054

- House, A. (2021). The Price Of A Cybersecurity Culture: How the CMMC should secure the department of defense's supply chain without harming small businesses and competition. *Public Contract Law Journal*, *50*(3), 449–470.

- Idemudia, U. (2018). Shell–NGO Partnership and Peace in Nigeria: Critical Insights and Implications. *Organization & Environment*, *31*(4), 384–405. https://doi.org/10.1177/1086026617718428

- Joseph, J., & Van Buren, H. J. (2022). Entrepreneurship, Conflict, and Peace: The Role of Inclusion and Value Creation. *Business & Society*, *61*(6), 1558–1593. https://doi.org/10.1177/00076503211040238

- Lim, G., Lee, H., & Kim, T. (2005). Formulating Business Strategies From A Stakeholder's Perspective: Korean Healthcare IT Business Cases. *International Journal of Information Technology & Decision Making*, 4(4), 541–566. https://doi.org/10.1142/S0219622005001714

- Looi, J. C., Allison, S., Bastiampillai, T., & Maguire, P. A. (2021). Clinical update on managing media exposure and misinformation during COVID-19: recommendations for governments and healthcare professionals. *Australasian Psychiatry*, *29*(1), 22–25. https://doi. org/10.1177/1039856220963947

- Ozsungur, A. (2022). Relativity Approach to the Strategic Cyber Conflict Management in Businesses. *Ege Akademik Bakis (Ege Academic Review)*. https://doi.org/10.21121/eab.1083229

- Silva, H. (2022). Information and misinformation about climate change: lessons from Brazil. *Ethics in Science and Environmental Politics*, *22*, 51–56. https://doi.org/10.3354/esep00201

- Shackelford, S. J. (2014). Managing Cyber Attacks In *International Law, Business, and Relations.* Cambridge University Press.

- Tăbuscă, A., & Tăbuscă, S.-M. (2019). Impact of 5G Technology In Global Economy. Cybersecurity And Legal Issues. *Journal of Information Systems & Operations Management*, *13*(2), 177–189. http://search.proquest.com.libaccess.sjlibrary.org/scholarly-journals/impact-5g-technology-global-economy-cybersecurity/docview/2449273124/se-2?accountid=10361

- Wallis, T., & Dorey, P. (2023). Implementing Partnerships in Energy Supply Chain Cybersecurity Resilience. *Energies*, *16*(4), 1868-. https://doi.org/10.3390/en16041868

- Wang, J. (2018). Strategies for Managing Cultural Conflict: Models Review and Their Applications in Business and Technical Communication. *Journal of Technical Writing and Communication*, *48*(3), 281–294. https://doi.org/10.1177/0047281617696985

- Wisniewski, R. (2021). Economic Sanctions as a Tool of China's Hybrid Strategies. *Polish Political Science/Polish Political Science Yearbook*, *50*(3), 91–103. https://doi.org/10.15804/ppsy202133

- Yu, W., & Shen, F. (2022). The relationship between online political participation and privacy protection: evidence from 10 Asian societies of different levels of cybersecurity. *Behaviour & Information Technology*, *41*(13), 2819–2834. https://doi.org/10.1080/014492 9X.2021.1953597

Environmental Studies

Focus: Environmental dimensions of grey zone conflicts, particularly in resource competition.

Topics: Water conflicts, territorial disputes, and environmental degradation as a strategic tool.

- Azad, T. M., Haider, M. W., & Sadiq, M. (2023). Understanding Gray Zone Warfare From Multiple Perspectives. *World Affairs*, *186*(1), 81–104. https://doi.org/10.1177/00438200221141101

- Chen, X., Zhang, A., & Yang, R. (2014). Modeling and Optimal Control of a Class of Warfare Hybrid Dynamic Systems Based on Lanchester (n,1) Attrition Model. *Mathematical Problems in Engineering*, *2014*(2014), 1–7. https://doi.org/10.1155/2014/481347

- Hussain, S., Roofi, Y., Faheem, F., & Qamar, M. T. R. (2023). Hybrid Warfare in Pakistan: How it's Effecting CPEC. *Pakistan Journal of Humanities and Social Sciences*, *11*(2). https://doi.org/10.52131/pjhss.2023.1102.0476

- Laine, J. E. (2022). War in Europe: health implications of environmental nuclear disaster amidst war. *European Journal of Epidemiology*, *37*(3), 221–225. https://doi.org/10.1007/s10654-022-00862-9

- Massingham, E., Almila, E., & Piret, M. (2023). War in cities: Why the protection of the natural environment matters even when fighting in urban areas, and what can be done to ensure protection. *International Review of the Red Cross (2005)*, *105*(924), 1313–1336. https://doi.org/10.1017/S1816383123000395

- Pan, L.; Wang,Y.; Sun, X.; Sadiq, M. & Dagestani. A.A. (2003). Natural resources: A determining factor of geopolitical risk in Russia? Revisiting conflict-based perspective, *Resources Policy,* Vol. 85, Part A.

History and generalities about Hybrid Warfare
Focus: Historical evolution of hybrid and grey zone conflicts.
Topics: Case studies from historical conflicts, such as Cold War-era strategies and modern applications.
Analysis: Continuities and changes in warfare.

- Andrei, C. (2022). The dimensions of military engineer support in the hybrid war. International Conference KBO, 28(3), 1-5. https://doi.org/10.2478/kbo-2022-0079

- Brânda, O. E., & Sauliuc, A. L. (2020). Hybrid Threats on NATO's Eastern Flank- A Comparative Analysis. International Conference KBO, 26(1), 33–41. https://doi.org/10.2478/kbo-2020-0005

- Dobias, P., & Christensen, K. (2022). The "Grey Zone" and Hybrid Activities. *Connections. The Quarterly Journal*, *21*(2), 41–54. https://doi.org/10.11610/Connections.21.2.03

- Dorosh, L. and Ivasechko, O. (2019). Comparative analysis of the hybrid tactics application by the Russian federation in conflicts with Georgia and Ukraine. Central European Journal of International and Security Studies, 13(2), 48-73. https://doi.org/10.51870/cejiss.a130202

- Duginets, G., & Busarieva, T. (2021). Hybrid War As A New Form Of Interstate Confrontation. Intellect XXI, 3, 2021. https://doi.org/10.32782/2415-8801/2021-3.1

- Ebbrecht-Hartmann, T. (2022). Media resonance and conflicting memories: Historical event movies as conflict zone. *Memory Studies*, *15*(5), 979–994. https://doi.org/10.1177/1750698020907948

- Echevarria, A. J. (2016). Operating in the Gray Zone: An Alternative Paradigm for U.S. Military Strategy. Strategic Studies Institute. https://press.armywarcollege.edu/monographs/425

- Freier, N. (2009). The Defense Identity Crisis: It's a Hybrid World. Parameters, 39(3), 81–94. https://doi.org/10.55540/0031-1723.2483

- Freier, N. (2009). Hybrid threats and challenges: Describe... Don't define. Small Wars Journal. https://smallwarsjournal.com/2010/01/07/hybrid-threats-and-challenges-describe-dont-define/

- Kazi, S. (2023). Conflict in Kashmir and Manipur: history, ethnicity, gender. *Journal of Aggression, Conflict and Peace Research*, *15*(1), 39–50. https://doi.org/10.1108/JACPR-01-2022-0667

- Murray, W., & Mansoor, P. R. (Eds.). (2012). Hybrid warfare: Fighting complex opponents from the ancient world to the present. Cambridge University Press.

- Najžer, B. (2020). Russia and Hybrid Warfare. In The Hybrid Age: International Security in the Era of Hybrid Warfare (pp. 113–146). London: I.B. Tauris. Retrieved November 28, 2024, from http://dx.doi.org/10.5040/9780755602544.0012

- Oprea, G. & Bercaru, R. G. (2023). Frozen conflicts as a tool of the Russian hybrid warfare in the post-Soviet space., 146-167. https://doi.org/10.18485/isimod_strint.2023.ch9

- Ryono, A., & Galway, M. (2015). Xinjiang under China: reflections on the multiple dimensions of the 2009 Urumqi uprising. *Asian Ethnicity*, *16*(2), 235–255. https://doi.org/10.1080/14631369.2014.906062

- Wang, B., & Xu, M. (2016). Interpreting conflicts and conflicts in interpreting: A micro-historical account of the interpreting activity in the

Korean Armistice Negotiations. *Linguistica Antverpiensia, New Series – Themes in Translation Studies*, *15*. https://doi.org/10.52034/lanstts. v0i15.402

- Wither, J. K. (2016). Making Sense of Hybrid Warfare. Connections. The Quarterly Journal (English Ed.), 15(2), 73–87. https://doi. org/10.11610/Connections.15.2.06

Legal Studies

Focus: International and domestic legal implications of hybrid warfare and grey zone activities.

Topics: Laws of armed conflict, attribution of cyber operations, and regulatory frameworks.

Key Areas: Humanitarian law and national security legislation.

- Ali, S. (2019). Cybersecurity support of insider threat operations: DoD regulation and constitutional compliance. *Geo. Mason UCRLJ*, *30*, 1.

- Allen, D. N. (2022). Deepfake Fight: AI-Powered Disinformation and Perfidy Under the Geneva Conventions. *Notre Dame J. on Emerging Tech.*, *3*, 1.

- Alstott, A., Olgun, M., Robinson, H., & McNamara, M. (2024). " Demons and Imps": Misinformation and Religious Pseudoscience in State Anti-Transgender Laws. *Yale JL & Feminism*, *35*, 223.

- Angelatos, D. (2021). Misinformation about Marijuana: Commercialization, Consolidation, and the New First Amendment. *Am. UL Rev.*, *71*, 2157.

- Ardia, D. S., & Ringel, E. (2022). First Amendment Limits on State Laws Targeting Election Misinformation. *First Amend. L. Rev.*, *20*, 291.

- Armel, A. (2021). Dangerous Speech: The Impact of Misinformation on Technological Advancements in Healthcare. *Annals Advance Directive*, *31*, 101.

- Balleste, R. (2021). Cyber Conflicts in Outer Space: Lessons from SCADA Cybersecurity. *Emory Corporate Governance and Accountability Review*, *8*(1), 1.

- Batinga, J. (2024). Reconciling the Global North-South Divide on the Use of Force: Economic Coercion and the Evolving Interpretation of Article 2 (4). *Wis. Int'l LJ*, *41*, 103.

- Blitt, R. C. (2021). Human Rights and Disinformation Under the Trump Administration: The Commission on Unalienable Rights. . *Louis ULJ*, *66*, 1.

- Bode, L. (2019). User correction as a tool in the battle against social media misinformation. *Geo. L. Tech. Rev.*, *4*, 367.

- Bowman, G. S. (2021). Securing the precipitous heights: US Lawfare as a means to confront China at sea, in space, and cyberspace. *Pace Int'l L. Rev.*, *34*, 81.

- Brown, N. I. (2020). Deepfakes and the Weaponization of Disinformation. *Va. JL & Tech.*, *23*, 1.

- Bui, N. S., & Lee, J. A. Comparative Cybersecurity Law in Socialist Asia'(2022). *Vand J Transnat'l L*, *55*, 631.

- Butler, A. (2020). Election Cybersecurity Amid a Global Pandemic. *Human Rights*, *45*(3), 9-11.

- Callamard, A. (2020). Challenges to, and Manifesto for, Fact-Finding in a Time of Disinformation. *Notre Dame J. Int'l Comp. L.*, *10*, 128. https://heinonline.org/HOL/LandingPage?handle=hein.journals/ndjicl10&div=12&id=&page=

- Calliess, C., & Baumgarten, A. (2020). Cybersecurity in the EU The Example of the Financial Sector: A Legal Perspective. *German Law Journal*, *21*(6), 1149–1179. https://doi.org/10.1017/glj.2020.67

- Chaisse, J., & Bauer, C. (2019). Cybersecurity and the Protection of Digital Assets: Assessing the Role of International Investment Law and Arbitration. *Vanderbilt Journal of Entertainment and Technology Law*, *21*(3), 549-589. http://libaccess.sjlibrary.org/login?url=https://search.ebscohost.com/login.aspx?direct=true&db=a9h&AN=136144845&site=ehost-live&scope=site

- Cheah, M. A. (2022). Section 230 and the Right to Remove Vaccine Misinformation. *Cardozo Arts & Ent. LJ*, *40*, 477. https://heinonline.org/HOL/LandingPage?handle=hein.journals/caelj40&div=23&id=&page=

- Chen, L. (2019). Chinese Crusaders' Lawfare Against Chinese Exclusion Laws. *UCLA Pacific Basin Law Journal*, *36*(2). https://doi.org/10.5070/P8362043776

- Civelek, C. (2023). Beyond lawfare: An analysis of law's temporality through Russian-doll urbanization from Turkey. *Political and Le-*

gal Anthropology Review, *46*(2), 241–263. https://doi.org/10.1111/plar.12543

- Coleman, C. H. (2022). Physicians Who Disseminate Medical Misinformation: Testing the Constitutional Limits on Professional Disciplinary Action. *First Amend. L. Rev.*, *20*, 113.

- Corbett, C. R. (2020). Chemtrails and Solar Geoengineers: Governing Online Conspiracy Theory Misinformation. *Missouri Law Review*, *85*(3), 633–686.

- Dawood, Y. (2020). Protecting elections from disinformation: A multifaceted public-private approach to social media and democratic speech. *Ohio St. Tech. LJ*, *16*, 639.

- Dell, M. (n.d.). Fake News, Alternative Facts, and Disinformation: The Importance of Teaching Media Literacy to Law Students. *SSRN Electronic Journal*. https://doi.org/10.2139/ssrn.3002720

- Desai, D. R., & Makridis, C. A. (2022). Identifying Critical Infrastructure in a World With Supply Chain and Cross-Sectoral Cybersecurity Risk. *Jurimetrics (Chicago, Ill.)*, *62*(2), 173–195.

- Didenko, A. N. (2020). Cybersecurity regulation in the financial sector: prospects of legal harmonization in the European Union and beyond. *Revue de Droit Uniforme*, *25*(1), 125–167. https://doi.org/10.1093/ulr/unaa006

- Dinstein, Y. (2017). *War, aggression and Self-Defence*. Cambridge University Press.

- Eichler, R. R. (2019). Cybersecurity, encryption, and defense industry compliance with united states export regulations. *Tex. A&M J. Prop. L.*, *5*, 5.

- Ellis, A. R. (2020). Bug or Feature: The Long-Intertwined Legacy of Disinformation, Race, and Voting. *BUL Rev. Online*, *100*, 238.

- Ellis, A. R. (2021). " This Lawsuit Smacks of Racism": Disinformation Racial Coding, and the 2020 Election. *La. L. Rev.*, *82*, 453.

- Epstein, M. M. (2023). Fiduciary Duty as a Shield for Social Media User Privacy and Platform Policing of Political Misinformation and Disinformation. *FIU L. Rev.*, *17*, 287.

- Fang, Y. (2021). Is the Current International Law a Good Fit for Cyber-security? A UN Charter-Based Analysis. *Wash. U. Global Stud. L. Rev.*, *20*, 549.

- Fischman, S. (2019). Redefining Law of War in the Wake of Gray-Zone Conflict's Ubiquity. *U. Pa. J. Int'l L.*, *41*, 491.

- Fogt, M. M. (2021). Legal challenges or "gaps" by countering hybrid warfare—Building resilience in *jus ante bellum*. *Southwestern Journal of International Law, 27*, 28.

- Furgalska, M., & de Londras, F. (2022). Rights, Lawfare and Repro-duction: Reflections on the Polish Constitutional Tribunal's Abortion Decision. *Israel Law Review, 55*(3), 285–301. https://doi.org/10.1017/S002122372100025X

- Garon, J. M. (2022). When AI Goes to War: Corporate Accountability for Virtual Mass Disinformation, Algorithmic Atrocities, and Synthetic Propaganda. *N. Ky. L. Rev.*, *49*, 181.

- Goldenziel, J. I. (2020). Law as a Battlefield: The US, China, and the Global Escalation of Lawfare. *Cornell L. Rev.*, *106*, 1085.

- Goldenziel, J. I. (2021). Information Lawfare: Messaging and the Moral High Ground. *J. Nat'l Sec. L. & Pol'y*, *12*, 233.

- Goldenziel, J. I. (2022). An Alternative to Zombieing: Lawfare between Russia and Ukraine and the Future of International Law. 108 Cornell L. Rev.

- Gordon, G. (2019). Contradiction & the Court: Heterodox Analysis of Economic Coercion in International Law. *Temp. Int'l & Comp. LJ*, *34*, 283.

- Gordon, A. (2023). Nondelegation Misinformation: A Reply to the Skep-tics. *Baylor L. Rev.*, *75*, 152.

- Gottlieb, M. J., & Governski, M. C. Truth Suits Litigating Against the Viral Spread. 48 Litigation 18

- Greenspan, R. L., & Loftus, E. F. (2020). Eyewitness confidence malle-ability: Misinformation as post-identification feedback. *Law and human behavior, 44*(3), 194.

- Griffin, M. (2022). Direct-to-Consumer Advertising of Prescription Drugs: Constitutionally Protected Speech or Misinformation? *Wm. & Mary L. Rev. Online, 64*, 89.

- Guernsey, J. (2023). The 'Natural' Disaster: How Americans' Obsession with' Natural' Foods Encourages Misinformation, Stifles Innovation, and Harms the Planet. *Hastings Env't LJ*, *29*, 81.

- Harbin, D. (2022). Lawfare and Sea Power: A Historical Perspective. *J. Nat'l Sec. L. & Pol'y*, *13*, 449.

- Heller, B. (2021). Enlisting useful idiots: The ties between online harassment and disinformation. *Colo. Tech. LJ*, *19*, 19.

- Henricksen, Wes (2022), Disinformation and the First Amendment: Fraud to the Public, 96 St. John's L. Rev. 543.

- Hopewell, K. (2022). Beyond U.S.-China Rivalry: Rule Breaking, Economic Coercion, and the Weaponization of Trade. *AJIL Unbound*, *116*, 58–63. doi:10.1017/aju.2022.3

- Irani, F. (2018). 'Lawfare', US military discourse, and the colonial constitution of law and war. *European Journal of International Security*, *3*(1), 113-133.

- Huq, A. Z. (2022). International Institutions and Platform-Mediated Misinformation. *Chi. J. Int'l L.*, *23*, 116.

- Jauregui, B. (2022). Lawfare and security labor: Subjectification and subjugation of police workers in India. *Law & social inquiry*, *47*(2), 420-448.

- Jones, R. A. (2023). Defamation, Disinformation, and the Press Function. *J. Free Speech L.*, *3*, 103.

- Kao, M. B. (2020). Cybersecurity in the Shipping Industry and English Marine Insurance Law. Tul. Mar. LJ, 45, 467.

- Karanicolas, M. (2021). A FOIA for Facebook: Meaningful Transparency for Online Platforms. Louis ULJ, 66, 49.

- Katz, E. (2020). Liar's war: Protecting civilians from disinformation during armed conflict. International Review of the Red Cross, 102(914), 659-682.

- Kaye, D., & Shaffer, G. (2021). Transnational legal ordering of data, disinformation, privacy, and speech. UC Irvine J. Int'l Transnat'l & Comp. L., 6, 1.

- Keitner, C. I., & Clark, H. L. (2019). Cybersecurity and Trade Agreements: The State of the Art. Harv. Bus. L. Rev. Online, 10, 1.

- Kiessling, E. K. (2021). Gray Zone Tactics and the Principle of Non-Intervention: Can" One of the Vaguest Branches of International Law" Solve the Gray Zone Problem?. Harv. Nat'l Sec. J., 12, 116.

- Kilovaty, I. (2020). An Extraterritorial Human Right to Cybersecurity. Notre Dame J. Int'l Comp. L., 10, 35.

- Kincaid, R. (2023). Mass incarceration and misinformation: The COVID-19 infodemic behind bars. U. St. Thomas LJ, 19, 323.

- Kornbluh, K., & Weiner, E. (2019). Public Safety and Disinformation. Geo. L. Tech. Rev., 4, 609.

- Krzywoń, A. (2021). Summary judicial proceedings as a measure for Electoral disinformation: Defining the European standard. German Law Journal, 22(4), 673-688.

- Labovitz, M. A. (2019). Your Natural Gas Is Not Cyber-Secure: A Two-Fold Case for Why Voluntary Natural Gas Pipeline Cybersecurity Guidelines Should Become Mandatory Regulations Overseen by the Department of Energy. NCJL & Tech., 21, 217.

- Leach, B. (2023). Lawfare for the Future. U. Ill. JL Tech. & Pol'y, 51.

- Levi, L. (2022). Disinformation and the Defamation Renaissance: A Misleading Promise of" Truth." U. Rich. L. Rev., 57, 1235.

- Liu, Z. (2022). The internet echo chamber and the misinformation of judges: The case of judges' perception of public support for the death penalty in China. International Review of Law and Economics, 69, 106028.

- Mangano, R. (2020). Cryptocurrencies, cybersecurity and bankruptcy law: how global issues are globalizing national remedies. University of Miami International and Comparative Law Review, 27(2), 355.

- Marrocco, A. J., Wasser, L., & Koczerginski, M. (2019). Data protection and cybersecurity in Canada. Franchise Law Journal, 39(1), 81-94.

- McLaughlin, R. (2022). The law of the sea and PRC gray-zone operations in the South China Sea. American Journal of International Law, 116(4), 821-835.

- Milanovic, M., & Schmitt, M. N. Cyber Attacks and Cyber (Mis) information Operations During a Pandemic'(2020). Journal of National Security Law & Policy, 11, 247.

- Mishra, N. (2020). Privacy, cybersecurity, and GATS Article XIV: a new frontier for trade and internet regulation?. World Trade Review, 19(3), 341-364.

- Moshirnia, A. (2020). Who will check the checkers? False fact checkers and memetic misinformation. Utah L. Rev., 1029.

- Mosquera, A. B. M., & Bachmann, S. D. (2016). Lawfare in hybrid wars: the 21st century warfare. Journal of International Humanitarian Legal Studies, 7(1), 63-87.

- Napoli, Philip M., and Chandlee A. Jackson. "Revisiting indecency: Considering a medium-specific regulatory approach to disinformation and hate speech on social media." Fed. Comm. LJ 75 (2022): 297.

- Newsome, E. C. (2019). Sorting Solutions: The Fix to the International Legal Framework on Cyberwarfare and Cyberterrorism Is a Decision Tree, Not a Magic Bullet. Rutgers JL & Pub. Pol'y, 17, 82.

- Noah, L. (2021). Censorship Is So Last Century: Therapeutic Products, Propaganda, and Compelled Speech. . Louis ULJ, 66, 79.

- Nunziato, D. C. (2020). Misinformation mayhem: social media platforms' efforts to combat medical and political misinformation. First Amend. L. Rev., 19, 32.

- O'Brien, R. (2022). Legalizing China's Economic Coercion Toolkit. UCLA Pac. Basin LJ, 39, 99.

- Ohlin, J. D. (2022). # Genocide: Atrocity as Pretext and Disinformation. Va. J. Int'l L., 63, 101.

- Omari, J. (2021). Taking Aim at" Fake News": Brazil's Legislative Agenda for Online Democracy. . Louis ULJ, 66, 115.

- Ono, A. (2023). Climate Change Disinformation Liability under the Federal Trade Commission Act. Env't L. Rep., 53, 10900.

- Orentlicher, D. (2020). Ensuring Access to Accurate Information and Combatting Misinformation about Pandemics. Am. U. Int'l L. Rev., 36, 1067.

- Panezi, A. (2021). A Public Service Role for Digital Libraries: A Case of Emergency Electronic Access to Library Material and the Unequal Battle Against Misinformation Through Copyright Law Reform. Cornell JL & Pub. Pol'y, 31, 65.

- Patterson, F. (2022). Feuding with Fauci: Towards a Tort of Reckless Dissemination of Medical Misinformation. U. Toronto Fac. L. Rev., 80, 264.

- Pecora, R. J. (2024). Weaponized Disinformation as a Use of Force in International Law.

- Pielemeier, J. (2020). Disentangling disinformation: What makes regulating disinformation so difficult? Utah L. Rev., 917.

- Poon, O. A., Garces, L. M., Wong, J., Segoshi, M., Silver, D., & Harrington, S. (2019). Confronting misinformation through social science research: SFFA v. Harvard. Asian Am. LJ, 26, 4.

- Quirk, S. (2021). Lawfare in the disinformation age: Chinese interference in Taiwan's 2020 elections. *Harvard International Law Journal*, *62*(2), 525–567.

- Qureshi, W. A. (2019). Lawfare: The weaponization of international law. Hous. J. Int'l L., 42, 39.

- Qureshi, W. A. (2019). Cyberwarfare: A Tortuous Problem for the Law of Armed Conflict? Tul. J. Int'l & Comp. L., 28, 1.

- Qureshi, W. A. (2020). The rise of hybrid warfare. Notre Dame J. Int'l Comp. L., 10, 173.

- Qureshi, W. A. (2020). The Future of Just War Theory in the Age of Cyberwarfare. Wis. Int'l LJ, 38, 1.

- Rajkovic, N. M. (2019). Performing 'Legality' in the Theatre of Hostilities: Asymmetric Conflict, Lawfare and the Rise of Vicarious Litigation. San Diego Int'l LJ, 21, 435.

- Reiss, D. R., & Diamond, J. (2019). Measles and Misrepresentation in Minnesota: Can There Be Liability for Anti-Vaccine Misinformation That Causes Bodily Harm. San Diego L. Rev., 56, 531.

- Reiss, D., & Ordonez, V. (2022). Law in the Service of Misinformation: How Anti-Vaccine Groups Use the Law to Help Spin a False Narrative. Nw. JL & Soc. Pol'y, 18, 51.

- Rodriguez, M. (2019). Disinformation Operations Aimed at (Democratic) Elections in the Context of Public International Law: The Conduct of the Internet Research Agency During the 2016 US Presidential Election. International Journal of Legal Information, 47(3), 149-197.

- Rubin, A. B. (2021). Disinformation on Trial: Fighting Foreign Disinformation by Empowering the Victims. Cardozo L. Rev., 43, 969.

- Rubinstein, I., & Kenneth, T. (2023). Taming Online Public Health Misinformation. Harv. J. on Legis., 60, 219.

- Rustad, M. L., & Koenig, T. H. (2021). Creating a Public Health Disinformation Exception to CDA Section 230. Syracuse L. Rev., 71, 1251.

- Rutschman, A. S. (2021). The COVID-19 vaccine race: Intellectual property, collaboration (s), nationalism and misinformation. Wash. UJL & Pol'y, 64, 167.

- Rychlak, R. J. (2020). Disinformation in Crossfire Hurricane. Nat'l Sec. LJ, 7, 112.

- Sackler, C. (2022). Misinformation Superhighway: The Real-World Consequences of Social Media Companies Profiting off Misinformation, and What the Federal Government Can Do to Address It. Rutgers JL & Pub. Pol'y, 20, 56.

- Sanz-Caballero, S. (2023). The concepts and laws applicable to hybrid threats, with a special focus on Europe. *Humanities & Social Sciences Communications*, *10*(1), 360–368. https://do.org/10.1057/s41599-023-01864-y

- Sari, A. (2020). Legal resilience in an era of grey zone conflicts and hybrid threats. Cambridge Review of International Affairs, 33(6), 846–867. https://doi.org/10.1080/09557571.2020.1752147

- Saver, R. S. (2023). Physicians Spreading Medical Misinformation: The Uneasy Case for Regulation. Minn. L. Rev., 108, 911.

- Scott, R. M. G. (2023). Managing Misinformation on Social Media: Targeted Newsfeed Interventions and Freedom of Thought. Nw. UJ Int'l Hum. Rts., 21, 109.

- Shackelford, S. J., Raymond, A., Stemler, A., & Loyle, C. (2020). Defending democracy: taking stock of the global fight against digital repression, disinformation, and election insecurity. Wash. & Lee L. Rev., 77, 1747.

- Shadmy, T. (2022). Content Traffic Regulation: A Democratic Framework for Addressing Misinformation. JURIMETRICS J., 63, 1.

- Shah, H.J., & Ehsan, M. (2023). Hybrid Warfare: Emerging Challenges for Pakistan. *The Journal of Contemporary Studies*, *11*(2), 69–85. https://doi.org/10.54690/jcs.v11i2.234

- Sloss, D. L. (2021). Stop electronic amplification of lies. . Louis ULJ, 66, 129.

- Smith, M. W. (2020). A Judicial Teaching Point: The Lesson of the Late Justice John Paul Stevens in Sony V. Universal City Studios as a Response to Civil Lawfare. Corp. & Bus. LJ, 1, 71.

- Sullivan, S. M. (2022). Fighting Destructive Dragons with Sea Turtles: Going on the Legal Offensive using" Info-Lawfare" against the People's Republic of China. Naval L. Rev, 68, 213

- Sun, H. (2022). Regulating algorithmic disinformation. Colum. JL & Arts, 46, 367.

- Sylvester, S. (2020). Don't Let Them Fake You Out: How Artificially Mastered Videos Are Becoming the Newest Threat in the Disinformation War and What Social Media Platforms Should Do About It. Fed. Comm. LJ, 73, 369.

- Tay, X. W. (2022). Reconstructing the Principle of Non-Intervention and Non-Interference-Electoral Disinformation, Nicaragua, and the Quilt-Work Approach. Berkeley J. Int'l L., 40, 39.

- Terry, C., Silberberg, E. J., Schmitz, S., Stack, J., & Sando, E. (2022). À la Carte Cable: A Regulatory Solution to the Misinformation Subsidy. Cath. UJL & Tech, 31, 33.

- Trachtman, J. P. (2022). Managing cybersecurity and technology appropriation threats to international investment: Trust or verify. *The International Lawyer*, *55*(2), 193–220. http://libaccess.sjlibrary.org/login?url=https://search.ebscohost.com/login.aspx?direct=true&db=a9h&AN=159458454&site=ehost-live&scope=site

- Tropin, Z. (2021). Lawfare as part of hybrid wars: The experience of Ukraine in conflict with Russian Federation. Security and Defence Quarterly, 33(1), 15–29. https://doi.org/10.35467/sdq/132025

- Unger, W. (2020). How the poor data privacy regime contributes to misinformation spread and democratic erosion. Colum. Sci. & Tech. L. Rev., 22, 308.

- Van der Vet, F. (2021). Spies, lies, trials, and trolls: Political lawyering against disinformation and state surveillance in Russia. Law & Social Inquiry, 46(2), 407-434.

- Van Hoboken, J., & Fathaigh, R. Ó. (2021). Regulating Disinformation in Europe: Implications for Speech and Privacy. UC Irvine J. Int'l Transnat'l & Comp. L., 6, 9.

- Van Loo, R. (2022). The Public Stakes of Consumer Law: The Environment, the Economy, Health, Disinformation, and Beyond. Minn. L. Rev., 107, 2039.

- Vegh Weis, V. (2023). What does Lawfare mean in Latin America? A new framework for understanding the criminalization of progressive political leaders. *Punishment & Society*, *25*(4), 909–933. https://doi.org/10.1177/14624745221116348

- Volini, A. G. (2020). A Deep Dive into Technical Encryption Concepts to Better Understand Cybersecurity & Data Privacy Legal & Policy Issues. J. Intell. Prop. L., 28, 291.

- Wang, X. (2023). Decoupling Trade and Cybersecurity: A Way to Recalibration?. *Asian J. WTO & Int'l Health L & Pol'y*, *18*, 39. https://heinonline.org/HOL/LandingPage?handle=hein.journals/aihlp18&div=5&id=&page=

- Wentz, J., & Franta, B. (2022). Liability for Public Deception: Linking Fossil Fuel Disinformation to Climate Damages. Env't L. Rep., 52, 10995.

- Werbner, P. (2021). Legal Mobilisation, Legal Scepticism and the Limits of 'Lawfare': Between law and politics in union activism in Botswana. *The Journal of Legal Pluralism and Unofficial Law*, *53*(3), 593-608. https://doi.org/10.1080/07329113.2021.1949898

- Wu, T. (2020). Disinformation in the Marketplace of Ideas. Seton Hall L. Rev., 51, 169.

- Yadin, S. (2021). Manipulating Disclosure: Creative Compliance in the Israeli Food Industry. . Louis ULJ, 66, 149.

- Yilma, K. M. (2021). On Disinformation, Elections, and Ethiopian Law. Journal of African Law, 65(3), 351-375.

- Zhao, W. (2020). Cyber disinformation operations (CDOs) and a new paradigm of non-intervention. *U.C. Davis Journal of International Law & Policy*, *27*(1), 35. https://jilp.law.ucdavis.edu/archives/27/1/cyber-disinformation-operations-cdos-and-new-paradigm-non-intervention

Media and Communication Studies

Focus: Role of media and communication in shaping perceptions and narratives. Topics: Misinformation campaigns, media literacy, and strategic communication.

- Abd, S. A. (2022). Social Media As A Threat To National Security: A Case Study Of Twitter In Pakistan. *Margalla Papers*, *26*(2), 96–107. https://doi.org/10.54690/margallapapers.26.2.117

- Bibi, N., Farhat, S. & Ud Din, M. (2022). Fifth-Generation Warfare and Challenges for Pakistan. *Journal of Management Practices, Humanities and Social Sciences*, *6*(6). https://doi.org/10.33152/jmphss-6.6.1

- Caliskan, M., & Cramers, P. A. (2018). What Do You Mean by "Hybrid Warfare"? A Content Analysis on the Media Coverage of Hybrid Warfare Concept. *Horizon Insights*, *1*(4), 23–35. https://doi.org/10.31175/hi.2018.04.02

- Dobias, P., & Christensen, K. (2022). The "Grey Zone" and Hybrid Activities. *Connections. The Quarterly Journal*, *21*(2), 41–54. https://doi.org/10.11610/Connections.21.2.03

- Fazal, M. S. (2022). India's Hybrid Warfare Strategy towards Pakistan in the Backdrop of Social Media (2018-2022). *Annals of Human and Social Sciences*, *3*(II). https://doi.org/10.35484/ahss.2022(3-II)80

- Huhtinen, A.-M., Kotilainen, N., Särmä, S., & Streng, M. (2019). Information Influence in Hybrid Environment: Reflexive Control as an Analytical Tool for Understanding Warfare in Social Media. *International Journal of Cyber Warfare and Terrorism*, *9*(3), 1–20. https://doi.org/10.4018/IJCWT.2019070101

- Hussain, S., Roofi, Y., Faheem, F., Qamar, M. T. R., & Ajmal, S. (2023). Role of Media in Hybrid Warfare in Pakistan: How to Convert Challenges into Opportunities. *Journal of South Asian Studies*, *11*(3), 231–241. https://doi.org/10.33687/jsas.011.03.4693

- Kaunert, C., & Wertman, O. (2020). The securitisation of hybrid warfare through practices within the Iran-Israel conflict - Israel's practices to securitize Hezbollah's Proxy War. *Security and Defence Quarterly*, *31*(4), 99–114. https://doi.org/10.35467/sdq/130866

- Lanoszka, A. (2016). Russian hybrid warfare and extended deterrence in eastern Europe. *International Affairs*, *92*(1), 175–195. https://doi.org/10.1111/1468-2346.12509

Military and Strategic Studies

Focus: Operational aspects of hybrid warfare, including tactics, strategies, and implications for national defense.

Topics: Doctrine development, military innovation, and counter-hybrid operations.

Key Institutions: War colleges, defense universities, and security think tanks.

- Batyuk, V. I. (2017). The US Concept and Practice of Hybrid Warfare. *Strategic Analysis*, *41*(5), 464–477. https://doi.org/10.1080/0970 0161.2017.1343235

- Benyamin, J., Mualim, M., & Duarte, E. P. (2023). Force development against irregular and hybrid warfare in Indonesia. *Defense and Security Studies (Online)*, *4*, 46–51. https://doi.org/10.37868/dss.v4.id234

- Fridman, O., Kabernik, V., Pearce, J. C., Kabernik, V., Pearce, J. C., & Fridman, O. (2022). Hybrid Conflicts and Information Warfare. In *Hybrid Conflicts and Information Warfare* (pp. 1–6). Lynne Rienner Publishers. https://doi.org/10.1515/9781626377622-002

- Gershaneck, K. K. (2020). *Political warfare: strategies for combating China's plan to "win without fighting"* (First edition, 2020.). Marine Corps University Press. https://www.usmcu.edu/portals/218/Political%20Warfare_web.pdf

- Hoffman, F. G. (2005). Small Wars Revisited: The United States and Nontraditional Wars. *Journal of Strategic Studies*, *28*(6), 913–940. https://doi.org/10.1080/01402390500441040

- Hoffman, F. G. (2007). *Conflict in the 21st century: The rise of hybrid wars*. Potomac Institute for Policy Studies. https://potomacinstitute.us/images/stories/publications/potomac_hybridwar_0108.pdf

- Hoffman, F. G. (2009). Hybrid vs. compound war: The Janus choice—Defining today's multifaceted conflict. Armed Forces Journal, 147(3), 14–21. http://armedforcesjournal.com/hybrid-vs-compound-war/

- Hoffman, F. G. (2009). *Hybrid threats: reconceptualizing the evolving character of modern conflict*. Institute for National Strategic Studies, National Defense University.

- Jordan, J. (2020). International Competition Below the Threshold of War: Toward a Theory of Gray Zone Conflict. *Journal of Strategic Security*, *14*(1), 1–24. https://doi.org/10.5038/1944-0472.14.1.1836

- Lesenciuc, A. (2023). Hybrid Warfare in Wartime – Concept and Action Operationalization Attempt. *Romanian Military Thinking*, *2023*(1), 48–69. https://doi.org/10.55535/RMT.2023.1.3

- Maisaia, V. (2022). Grand Strategy and Military Implications Of New Russia's Military Doctrine In 21st Century: Geostrategic Aspects Of Hybrid Warfare Strategy Against Georgia And Ukraine. *International Scientific Conference "STRATEGIESXXI,"* *18*(1), 11–21. https://doi.org/10.53477/2971-8813-22-01

- Matisek, J. W. (2017). Shades of gray deterrence: Issues of fighting in the gray zone. *Journal of Strategic Security*, *10*(3), 1-26. https://www.jstor.org/stable/26466832

- Mazarr, M. J. (2015). Mastering the gray zone: understanding a changing era of conflict. *Strategic Studies Institute and US Army War College Press*. https://press.armywarcollege.edu/monographs/428

- Morris, L. J., Mazarr, M. J., Hornung, J. W., Pezard, S., Binnendijk, A., & Kepe, M. (2019). *Gaining competitive advantage in the gray zone: Response options for coercive aggression below the threshold of major war.* RAND Corporation. https://www.rand.org/pubs/research_reports/RR2942.html

- Mumford, A. (2020). Understanding hybrid warfare. *Cambridge Review of International Affairs*, *33*(6), 824–827. https://doi.org/10.1080/09557571.2020.1837737

- Qiao, L. and Wang, X. 1999. Unrestricted Warfare. Beijing: People's Liberation Army Publishing House. (For recommendations of English translations of Qiao and Wang, see "Précis: Unrestricted Warfare," Military Review, Sept.–Oct. 2019, available at https://www.armyupress.army.mil/Journals/Military-Review/English-Edition-Archives/September-October-2019/Precis-Unrestricted-Warfare/)

- Reichborn-Kjennerud, E., & Cullen, P. (2016). *What is Hybrid Warfare?* Norwegian Institute of International Affairs (NUPI). http://www.jstor.org/stable/resrep07978

- Renz, B., & Smith, H. Russia and hybrid warfare–going beyond the label. Project «Russia and Hybrid Warfare: definitions, capabilities, scope and possible responses». Funded by the Finnish Prime Minister's Office, government's analysis, assessments and research activities [Електронний ресурс].–January 2016.–P. 2–4. *Режим доступу:*

https://researchportal.helsinki.fi/en/publications/russia-and-hybrid-warfare-going-beyond-the-label

- Schmidt, N. (2014). Neither Conventional War, nor a Cyber War, but a Long-Lasting and Silent Hybrid War. *Obrana a Strategie, 14*(2), 73–86. https://doi.org/10.3849/1802-7199.14.2014.02.073-086

- Solmaz, M. (2022). 'Hybrid warfare': National security and the future. *National Security and the Future*, 23(1), 1–10. https://doi.org/10.37458/nstf.23.1.5

- Theodoss, C. M. D. (2010). Technology Transition for Hybrid Warfare. *Senior Service College Fellowship Civilian Research* (Doctoral dissertation, US Army). https://apps.dtic.mil/sti/citations/ADA561212

- Troeder, E. (2019). *A whole-of-government approach to grey zone warfare. Strategic Studies Institute and U.S. Army War College Press.* https://press.armywarcollege.edu/monographs/937

- Weissmann, M. (2019). Hybrid warfare and hybrid threats today and tomorrow: towards an analytical framework. *Journal on Baltic Security (Warsaw, Poland)*, 5(1), 17–26. https://doi.org/10.2478/jobs-2019-0002

- Wither, J. K. (2023). Hybrid Warfare Revisited: A Battle of 'Buzzwords.' *Connections. The Quarterly Journal, 22*(1), 7–27. https://doi.org/10.11610/Connections.22.1.02

Political Science, International Relations, and Security Studies
Focus: Theoretical frameworks for understanding state behavior, power dynamics, and international law in grey zone and hybrid contexts.
Topics: Sovereignty challenges, strategic competition, and global governance.
Key Disciplines: International security, geopolitics, and foreign policy analysis.

- Arcos, R., Gertrudix, M., Arribas, C., & Cardarilli, M. (2022). Responses to digital disinformation as part of hybrid threats: A systematic review on the effects of disinformation and the effectiveness of fact-checking/debunking. Open Research Europe, 2, 8–8. https://doi.org/10.12688/openreseurope.14088.1

- Ardita, N. D., Prakoso, S. G., Putra, F. A. A., Sulistiobudi, A., & Satria, R. (2023). Cyberwarfare between the United States and China 2014-2022: in Retrospect. *Jurnal Pertahanan, 9*(1), 17–29. https://doi.org/10.33172/jp.v9i1.1869

- Arribas, C. M., Arcos, R., Gértrudix, M., Mikulski, K., Hernández-Escayola, P., Teodor, M., Novăcescu, E., Surdu, I., Stoian, V., & García-Jiménez, A. (2023). Information manipulation and historical revisionism: Russian disinformation and foreign interference through manipulated history-based narratives. Open Research Europe, 3, 121–121. https://doi.org/10.12688/openreseurope.16087.1

- Atkinson, R. (2018). Hybrid Warfare And Societal Resilience: Implications for democratic governance. *Information & Security: An International Journal*, 41, 1–16. https://doi.org/10.11610/isij.3906

- Avant, D. (2000). From mercenary to citizen armies: Explaining change in the practice of war. International Organization, 54(1), 41–72. https://doi.org/10.1162/002081800551118

- Avant, D., & Nevers, R. (2011). Military contractors and the American way of war. Daedalus, 140(3), 88–99. https://doi.org/10.1162/DAED_a_00100

- Blažic, B. J. (2022) - Changing the Landscape of Cybersecurity Education in the EU: Will the New Approach Produce the Required Cybersecurity Skills? By: Education and Information Technologies, v27 n3 p3011-3036.

- Burkle, F. M., et al. (2022). Bastardizing Peacekeeping And The Birth Of Hybrid Warfare. *Prehospital and Disaster Medicine*, 37(2), 143–149. https://doi.org/10.1017/s1049023x22000425

- Cilizoglu, M., & Bapat, N. A. (2020). Economic coercion and the problem of sanctions-proofing. *Conflict Management and Peace Science*, *37*(4), 385-408.

- Cipers, S., Meyer, T., & Lefevere, J. (2023). Government responses to online disinformation unpacked. *Internet Policy Review*, *12*(4), 1-19.

- Cover, R, Haw, A.., Thompson, J.D. (2023) - Remedying disinformation and fake news? The cultural frameworks of fake news crisis responses and solution-seeking. International Journal of Cultural Studies, Vol. 26 Issue 2, p216-233, 18p.

- Dawson, M. (2020), National Cybersecurity Education: Bridging Defense to Offense. *Revista Academiei Fortelor Terestre*, Vol. 25 Issue 1, p68-75. 8p. DOI: 10.2478/raft-2020-0009.

- Digmelashvili, T. (2023). The Impact of Cyberwarfare on the National Security. Future Human Image, (19), 12-19. https://www.ceeol.com/search/article-detail?id=1205984

- Dossi, S. (2020). On the asymmetric advantages of cyberwarfare. Western literature and the Chinese journal Guofang Keji. Journal of Strategic Studies, 43(2), 281–308. https://doi.org/10.1080/01402390.2019.1581613

- Dov Bachmann, S., Putter, D., & Duczynski, G. (2023). Hybrid warfare and disinformation: A Ukraine war perspective. *Global Policy*, *14*(5), 858–869. https://doi.org/10.1111/1758-5899.13257

- Dowling, M.-E., & Legrand, T. (2023). "I do not consent": political legitimacy, misinformation, and the compliance challenge in Australia's Covid-19 policy response. Policy & Society, 42(3), 319–333. https://doi.org/10.1093/polsoc/puad018

- Flynn, D.J.; Horiuchi, Y.; & Zhang, D. (2020) Replication Data for: Misinformation, Economic Threat, and Public Support for International Trade." Harvard Dataverse, V1. https://doi.org/10.7910/DVN/5HNLJ6

- Gu, J., Dor, A., Li, K., Broniatowski, D. A., Hatheway, M., Fritz, L., & Abroms, L. C. (2022). The impact of Facebook's vaccine misinformation policy on user endorsements of vaccine content: An interrupted time series analysis. Vaccine, 40(14), 2209–2214. https://doi.org/10.1016/j.vaccine.2022.02.062

- Gueorguiev, D., McDowell, D., & Steinberg, D. A. (2020). The Impact of Economic Coercion on Public Opinion: The Case of US–China Currency Relations. The Journal of Conflict Resolution, 64(9), 1555–1583. https://doi.org/10.1177/0022002720912323

- Hadzhiev, B. (2020). Enablers of Hybrid Warfare: The Bulgarian Case. Journal of International Studies (Kyiv), 13(1), 28–43. https://doi.org/10.14254/2071-8330.2020/13-1/2

- Irwin, R..E. (2020). Misinformation and de-contextualization: international media reporting on Sweden and COVID-19. Globalization and Health, Vol 16, Iss 1, Pp 1-12.

- Janičatová, S., & Mlejnková, P. (2021). The ambiguity of hybrid warfare: A qualitative content analysis of the United Kingdom's political–military discourse on Russia's hostile activities. Contemporary security policy, 42(3), 312-344. https://doi.org/10.1080/13523260.2021.1885921

- Jiang, T. (2023). The Shift of China's Strategic Thinking on Cyberwarfare Since the 1990s. Chinese Journal of Political Science, 28(1), 127–149. https://doi.org/10.1007/s11366-022-09813-3

- Kardaś, S. (2019). The great troublemaker: Nord Stream 2 in Russia's foreign energy policy. *International Issues & Slovak Foreign Policy Affairs*, *Vol. 28(3/4)*: 25–44. https://www.jstor.org/stable/26905904

- Khan, T. F. (2023). Hybrid Warfare: India's New Policy Instrument. *NUST Journal of International Peace & Stability*, 14-30. http://doi.org/10.37540/njips.v6i2.149

- Kilinskas, K. (2016). Hybrid Warfare: an Orientating or Misleading Concept in Analysing Russia's Military Actions in Ukraine? Lithuanian Annual Strategic Review, 14(1), 139–158. https://doi.org/10.1515/lasr-2016-0006

- Kormych, B., Malyarenko, T., & Wittke, C. (2023). Rescaling the legal dimensions of grey zones: Evidence from Ukraine. *Global Policy*, *14*(3), 516–530. https://doi.org/10.1111/1758-5899.13233

- Kozyreva, A., Smillie, L., Lewandowsky, S., & Ecker, U. K. H. (2023). Incorporating Psychological Science Into Policy Making: The Case of Misinformation. European Psychologist, 28(3), 206–224. https://doi.org/10.1027/1016-9040/a000493

- Kurylo, B. (2016). Russia and Carl Schmitt: The hybridity of resistance in the globalised world. Humanities & Social Sciences Communications, 2(1), 16096-. https://doi.org/10.1057/palcomms.2016.96

- Lancelot, J. F. (2020). Cyber-diplomacy: cyberwarfare and the rules of engagement. Journal of Cyber Security, 4(4), 240–254. https://doi.org/10.1080/23742917.2020.1798155

- Laurenceson, J., Zhou, M., & Pantle, T. (2020). Interrogating Chinese economic coercion: the Australian experience since 2017. Security Challenges, 16(4), 3–23. https://www.jstor.org/stable/26976255

- Marecos, J., Shattock, E., Bartlett, O., Goiana-da-Silva, F., Maheswaran, H., Ashrafian, H., & Darzi, A. (2023). Health misinformation and freedom of expression: considerations for policymakers. *Health Economics, Policy and Law*, *18*(2), 204–217. https://doi.org/10.1017/S1744133122000263

- Naz, I. H. (2021). Foreign Policy In Hybrid Warfare Environment – Way Forward For Pakistan. *Margalla Papers, 25*(1), 1–11. https://doi.org/10.54690/margallapapers.25.1.46

- Niemiec, E. (2020). COVID-19 and misinformation: Is censorship of social media a remedy to the spread of medical misinformation? *EMBO Reports, 21*(11), e51420–e51420. https://doi.org/10.15252/embr.202051420

- Peterson, T. M. (2020). Reconsidering economic leverage and vulnerability: Trade ties, sanction threats, and the success of economic coercion. *Conflict Management and Peace Science, 37*(4), 409–429. https://doi.org/10.1177/0738894218797024

- Rauta, V. (2020). Towards a typology of non-state actors in "hybrid warfare": proxy, auxiliary, surrogate and affiliated forces. *Cambridge Review of International Affairs, 33*(6), 868–887. https://doi.org/10.1080/09557571.2019.1656600

- Samadashvili, S. (2015). Muzzling the Bear: Strategic Defence against Russia's Undeclared Information War on Europe. *European View, 14*(1), 141–141. https://doi.org/10.1007/s12290-015-0361-7

- Sarjito, A. (2024). Countering hybrid threats: Challenges and the role of defense science. *Publicness: Journal of Public Administration Studies,* 3(1), 1–15. https://doi.org/10.24036/publicness.v3i1.188

- Shah, M., & Ehsan, M. (2023). Hybrid warfare: Emerging challenges for Pakistan. *Journal of Contemporary Studies, 11*(2), 1–15. https://doi.org/10.54690/jcs.v11i2.234

- Simons, G. (2021). Operational implications and effects of informational and political dimensions of Western hybrid warfare. *Vestnik Moskovskogo Gosudarstvennogo Oblastnogo Universiteta, 3,* 106-. https://doi.org/10.18384/2224-0209-2021-3-1078

- Smith, K., & Parker, L. (2021). Reconfiguring Literacies in the Age of Misinformation and Disinformation. Journal of Language and Literacy Education, 17(2), n2. https://eric.ed.gov/?id=EJ1342485

- Suchkov, M. A. (2021). Whose hybrid warfare? How "the hybrid warfare" concept shapes Russian discourse, military, and political practice. *Small Wars & Insurgencies, 32*(3), 415–440. https://doi.org/10.1080/09592318.2021.1887434

- Thompson, T. L. (2020). No Silver Bullet: Fighting Russian Disinformation Requires Multiple Actions. *Georgetown Journal of International Affairs*, *21*(1), 182–194. https://doi.org/10.1353/gia.2020.0033

- Tyushka, A. (2019). HYBRID WAR(FARE): THE CHALLENGE OF CONTAGION. *Torun International Studies*, *1*(12), 5–29. https://doi.org/10.12775/TIS.2019.001

- Ucko, D. H., & Marks, T. A. (2018). Violence in context: Mapping the strategies and operational art of irregular warfare. Contemporary Security Policy, 39(2), 206–233. https://doi.org/10.1080/13523260.2018.1432922

- Vračar, M., & Ćurčić, M. (2018). The evolution of European perception of the term "hybrid warfare." *Vojno Delo*, *70*(1), 5–21. https://doi.org/10.5937/vojdelo1801005V

- Westhoff, M.-A., Posovszky, C., & Debatin, K.-M. (2023). How to Respond to Misinformation From the Anti-Vaccine Movement. *Inquiry (Chicago)*, *60*, 469580231155723–469580231155723. https://doi.org/10.1177/00469580231155723

- Whyte, J. (2023). Economic Coercion And Financial War. The Journal of Australian Political Economy, (90), 5-25. http://search.proquest.com.libaccess.sjlibrary.org/scholarly-journals/economic-coercion-financial-war/docview/2758124309/se-2

- Yeo, Y. (2023). The limits of pressure: China's bounded economic coercion in response to South Korea's THAAD. *Australian Journal of International Affairs*, *77*(3), 276–298. https://doi.org/10.1080/10357718.2023.2216642

- Zhang, B. (2023). Rethinking China's 'economic coercion': The case of the UK leaders' meeting with the Dalai Lama in 2012. *British Journal of Politics & International Relations*, *25*(4), 723–739. https://doi.org/10.1177/13691481221126914

- Ziegler, C. E. (2017). International dimensions of electoral processes: Russia, the USA, and the 2016 elections. *International Politics, 55*(5), 557–574. https://doi.org/10.1057/s41311-017-0113-1

Public Health

Focus: Public health consequences of hybrid warfare, including bioterrorism and societal disruption.

Topics: Pandemic responses as a grey zone tactic and resilience building.

- Baker, M. S., Baker, J., & Burkle, J. (2023). Russia's Hybrid Warfare in Ukraine Threatens Both Healthcare & Health Protections Provided by International Law. *Annals of Global Health*, *89*(1), 3–3. https://doi.org/10.5334/aogh.4022

- Behboudi-Gandevani, S., Bidhendi-Yarandi, R., Panahi, M. H., Mardani, A., Prinds, C., & Vaismoradi, M. (2022). Perinatal and Neonatal Outcomes in Immigrants From Conflict-Zone Countries: A Systematic Review and Meta-Analysis of Observational Studies. *Frontiers in Public Health*, *10*, 766943–766943. https://doi.org/10.3389/fpubh.2022.766943

- Burkle, F. M., Goniewicz, K., & Khorram-Manesh, A. (2022). Bastardizing Peacekeeping and the Birth of Hybrid Warfare. *Prehospital and Disaster Medicine*, *37*(2), 147–149. https://doi.org/10.1017/S1049023X22000425

- Devkota, B., & van Teijlingen, E. R. (2010). Understanding effects of armed conflict on health outcomes: the case of Nepal. *Conflict and Health*, *4*(1), 20–20. https://doi.org/10.1186/1752-1505-4-20

- Gele, A. A., & Bjune, G. A. (2010). Armed conflicts have an impact on the spread of tuberculosis: the case of the Somali Regional State of Ethiopia. *Conflict and Health*, *4*(1), 1–1. https://doi.org/10.1186/1752-1505-4-1

- Kokori, E., Olatunji, G., Yusuf, I. A., Isarinade, T., Moradeyo Akanmu, A., Olatunji, D., Akinmoju, O., & Aderinto, N. (2024). A mini-review on safeguarding global health amidst a "Pandemic" of armed conflicts. *Medicine (Baltimore)*, *103*(20), e37897–e37897. https://doi.org/10.1097/MD.0000000000037897

- Kraemer, M. U. G., Pigott, D. M., Hill, S. C., Vanderslott, S., Reiner, J., Stasse, S., Brownstein, J. S., Gutierrez, B., Dennig, F., Hay, S. I., Wint, G. R. W., Pybus, O. G., Castro, M. C., Vinck, P., Pham, P. N., Nilles, E. J., & Cauchemez, S. (2020). Dynamics of conflict during the Ebola outbreak in the Democratic Republic of the Congo 2018-2019. *BMC Medicine*, *18*(1), 113–10. https://doi.org/10.1186/s12916-020-01574-1

- Marecos, J., Shattock, E., Bartlett, O., Goiana-da-Silva, F., Maheswaran, H., Ashrafian, H., & Darzi, A. (2023). Health misinformation and freedom of expression: considerations for policymakers. *Health Economics, Policy and Law, 18*(2), 204–217. https://doi.org/10.1017/S1744133122000263

- Meagher, L., et al. (2021). Exploring the role of gender and women in the political economy of health in armed conflict: A narrative review. Globalization and Health, 17(1), Article 38. https://doi.org/10.1186/s12992-021-00738-9

- Reñosa, M. D. C., Wachinger, J., Bärnighausen, K., Endoma, V., Landicho-Guevarra, J., Landicho, J., Bravo, T. A., Aligato, M., & McMahon, S. A. (2022). Misinformation, infighting, backlash, and an "endless" recovery; policymakers recount challenges and mitigating measures after a vaccine scare in the Philippines. *Global Health Action, 15*(1), 2077536–2077536. https://doi.org/10.1080/16549716.2022.2077536

- Van Hout, M. C., & Wells, J. S. G. (2021). The right to health, public health and COVID-19: a discourse on the importance of the enforcement of humanitarian and human rights law in conflict settings for the future management of zoonotic pandemic diseases. *Public Health, 192*, 3–7. https://doi.org/10.1016/j.puhe.2021.01.001

- Wells, J. (2022). Preparing for hybrid warfare and cyberattacks on health services' digital infrastructure: What nurse managers need to know. Journal of Nursing Management, 30(3), 657–664. https://doi.org/10.1111/jonm.13633

Psychology

Focus: Psychological operations and the human impact of hybrid tactics.

Topics: Influence of propaganda, cognitive biases in conflict responses, and mental health impacts.

Applications: PSYOPS (Psychological Operations) and counter-disinformation efforts.

- Eberle, J., & Daniel, J. (2019). "Putin, You Suck": Affective Sticking Points in the Czech Narrative on "Russian Hybrid Warfare." *Political Psychology, 40*(6), 1267–1281. https://doi.org/10.1111/pops.12609

- Karaman, A., & Yurkiv, O. (2020). Deformation of personality as a consequence of a hybrid warfare. *Postmodern Openings, 11*(1), 45–58. https://doi.org/10.18662/po/107

- Kwiat, M. (2020). Pandemics, Grey Zone Warfare, and (Inter)National Security. *Israel Journal of Foreign Affairs*, *14*(2), 259–274. https://doi.or g/10.1080/23739770.2020.1815388

- Payo, N., & Askandar, K. (2024). (Re)Thinking Resilience: The Multi-faceted Impact of Conflict on Southern Thailand's Youth. *International Journal of Academic Research in Business & Social Sciences*, *14*(4). https://doi.org/10.6007/IJARBSS/v14-i4/21069

- Roozenbeek, J., Culloty, E., Suiter, J., & Ecker, U. K. H. (2023). Countering Misinformation: Evidence, Knowledge Gaps, and Implications of Current Interventions. *European Psychologist*, *28*(3), 189–205. https://doi. org/10.1027/1016-9040/a000492

Sociology and Anthropology

Focus: Impact of hybrid and grey zone conflicts on societies and cultures.
Topics: Civil resilience, public opinion manipulation, and societal polarization.
Methods: Ethnographic studies, surveys, and community resilience frameworks.

- Denisova, O. (2022). Africa in the 21st century: New insights into the problem of security. Asia and Africa Today, 22(1), 81-84. https://doi. org/10.31857/s032150750022722-6

- Dieuaide, P., & Azaïs, C. (2020). Platforms of Work, Labour, and Employment Relationship: The Grey Zones of a Digital Governance. *Frontiers in Sociology*, *5*(2), 2–2. https://doi.org/10.3389/fsoc.2020.00002

- Oleksandr, K., & Olga, K. (2022). Sociological aspect in the content of the modern hybrid warfare. The Bulletin of Yaroslav Mudryi National Law University, Series: Philosophy, Philosophies of Law, Political Science, Sociology, 52, 249–258. https://doi.org/10.21564/2663-5704.52.249948

- Santos, A. (2024). State violence in the production of territories, informality, and protection networks. Cadernos Metrópole, 26(1), 1–20. https://doi.org/10.1590/2236-9996.2024-5913.e

- Savchenko, O., & Kurylo, O. (2018). Patriotic education in the process of youth socialization in conditions of hybrid warfare. The Journal of Social Sciences Research, 5, 1121–1125. https://doi.org/10.32861/jssr. spi5.1121.1125

- Tomo, M., Ricci, P., & Carillo, F. (2020). Stories of grey zone between corruption and whistleblowing: Insights from the Italian public administration. Meditari Accountancy Research, 28(1), 1–15. https://doi.org/10.1108/medar-11-2018-0405

- Velychko, O. (2023). The assessment of social work needs and priorities in the context of the armed conflict in Ukraine. Scientific Annals of the Alexandru Ioan Cuza University Iasi, New Series: Sociology and Social Work Section, 12(2), 45–60. https://doi.org/10.47743/asas-2023-2-741

- Yatchenko, O., & Oliinyk, O. (2019). Social trauma as a conflicto-genic factor in Ukrainian studies and in Ukrainian history. Almanac of Ukrainian Studies, 25, 21–30. https://doi.org/10.17721/2520-2626/2019.25.21

Technology and Engineering

Focus: Development and application of technologies in hybrid warfare.
Topics: Autonomous systems, artificial intelligence in conflict, and weaponized technologies.

- Adnasi, I. N. (2022). An Appraisal of The Legal Framework for The Protection of Civilians in Cyber-Warfare Under International Humanitarian Law. (n.d.). International Journal of Research and Scientific Innovation. https://doi.org/10.51244/ijrsi.2022.9702

- Bachmann, S. D. (2011). Hybrid threats, cyber warfare and NATO's comprehensive approach for countering 21st century threats-mapping the new frontier of global risk and security management. *Amicus Curiae*, *88*, 24.

- Bouke, M. A., & Abdullah, A. (2024). Smrd: A novel cyber warfare modeling framework for social engineering, malware, ransomware, and distributed denial-of-service based on a system of nonlinear differential equations. *Journal of Applied Artificial Intelligence*, *5*(1), 54-68.

- Fedotenko, K. (2023). Cyber Warfare As Part of Information Warfare of Russia Against Ukraine Since the Beginning of the 2022 Russian Invasion. *Věda a Perspektivy*, *8(27)*. https://doi.org/10.52058/2695-1592-2023-8(27)-351-357

- Gabrielli, G. (2023). Individual Criminal Responsibility of Non-State Actors Operating in Cyberspace for War Crimes Under the ICC Statute. EU and comparative law issues and challenges series (ECLIC), 7, 286-315. https://doi.org/10.25234/eclic/28268

- Grobler, M., & Swart, I. (2014). On the probability of predicting and mapping traditional warfare measurements to the cyber warfare domain. In ICT and Society: 11th IFIP TC 9 International Conference on Human Choice and Computers, HCC11 2014, Turku, Finland, July 30–August 1, 2014. Proceedings 11 (pp. 239-254). Springer Berlin Heidelberg. https://doi.org/10.1007/978-3-662-44208-1_20

- Ibrahim, A., Mahmud, N., Isnin, N., Hazelbella Dillah, D., & Nurfauziah Fauz Dillah, D. (2019). Cyber Warfare Impact to National Security - Malaysia Experiences. KnE Social Sciences. https://doi.org/10.18502/kss.v3i22.5052

- Kumar, S., & Nagar, G. (2024). Threat Modeling for Cyber Warfare Against Less Cyber-Dependent Adversaries. European Conference on Cyber Warfare and Security, 23(1), 257–264. https://doi.org/10.34190/eccws.23.1.2462

- Kuntsman, A. (2010). Webs of hate in diasporic cyberspaces: the Gaza War in the Russian-language blogosphere. Media, War & Conflict, 3(3), 299–313. https://doi.org/10.1177/1750635210378948

- Kwiat, M. (2020). Pandemics, Grey Zone Warfare, and (Inter)National Security. Israel Journal of Foreign Affairs, 14(2), 259–274. https://doi.org/10.1080/23739770.2020.1815388

- Maskun, M., & Rum, A. R. (2021). Cyber Warfare: National Security In Dealing With Changing Method of War. Kanun (Banda Aceh), 23(3), 477–490. https://doi.org/10.24815/kanun.v23i3.22371

- Mtsweni, J., & Thaba, M. (2024). Bibliometric Analysis of Cyber Warfare Research in Africa: Landscape and Trends. International Conference on Cyber Warfare and Security, 19(1), 208–218. https://doi.org/10.34190/iccws.19.1.2242

- Robinson, M., Jones, K., Janicke, H., & Maglaras, L. (2018). An introduction to cyber peacekeeping. Journal of Network and Computer Applications, 114, 70–87. https://doi.org/10.1016/j.jnca.2018.04.010

- Safdar, M.A., Bakhsh F., Nadeem, S.A., & Habib, R.I. (2024). Common Article 3 and Asymmetric Warfare in the Context of Cyber Operations. Pakistan Journal of Criminal Justice, 4(1), 15–23. https://doi.org/10.62585/pjcj.v4i1.36

- Sholikah, D. I., Harbriyana Putra, T., & Fauzan Hidayat, M. (2024). Cyber Warfare Is The Newest Challenge To Support Indonesian National

Resilience. Asian Journal of Social and Humanities, 2(9), 2000–2006. https://doi.org/10.59888/ajosh.v2i9.332

- Stoddart, K. (2024). Russia's Cyber Campaigns and the Ukraine War: From the 'Gray Zone' to the 'Red Zone. Applied Cybersecurity & Internet Governance, 3(1), 5–33. https://doi.org/10.60097/ACIG/189358

- Wang, Q. (2014). Applicability of Jus in Bello in Cyber Space: Dilemmas and Challenges. International Journal of Cyber Warfare and Terrorism, 4(3), 43–62. https://doi.org/10.4018/ijcwt.2014070104

A concluding note: This diversity of disciplines highlights the complexity of hybrid warfare and grey zone conflicts, necessitating collaboration across academic fields, as well as collaboration between academics and practitioners to address their challenges fully.

PRINCIPAL CHAPTER AUTHORS

Listed here are those contributors who volunteered to take primary responsibility for drafting, and/or for final editing of a case or other chapter. However, many others served as drafting team members and made substantive contributions to those discussions. Some 50 people in all were involved. Those not named here are thanked in notes in each chapter.

Adler, Peter S.

Peter S. Adler is a partner in GUILD Strategies, a strategic analysis and planning consulting group. He is the former president and CEO of The Keystone Center. He has long experience as a mediator, arbitrator and hearings officer. He specializes in multi-party problem-solving for policy and governance disputes and for enterprises seeking operational alignment, excellence, and strategy. He has extensive national and international experience with business and policy negotiations and writes, trains, and teaches in areas of conflict management. He is a former Peace Corps volunteer and has held executive positions with the Hawaiʻi Supreme Court, Hawaiʻi Justice Foundation, and the Neighborhood Justice Center and served as president of the Society of Professionals in Dispute Resolution. He is the author of 5 books including the recently released *Calming the Storm: A Leader's Handbook for Resolving Unproductive Conflicts*, Rowman and Littlefield, 2024.

Ajaja, Oluwaseun

Oluwaseun Ajaja is a dynamic lawyer and strategic advisor with expertise in public policy, social justice, and organizational strategy. With a strong foundation in law, change management, and intergovernmental affairs, Oluwaseun excels in navigating complex organizational and governmental challenges to foster collaboration and drive sustainable solutions. Committed to advancing systemic change, Oluwaseun addresses workplace dynamics, resolves conflicts, and shapes policies that promote social justice and economic innovation. Known for a strategic, solutions-oriented approach, Oluwaseun empowers organizations and governments to build resilient and inclusive frameworks that create lasting societal impact.

Borbély, Adrian

Adrian Borbély is Associate Professor of Negotiation at emlyon business school in France. A litigation lawyer by training, he has been teaching and developing negotiation theory and pedagogy for over 15 years. He is a trained mediator, an entrepreneur and an administrator of the French Non-Profit Organization PRONEGO-DBS, which gathers negotiation and conflict management practitioners, trainers and theoreticians. He has been writing on hybrid warfare for a few years and is a founding member of the Council for Countering Hybrid Warfare. His research interests cover agency in dispute resolution, the organization as a negotiator, negotiation theory and the adaptation of negotiation thinking in hybrid warfare situations. He holds a Ph.D. from ESSEC business school, a French master's in law and a master's degree in public affairs from Indiana University's O'Neill school of public and environmental affairs.

Burgess, Guy

Guy Burgess (and his wife, Heidi Burgess) are Co-Directors of the Beyond Intractability Project (https://www.beyondintractability.org/). Constructed with contributions from over 500 conflict experts, BI is a large, online knowledge base system focused on assembling what we collectively know about ways of more constructively handling difficult and intractable conflicts at all levels of social organization, from the interpersonal to the international. They helped found and co-directed from 1988 to their retirement in 2019 the Conflict Information Consortium at the University of Colorado. Guy has taught in the Conflict and Peace Studies program at the University of Colorado, at the Carter School of Peace and Conflict Resolution at George Mason University, and at the University of Denver. Before that, he earned a Ph.D. in Sociology from the University of Colorado and did postdoctoral work at the Massachusetts Institute of Technology.

Chrustie, Calvin

Calvin Chrustie is a Canadian senior security and critical risk consultant who advises and coaches executives, law offices, diplomats, politicians, community leaders in negotiations (ransom), intelligence, investigations, crisis response, and management. His work is often described as 'asymmetrical problem solving' and often touches on national security related issues, transnational crime actors and/or geopolitical dynamics. Calvin served 33 years with the Royal Canadian Mounted Police. He specialized in complex transnational organized crime investigations, kidnap / extortion negotiations, illicit finance, crisis, and conflict management. He has extensive experience in intelligence operations and international investigations with transnational organized crime networks, including those affiliated with state actors. He has extensive experience in the design and delivery of scenario-based and simulation training for crisis-related incidents. Calvin was the Team

Leader of Canada's International Negotiation Group, a group of highly specialized negotiators tasked with terrorist and hostage situations.

Cooper, Sam

Sam Cooper is an award-winning investigative journalist and best-selling author, who founded the investigative journalism platform TheBureau.news in June 2023, after reporting for 17 years with Canadian newspapers and television media. Cooper has presented his anti-corruption and financial integrity investigations findings to Canadian law enforcement agencies, U.S. government officials, financial and legal professionals, and academics internationally. Cooper graduated with a degree in history, philosophy and English from the University of Toronto and a certificate in Journalism from Langara College, before reporting for The Province and Vancouver Sun in British Columbia, and Global News in Ottawa. He has won several awards for narrative reporting and his first book, Wilful Blindness, debuted as a #1-seller on Amazon, in Canada. Cooper has researched the threat of lawfare in relation to hybrid warfare activities and directly experienced suspected personal, reputational, and legal threats in the field.

Corpora, Christopher A.

Christopher A. Corpora, Ph.D. currently serves as a Civilian Observer with the Multinational Force and Observers (MFO) and as a Board Member with the International Coalition Against Illicit Economies (ICAIE). He is an international security expert with over 30 years of experience in the field and classroom. He served as a senior analyst and advisor with multiple U.S. government agencies and private companies, focused on conflict stabilization and countering transnational threats – global illicit trafficking, transnational organized crime, corruption and violent extremism. He received his Ph.D. from American University's School of International Service and is an alumni of the Woodrow Wilson Center's Junior Scholars Seminar. Most importantly, he is the proud father of three creative and remarkable daughters.

Druckman, Daniel

Daniel Druckman is Professor Emeritus of Public and International Affairs at George Mason's Schar School of Policy and Government in Arlington Virginia and an Honorary Professor at Macquarie University in Sydney and at the University of Queensland in Brisbane, Australia. Two of his books, *Doing Research: Methods of Inquiry for Conflict Analysis* (Sage, 2005) and, with Paul F. Diehl, *Evaluating Peace Operations* (Lynne Reinner, 2010) received the outstanding book award from the International Association for Conflict Management (IACM). His co-authored article on robot mediation (2021) received a best article of the year award from Group Decision and Negotiation. He is the recipient of six lifetime achievement awards. His recent career book is "Negotiation, Identity, and Justice: Pathways to Agreement" (Routledge, 2023).

Ebner, Noam

Over the past twenty-five years, Noam Ebner has resolved disputes, consulted to organizations and businesses, and taught conflict resolution skills to thousands of people. Ebner has taught at universities in the U.S, Israel, Turkey, and Costa Rica. In his 15-year tenure as a professor in Creighton University's law and business schools, he designed, taught in, and chaired Creighton's online graduate degree program in Negotiation and Conflict Resolution. He has practiced as an attorney, negotiator, and mediator, and conducted hundreds of workshops on negotiation and conflict resolution for private sector industries, governmental agencies, universities and non-profits around the world. Ebner holds LL.B and LL.M degrees from Hebrew University (Israel) and a postgraduate diploma in social science research from the University of Bradford (U.K).

Galeotti, Mark

Dr Mark Galeotti is an honorary professor at University College London and director of the Russia-focused consultancy Mayak Intelligence. He is also a senior fellow with the Royal United Services Institute and the Council on Geostrategy in London, the University of Kent and the Institute of International Relations Prague. He is one of the world's leading experts on Russian politics, crime and security (which are often one and the same), which may explain why Moscow banned him in 2022. He read History at Cambridge University and Politics at the LSE and has travelled extensively across Russia and the post-Soviet states. He has briefed widely, from prime ministers and CEOs to generals and intelligence chiefs and is a prolific author: his more than 30 books include *Forged in War* (2024), *Downfall: Prigozhin, Putin and the new fight for the future of Russia* with Anna Arutunyan (2024), *Putin's Wars* (2022), *The Weaponisation of Everything* (2022), and *The Vory: Russia's super mafia* (2017).

Honeyman, Chris

Chris Honeyman is Managing Partner of Convenor Conflict Management, a consulting firm based in Washington, DC. Chris served as Project Seshat's Principal Investigator and chaired its steering committee from 2019 to 2023. Among other roles, he was primary designer of the case specifications and of five project teams, which wrote eight cases that became the foundation for this book. Previously he directed or co-directed a 30-year succession of conflict management research-and-development projects of national or international scale; wrote or co-authored more than 100 articles, book chapters and monographs; and co-edited seven books, including the most comprehensive work in the field, the two-volume Negotiator's Desk Reference. As a practitioner he has served as a mediator, arbitrator or in other neutral capacities in more than 2,000 disputes, including issuing some 500 arbitration awards and administrative law decisions.

Jordaan, Barney

Barney Jordaan is Professor of Negotiation and Conflict Management at Vlerick Business School in Belgium and Professor Extraordinaire at the University of Stellenbosch Business School, South Africa. Prior to moving to Belgium in 2014 to take up his current position, he held several academic appointments in South Africa, including 14 years as Professor of law at Stellenbosch University and thereafter as Professor of negotiation and conflict management at the University of Stellenbosch Business School and the Graduate School of Business, University of Cape Town. He also practised as a human rights lawyer in South Africa during the apartheid era before co-founding a consulting firm which advised clients on conflict management strategies, negotiation and related matters. As an internationally certified mediator, he has been involved in mediation since 1989. He is the author and co-author of several book chapters, conference papers, cases and articles and is a founding member of Project Seshat.

Kaufman, Sanda

Sanda Kaufman is Professor Emerita of Planning, Public Policy and Administration, Cleveland State University and member of the Council on Countering Hybrid Warfare. Her research spans negotiations / intervention in environmental and other public conflicts; dynamic modeling of conflicts and of social polarization; hybrid warfare; social-environmental systems resilience; disaster preparedness; and negotiation pedagogy. Some of her recent publications include "How Should the Whole-of-Society Respond to Hybrid Warfare?" (On track, Canada's global defence and security e-magazine 2023); with social scientists G. and H. Burgess "Applying conflict resolution insights to the hyper-polarized, society-wide conflicts threatening liberal democracies" (Conflict Resolution Quarterly 2022, feature article); with law scholar C. Alkon, "A Theory of Interests in the Context of Hybrid Warfare: It's Complex" (Cardozo Journal of Conflict Resolution, Special Melnick Symposium Issue 2023); with physicists H. Diep and M. Kaufman, "An Agent-based Statistical Physics Model for Political Polarization" (Entropy 2023, Special issue: Statistical Physics of Opinion Formation and Social Phenomena) and "Social Depolarization: Blume-Capel Model." (Physics 2024. Special Issue).

LeBaron, Michelle

Michelle LeBaron is a tenured faculty member at the University of British Columbia Allard Law School and a scholar / practitioner of conflict transformation. Professor LeBaron has written and practiced in many international contexts. Her books include *Changing Our Worlds: Art as Transformative Practice; The Choreography of Resolution: Conflict,*

Movement and Neuroscience; Conflict Across Cultures: A New Approach for a Changing World; Bridging Cultural Conflicts; and *Bridging Troubled Waters*. Professor LeBaron's articles on alchemy and arts-informed research / practice in conflict have appeared in *Organizational Aesthetics,* the *International Journal of Professional Management, Non Liquet* (Westminster Law and Theory Lab Law and the Senses Series) and the *Journal of Law and Society.*

Leslie, Anne

Anne Leslie is Cloud Risk & Controls Leader at IBM Cloud covering the EMEA region, based in Paris (France). She has over 18 years of experience in international roles in banking and related technology businesses, spanning the intersection of digital transformation, information security, risk management, and regulatory policymaking. Widely known for her public speaking, Anne regularly contributes her thought leadership to industry conferences and working groups on topics related to the digitization of financial services, operational resilience, cybersecurity, and the growing impact of hybrid warfare on the conduct of business. A recognized trusted advisor, she has a proven ability to orchestrate outcome-oriented dialogue on complex industry issues by cultivating positive relationships across diverse public-private stakeholder groups.

Levine, Joshua F.

Joshua F. Levine is Librarian – Law and Adjunct Professor at Benjamin N. Cardozo School of Law, Yeshiva University, in New York City. He provides reference and research services to the law school community and teaches Advanced Legal Research to upper-level students. His research into articles on hybrid warfare and cyberwarfare, on behalf of Professor Andrea Schneider at Cardozo School of Law, forms a major portion of the selected readings chapter. He greatly appreciates the support both of his library colleagues at Cardozo and of his family.

Lira, Leonard L.

Leonard L. Lira is the Chair of the Department of Public Policy and Service at San Antonio College, San Antonio, TX. He also was the founding Director of the Center for Teaching and Learning Excellence at the Army University. His teaching experiences include teaching Strategic and Operational Studies, Enterprise Leadership and Management to Army Command and Management Staff, as well as American Politics at West Point. He has over 30 years of public service with direct, organizational and enterprise management and leadership experience. He served as a Colonel in the US Army, having deployed to Iraq twice and Afghanistan once. He received a Ph.D. in Public Administration from the University of Kansas in 2016. In 2003, he received an M.A. in International Relations, a Master of Public Administration, and a Certificate of Advanced Study in Conflict Resolution from the Maxwell School of Public Affairs and Administration, Syracuse University. He received a B.A. from Sam Houston State University in Criminal Justice and Police Administration in 1994.

McGregor, Scott

Scott McGregor is a highly accomplished Canadian intelligence professional. A combat veteran and former diplomatic defence attaché, he served in the Canadian Armed Forces as a senior domestic intelligence analyst, where he uncovered the nexus between terrorism and transnational organized crime (TNOC) in the Middle East. As a special intelligence advisor to the RCMP Federal Serious Organized Crime unit, Scott advanced awareness of the intersections between TNOC and national security, introducing the concept of hybrid warfare to law enforcement. At the provincial level, he served as a senior intelligence officer and policy analyst with the Attorney General of British Columbia, exposing how TNOC and state threat actors exploit the gaming and real estate sectors. In the private sector, Scott led intelligence operations as the head of Canada's largest private security company and now serves as CEO and managing partner of Close Hold Intelligence Consulting Inc., where he continues to address emerging global security challenges.

Mikulski, Kamil

Kamil Mikulski is a Senior Innovation Research Analyst at IN2 and a doctoral student at Rey Juan Carlos University and the European Doctoral School on CSDP. He graduated in International Relations and Diplomacy from the College of Europe, as well as in law from Wroclaw University. He is an alumnus of the James S. Denton Transatlantic Fellowship. Kamil Mikulski is the founder of the Emerging Threats Observatory Foundation, which researches new methods of countering hybrid threats. He was a member of the European Commission's Expert Group on tackling disinformation and promoting digital literacy through education and training. He is associated with the Kosciuszko Institute and European Academy of Diplomacy. He speaks five languages and is passionate about the Nordic-Baltic Eight countries and Central Europe.

Omotor, Stanley Oghenevwairhe

Stanley Oghenevwairhe Omotor is a lawyer called to the Bar both in Nigeria and Canada. Before moving to Canada, Stanley lived in the Niger Delta area of Nigeria. Growing up in the Niger Delta, Stanley witnessed some of the various conflicts in the oil-rich area, including communal crises and those involving the Nigerian military. Stanley's lived experiences resulted in his interest in conflict resolution and negotiations. Stanley holds a Master of Laws degree from the University of British Columbia.

Omotosho, Mariam

Mariam Omotosho is an experienced policy and program advisor with a strong academic background in law and expertise in legislative analysis, policy development, stakeholder engagement, and issues management. She is passionate about shaping policies at the intersection of sustainable transportation and capital infrastructure development. Currently, Mariam is a Senior Advisor at Metrolinx, Ontario's leading transit agency. In her role, she specializes in negotiation, conflict resolution, and stakeholder management, ensuring effective communication among diverse groups. Mariam's work focuses on fostering collaboration, building consensus, and creating solutions that support long-term growth and sustainability in transportation and infrastructure projects.

Reyes, Bryan R.

Bryan R. Reyes is an undergraduate student at Santa Clara University where he is studying Political Science and pursuing a minor in Applied Computing for Behavioral and Social Studies, and is a research assistant. In addition, he is a scholar student in the SJSU Intelligence Center for Academic Excellence (ICCAE) and has concentrated his studies in international relations, conflict management, and hybrid warfare over the past four years. In recent years, Bryan has attended conferences and university classes to speak on the impact and importance in addressing hybrid conflicts.

Schneider, Andrea K.

Andrea K. Schneider is a Professor of Law and the director of the Kukin Program for Conflict Resolution of Benjamin N. Cardozo School of Law in New York. She is also the Executive Director of the Council for Countering Hybrid Warfare. She has taught dispute resolution, negotiation, ethics, and international conflict resolution for 25 years. She previously served as the inaugural director of the Institute for Women's Leadership at Marquette University and as the Director of the nationally ranked Dispute Resolution Program at Marquette University Law School. She authored or co-authored numerous books, including leading textbooks on dispute resolution generally, negotiation, mediation, and dispute resolution in the criminal context. She has also edited multiple volumes focusing on interdisciplinary approaches to negotiation, including *Negotiation Essentials for Lawyers* and *The Negotiator's Desk Reference,* both co-edited with Chris Honeyman.

Senger, Jeffrey M.

Jeffrey M. Senger is a mediator and arbitrator at JAMS who teaches at Harvard and Columbia law schools. He served as FDA's acting General Counsel and was a life sciences partner at Sidley Austin. As Senior Counsel in the Office of Dispute Resolution at the U.S. Department of Justice, he coordinated dispute resolution for the federal government. He wrote the award-winning book, Federal Dispute Resolution (Wiley), along with many journal articles and book chapters. He testified as an expert witness on ADR before the U.S. Congress, has spoken about dispute resolution on behalf of the U.S. government on five continents, and is an honors graduate of Harvard College and Harvard Law School.

Sourdin, Tania

Professor Sourdin is President of the Academic Senate at the University of Newcastle in Australia. She is the author of more than 140 publications that include books, articles, and papers that are focused on justice reform issues and has presented on a range of topics including dispute resolution, justice innovation, artificial intelligence and technology and law. She has worked as a mediator, conciliator, tribunal member and continues to work in these areas internationally and within Australia. She has had several projects that have explored the use of dispute resolution and mediation in the justice field.

Zartman, I. William

The late I. William Zartman (1932-2025) was the Jacob Blaustein Distinguished Professor Emeritus of International Organization and Conflict Resolution at the School of Advanced International Studies of The Johns Hopkins University in Washington, and a founding member of the Processes of International Negotiation (PIN) Program. His doctorate is from Yale and doctorates honoris causa from Louvain and Uppsala. He is author and co-author/editor of numerous works on the Middle East and North Africa and on negotiation and mediation, including *Practical Negotiator* (Yale 1982*), Ripe for Resolution* (Oxford 1989), *Elusive* Peace (Brookings 1995), *Cowardly Lions* (Rienner 2005), Preventing *Deadly Conflict* (Polity 2015), *Negotiating in the Shadow of the Intifadat (Georgia 2015), How Negotiations End* (Cambridge 2019), and *Rethinking Conflict Management and Resolution* (Edgar 2023).